Wasn't Love Supposed To Be Enough?

Biographies of a Long-Term Adoptive Parent Support Group

and

Services for Adoptive Families

Barbara D. VanSlyck, M.S.Ed.
Ellen Wristen, J.D.
Alan Dupre-Clark, D.Min.
Richard Mague, Ph.D.
Rosemary Haggerty

Printed in the United States of America

Wasn't Love Supposed to be Enough?

ISBN   0-9668752-0-6

Address inquiries to:
Barbara D. VanSlyck
3915 Patricia Drive
Columbus, Ohio 43220-4914

First Edition: November 1998

Cover design by:
Internet Media Properties

Reproduction and *Binding* by:
General Binding Corporation

This book is dedicated to the adoptive parents
who contributed their stories, feelings,
and emotions to make this project possible.

Table of Contents

Acknowledgments

This book was truly a collaborative effort that extends far beyond the listed authors. Every parent who wrote a biography for the book deserves the title of author. One group member, Rosemary Haggerty, put her own book on hold to review, edit, give suggestions, and write the introduction to the adoptive family stories. She made many trips across town for meetings and called all of the families to obtain information for the survey section. The short descriptions of each family in the survey section were compiled and written by Rosemary.

Ellen Wristen is an adoptive parent and an attorney who has learned much about the difficulties adoptive children can have in achieving their educational needs. She contributes a practical guide to obtaining educational services.

Dr. Alan Dupre-Clark has been a counselor for adoptive families for many years and has assisted in writing of training manuals we use for adoptive families. He leads the parent groups, does all of our assessments, and has developed treatment modalities for adopted children.

Dr. Richard Mague is a counselor for families and children who brings a fresh approach for assessment and treatment to our objectives. He works with families in crisis and co-leads the newer parent support group.

The authors are grateful to the families of our support group who shared their lives to help other adoptive families and to enlighten professionals who work in the field of adoption. So we wish to thank the parent authors who wrote about their lives as adoptive families and the other adoptive parents who participated in the survey and encouraged us to follow through with this journey. We are grateful for the confidence and faith expressed by the families who wrote about their life experiences and then relied on us to complete the book around their stories. The parents who chronicled their lives found the experience emotionally draining. Many of the parents found themselves reliving painful times from the past. Every one found the writing much more challenging and difficult than they had imagined before they began.

I had wanted to write a book that emphasizes the need for post finalization services and pre-adoptive education, but without the impact of the family profiles, it would have been just another professional expressing the need for better services for adoptive families.

Few support groups remain healthy and intact for ten years. These families came to group when their need was great and they stayed to help others. I will be forever grateful that I had the opportunity to meet and be a part of their support group. Their kindness to me over the years have nurtured me in times of need.

We asked teens who participated in our education series to write poetry reflecting their feelings about adoption. Six poems are located throughout the book. Thanks also go to two teen artists who gave us drawings of their depictions of adopted children and families. They had not read the poetry prior to creating the drawings.

Thanks to the insightful caregivers at Parenthesis Family Advocates who recognized a need for adoptive families and formed the post adoption program in 1986. Thanks to Bob and Jan Davis who were instrumental in forming the first support group and who always made sure we had a place to meet.

A special thanks to Marilyn Wilson, an adoptive parent and adoption educator, for her careful review and important contributions. She was always available and understanding of the stresses and strains from a work in progress.

Time and time again we sent the manuscript sections for review and edit to Rosemary Haggerty, Marilyn Wilson, Steve VanSlyck, and others. Each time hours of reading and meetings to agree on changes, additions, and clarification required a good deal of volunteered time.

Thanks to Steve VanSlyck who reviewed the manuscript for all of those typos and errant commas and kept me busy with all of his suggestions. Also to my husband, Lou, for his invaluable concrete advise and counsel. He was very understanding and protective of my need for uninterrupted concentration. He also used his computer facilities to typeset the book and prepare every page for camera-ready reproduction.

Last, a special thanks to John Shannon, Executive Director of Parenthesis Family Advocates, for his commitment to post adoptive services.

All of the authors and members of the support group wish to thank those who have formed grass roots support groups across the country and agencies who have had the foresight to maintain a commitment to the health of the adoptive family. We wish to thank the parents who adopt special needs children knowing that their children will require intensive guidance and a commitment that few envisioned when the decision to adopt was made.

Barbara D. VanSlyck
Upper Arlington, Ohio
November, 1997

Contributors

Most of all, this book represents the efforts, emotional input and love from the following people. They made this project possible by their contributions and encouragement. They gave their stories, quotes, survey responses, poetry, drawings and inspiration for this project.

Adoptive Parents

Jan and Bob Davis

Cathy and Jim Gauchel

Rosemary and Tom Haggerty

Karen Hamill

Lynne and David Henderson

Carolyn and Peter Hendey

Ann and Allen Isenberg

Paul Keaveney

Pat and Rich Link

Judy and Tom Moore

Barbara and Dan Rankin

Carol and Greg Roddy

Poetry

Patrick Gauchel

Kelly Haggerty

Alicia Shelton

Brian Wildenthaler

Jennifer VanSlyck

Anonymous

Illustrations

Jamie Hamill

Aaron Wristen

Editing, Writing, and Review Assistance

Steven B. VanSlyck, J.D.

Marilyn Wilson

Typesetting and Print Preparation

Louis S. (Lou) VanSlyck, P.E., Ph.D.

Introduction

This book chronicles in detail the life experiences of several adoptive families who have participated in a support group for adoptive families. It contains a compilation of information and advice for other families and professionals who are touched by adoption.

I first became acquainted with the support group in 1992 when I accepted the position of Post Adoption Program Coordinator for Parenthesis Family Advocates. As an adoptive parent of two children (one with fetal alcohol effect and attention deficit hyperactivity disorder; and a second who was adopted at age 11 after much abuse, and a disruption, who was diagnosed with depression, and post traumatic stress disorder, [PTSD]), I knew first hand the challenges of parenting without specialized education or support.

As I managed the "warmline," I heard day after day the tragedy of families who, after years of seeking help for severe behavioral problems, found themselves frustrated in their efforts to find answers for their children and themselves. These families, who were ready to give up, found the help they needed from each other in our support group aimed at the specific issues of adoptive children and parents.

The original parent support group has been together since 1986. There are now three such adoptive parent support groups. We formed a second group for parents of teens in 1992 and yet another for parents of younger children in 1996. Most of the parents came to our attention during times of crisis and were first assisted via our ten-week parallel education series. A number remained to join an ongoing support group which sustained them until their adopted youth were stabilized. Many have stayed on to help others.

After three years of discussion about the needs of adoptive parents who lack the support and information that these group members have found, we made the decision to move forward with the writing of this work.

Most of the persons who contributed significantly to this book are adoptive parents who have been part of a monthly support group for over ten years. Other contributing parents belong to a monthly group that has been meeting for five years. Most of them first came to know one another while attending our ten-week parallel education series.

Contributing clinicians who have worked with these families are aware that it is not possible for them to adequately portray the families' anguish and the struggles they have lived through and may still be enduring. These families came to the series or groups as parents who had borne terrible grief and pain for many years and had lost hope for any real assistance. When they attended their first meeting and felt the empathy and understanding of the others envelop them, they realized they would never feel so alone or helpless again. The group provided a lifeline.

We cannot fully express how even small victories were celebrated by the group as a whole. The group members have become friends who call just to check on one another. They are available to each other in times of trouble and in times of joy. As the years went by the members began to develop a concern for families who needed and did not have a support group to help them. The members believe that all adoptive parents should have the opportunity to share such a rewarding experience. They want to share the knowledge they have labored so long to acquire.

Many times the idea of writing a book arose during group sessions, but the thought of reliving painful past struggles made such a project daunting.

However, as the years passed and more and more people came for help, it became apparent just how much such groups were needed by adoptive families. Parents would drive from two counties away because the need was so great and no groups were available close to their homes.

The benefits were quickly apparent to all who came. Parents were able to stay connected to children who were acting out and unreachable by counselors, medication, or even juvenile authorities. They saw other families who did not seek out the group, giving up on their commitments to their teenage youth who were in trouble. A research paper by Denise Goodman, Ph.D. studied the differences between children who were placed out of the home and those who were maintained in the home. She found that parents who were educated about adoption issues and receiving support were more likely to remain connected to their child and maintain them at home even when their behaviors were more extreme than those who were placed. The majority of adoptive parents who placed children out of the home had experienced little or no adoption education or support systems.

After long discussion and some concern that this book might be seen as unsupportive of adoption, the support group families made the commitment to tell their stories so that other adoptive parents could take solace in knowing that conditions can improve if the parents can hang on during the problem years. They wanted to say that the commitment is forever, not just till the going gets tough. They want others to know that over a lifetime with your adoptee, the difficult years of adolescence comprise only a short space in their lives.

None of the stories have really ended. Not all of the families' stories have happy endings to date. It would be dishonest to portray them as such. Some of the families are still struggling and in pain. We wanted to provide a cross section of the members' experiences. Many families who wanted their stories to be told found they were unable to make themselves relive past events in order to write about them. We have conducted interviews in order to include some of that group and surveyed others just to get their comments about adoption. A few found even a two-page survey too emotionally difficult to complete.

We had several discussions in group about the possible negative impact that the reported histories could have on those considering adoption or those with young children. However, we reached a consensus that we had to inform parents that:

1. It is essential to inform pre-adoptive individuals about the need for support, education, and a lifelong commitment.
2. There is hope for families engaged in struggles.
3. A good support system, knowledgeable professional assistance, and time can help in the healing.

Another reason for this project was to sensitize and educate adoption agency personnel about the importance of parent education and appropriate preparation of older children for adoption. It is our wish to encourage those who choose adoption as a way to build a family and to assist children who need permanent homes.

Therefore, we want this project to serve as a teaching tool for those attempting to create and maintain healthy adoptive families and help children who have already endured abusive histories. Adoptive children deserve to be raised by well-prepared parents who are ready and able to stand with children who need nurturing, tolerance, and the knowledge that mom and dad will be their forever family.

Barbara D. VanSlyck

Our Goals

- To encourage ongoing support of the adoptive family
- To help adoptive parents accept that there may be some struggles in the developmental years and that some of the child's behaviors are normal and not an indication of poor parenting
- To stress the need for pre- and post-adoptive education
- To help families understand that asking for help is not a sign of failure or poor parenting

We Hope

We hope that those parents who read this book will take hope from it and attend or create support groups.

We hope that parents will feel less guilt about the actions of their child and the feelings of ambivalence that can arise in times of turbulence.

We hope that therapists, caseworkers, and other professionals who read this book will study more about the feelings, adversities, environmental histories, and treatment needs of children who come to adoption, whether as infants or as older children.

We hope that all professionals who work with foster children, prospective parents, and adoptive families will press for first-rate parental education, and applicable, relevant counseling for the children.

We hope that adoptees who read this book will take heart and know the real commitment that each of the parents who contributed to this book maintained in the face of great odds.

We hope that adoptees who read this book understand that we are not categorizing all adopted children as troubled. Current research indicates that 75% of adopted children adjust well.

An Historical Overview
of our
Post-Adoptive Services

It is hard to find structured post adoptive services that existed before the creation of the Post Adoption Project at Parenthesis Family Advocates. Parenthesis' program began when the staff, who were foster parents realized that a large percentage of youth entering substitute care were coming out of adoptive homes. They searched for a way to serve the families in order to help prevent their breakup. When no programs or services could be found the agency decided to form its own post-adoption program. They created an education series for adoptive parents and teens. The goals were to:

1. Teach parents how adopted youth may experience grief, anger and a large range of emotions that can lead to negative action and
2. Help the teens explore their feelings and talk to each other to help normalize those feelings.

The agency personnel could find no teaching guide and drafted their own. The manual included ten structured sessions, to cover grief, commitment, understanding feelings and behaviors, the birth parent connection and other concepts about separation and loss and the lifelong adjustments to adoption.

To accompany that series, a "warmline" was set up. Warm rather than hot because it was only manned during the workday. (The warmline was initiated to respond quickly to questions and concerns of adoptive families. Although we would have preferred to provide prevention services, the calls came and continue to come from families under extreme stress or in crisis. The callers received empathy, as well as practical information.) The staff consisted of two social workers, who managed the warmline and facilitated the classes. Later a quarterly newsletter was added, followed by a support group for parents who were having severe struggles in the home with their children.

The first support group had a grass roots beginning. Several fathers of transracially adopted youth began meeting and bringing their children together in social settings. Several of the youth had emotional problems and behaviors that became so severe that they needed residential care. It was at this time that the parents met with the former Parenthesis Post Adoption Coordinator, Betsy Keefer. The parents expressed a need for a support group for adoptive parents of youth in substitute care. That group has met monthly since 1986. Some of the "children" are now in their mid-to late twenties.

Many of the families who came in the beginning are still attending. A profile of those families follows (see Chapter 5) and the chapter about the parents of our support group includes information about others who joined a second group that was formed four years ago. Members of that group have children ranging in age from 12 to 22. And we now have a third group that formed in 1996. Parents in the new group have children ranging in age from toddler to teen.

The current post-adoptive program, called Charting the Course, now includes four training series used to educate pre-adoptive parents, parents of pre-school children, a non-crisis oriented series for families with school-age children, and the parallel series for teens, parents and latency age children that addresses issues of struggling families.

We also train agency personnel, using our manuals, to provide post-adoptive services outside our service area.

PART ONE

THE RATIONALE FOR ADOPTIVE FAMILY SERVICES

Being adopted

*Being adopted is meaning that
  you're loved.
Being adopted means your best
  interest was at heart.
Being adopted means sometimes
  being unhappy.
Being adopted can sometimes mean
  being confused.
Being adopted sometimes means
  being happy.
Being adopted sometimes means
  being sad.*

That's what I feel about being
adopted.   Tom — 17

1

The Need for Services

As we approach the year 2000, there are many more children in need of permanency than ever before. Since the 1980s the challenge of child welfare has been to locate permanent homes for a growing number of children who have histories of abuse and neglect, and for those who suffer from congenital and genetic disabilities. Only a generation ago these same children would have been categorized as unadoptable and raised in foster care or orphan homes.

Special needs adoption recruitment efforts have been relatively successful in finding placements with dedicated, committed parents. However, the number of children needing qualified homes far exceeds current resources. The recent attention by those in government at the federal level may create placement opportunities for large numbers of waiting children. Unfortunately, the same parties who are promoting the adoptions have neglected to give any attention to the challenges that will be faced by the adoptive families or provide for services after finalization.

The need for change is evident when one looks at the trends:

1. An increase in abused, neglected, and sexually victim-

ized children moving to adoption. These children are at increased risk for ongoing psychological problems, substance abuse, criminal behaviors, and sexual promiscuity leading to adolescent parenthood.

2. The lack of healthy newborns available for adoption in the United States is leading to the rise in adoptions from other countries. In 1996, 11,340 children were adopted from abroad. Many of these children have lived all their lives in institutions and have difficulty adjusting to life in a family setting. Issues of culture and identity arise over time. Early intervention is needed for loss of language, culture shock, and adjustment to a family setting.

3. This same lack of healthy infants has caused eager potential parents to accept children with no birth history information. Many parents who are expecting to raise a healthy child find they are ill prepared for the severity of the health and emotional issues they must later accept as the reality.

4. Attorneys and small private agencies offering infant adoptions often obtain extensive birth family histories but provide little if any information to the adoptive parents. They do little or no preparation or education about adoption issues.

5. The growing problem of substance abuse is leaving many children in need of permanent families. Mothers who have abused alcohol and their bodies during the pregnancies give birth to babies who have a questionable future. Fetal alcohol syndrome affects far more children than previously thought. This syndrome impairs the ability to learn and to function as children and adults.

Clearly, the demand for post-adoptive services will rise as these thousands of children are growing and developing toward adulthood. Too often the adoptive parent enters into adoption with little or no adoption related education but high expectations that the child will soon become "just like their dream child." They are unprepared for the challenges that will face them and their commitment to the child may waver and break if appropriate services are not readily available.

The prospective adoptive parent needs extensive education prior to placement and ongoing education for each developmental stage. The parent who is realistic about expectations is a better and more committed parent.

While we mention the many issues of behavioral, developmental, and emotional difficulties that may be experienced by a child who comes to adoption, it is not meant to infer that all adopted children have extreme difficulties during adolescence. The majority of adopted children exhibit no more difficulties than children raised in birth homes.

What we wish to convey is that the older child who comes to adoption, or the child from another country who is transplanted to America, has already experienced trauma through separation, abandonment, and loss. We believe that the system should not compound the negative history with an absence of services, inadequate services, or by denying education and financial support for the families who have made such a profound commitment to these children.

We have utilized the advice and expertise of the parents in our support groups to prepare suggested specific needs and services.

There are many reasons children (and the families who adopt them) may need long-term services. We are citing a few of these reasons by looking at children with fetal alcohol effects and those in residential care.

Foster care figures

The North American Council on Adoptable Children in St. Paul, Minn., a support and advocacy group, found the numbers of children in foster care:

1990 — 404,407
1993 — 442,210
1996 — 600,000 (estimated)

Outcomes for children in foster care:

About 66% eventually return to birth relatives, 6.5% reach 18 while in placement care, 7.7% are adopted, 15.7% have "other" outcomes (run away, get married, die or are put under legal guardianship), and 3.5% have an unknown outcome.

If 7.7% of the estimated 600,000 children in foster care enter adoptive homes, over 47,000 homes will be needed for them. Many of these children have endured much and have developed psychological problems that will be long-lasting and require extensive support services from the placing agency.

Fetal alcohol syndrome and fetal alcohol effects

We interject the following statistics, as many of the families who come to us for services have children with confirmed or suspected fetal alcohol syndrome or fetal alcohol effect (FAS/FAE).[†]

4000 to 8000 babies are born yearly with FAS
55,000 babies are born yearly with FAE
66% of pregnant women drink

If the new stress on permanent homes and quicker resolutions for children results in more permanent custody cases, and the outcome numbers are doubled in the adoption columns, the need for follow-up services will explode. A

[†] Data from Federal Offices of Substance Abuse and Prevention

larger number of children who will be available for adoption
are those with serious emotional, developmental, and behavioral problems. One of those possible problems is FAS. Many
more children are coming into care from homes where there
is alcohol and drug abuse. The mothers of a large number
of the children in care used substances during pregnancy,
leading to developmental disabilities in many of the children needing placements. Families who make commitments
to children with such histories need a great deal of information, support, and services to help the children toward a
healthy future.

Needs of the children

While every child who comes to adoption is a unique
individual, common issues have emerged. Grief and loss are
the central themes of adoption. Every adoptee has lost a
birth family and the accompanying culture. The adopted
person must revisit the efforts of grief resolution throughout
life. Many youth resent the loss of control and that decisions
were made involving life altering changes that were not of
his or her making. Divided loyalties often create long-lasting
conflicts for the youth and the families.

Although it is recognized that forming attachment to
the new adoptive family may be difficult and take many
years to accomplish, it is not often recognized that the child
who was adopted in infancy or the toddler years may become
unattached at some levels once he or she has reached an understanding of the losses incurred, and may then experience
the grief and identity confusion surrounding the losses.

Regardless of the circumstances surrounding the move
from birth family to adoptive family, the child may struggle
with feelings of rejection, believing the reason for the loss to
be a flaw in his or her own makeup. Repeated assurances
of commitment by the adoptive family may not quell the
child's fears of future losses.

—

As the child grows and develops an identity, he or she may experience much confusion about who he or she is to emulate: the adoptive family or the birth family. In closed adoptions the child may create imaginary birth parents from which to follow and mold his or her personality. Counseling may be needed if the issues interfere with normal development.

Group counseling with adolescent adoptees is a particularly potent modality because it mitigates the sense of difference and alienation that they may feel and allows them to identify with others who share their experiences (Cordell *et al.*, 1995).

Issues may appear, be resolved and re-appear in many life stages. Normal developmental tasks are more complex and emotional upheavals deeper, especially in the adolescent years. Most of our earlier group members first sought care for their children before age ten, although research shows that most adoptive families begin to seek services between ages 12 and 16, (Fales, 1986). This need to seek services may come several years after finalization. Consequently, parents, and even many therapists, do not recognize the issues as related to the separation or loss of the birth family. Most of our parents wish that they had begun seeking help much earlier—by grade school at the latest.

Over half of the children from our series and support groups have needed residential treatment. There has been concern among adoption professionals for some years that 15 to 25 percent of the population in residential treatment centers are adopted, when they comprise less than five percent of the general population. Many of the children in such centers were adopted as infants. The percentages of youth from our support group who have spent some time in residential care showed a high number of infant placements. Families who seek residential care for their children are often frustrated by limited options and significant costs. To gain residential care assistance from children services they often must give temporary custody through the courts to accomplish the proper placement. The parent who does not seek out the best placement and obtain legal counsel prior to a court hearing, may find their child not placed in the best environment for his or her needs. The lack of residential treatment space and high costs are leading to more serious family crises. Managed care and other insurance plans are reluctant to cover any but the most dire emergencies. Adoption subsidies are too small and the application process too slow.

Thus, youth who are in need of protective environments and intensive treatment are being denied access to appropriate care and the parents find themselves unable to cope as conditions worsen. Early intervention and timely placement in appropriate facilities could prevent situations that are potentially catastrophic to the family and the child.

Needs of the adoptive parents

Most adoptive parents enter adoption with great anticipation that their family will be just like any other.

Potential adoptive parents come to adoption with expectations of future family life that might not be met if the child is very different from themselves in personality, temperament or values. Parents who are uninformed about the child's emotional state and potential future problem behaviors prior to placement may later react to the child in a less than nurturing manner. For example, their own infertility issues may resurface if their adopted teen daughter becomes pregnant. The acting out behaviors and emotions of their adopted children may be shocking to friends or family. The parents may feel embarrassment or guilt at not raising the "perfect" child that they expected.

When and if issues and problems do develop, parents often do not identify loss, grieving, adoption, or the child's pre-adoptive experiences as a root cause.

When parents take the child for help, they are often told their problems stem from a lack of basic parenting skills. They are subsequently sent to generic parenting classes that naively teach parents how to manage average behaviors. The parents leave the classes with useless skills that do not begin to address their child's behaviors or disciplinary needs.

Many times when parents seek the assistance of a therapist, the "treatment" does not address adoption, loss, abandonment fears, or attachment. The parents from our groups said over and over that they needed knowledgeable therapists, physicians, teachers, and school counselors. Their pastors and priests were naively quick to judge them as poor parents, as were uninformed friends, neighbors, and extended family.

Too often the behaviors of the children were mis-read as "normal" or "growing stages" when the children were suffering greatly from conditions such as depression, post traumatic stress disorder (PTSD), fetal alcohol syndrome or effect (FAS/FAE), and attention deficit disorder (ADD). Attachment issues went undiagnosed as did severe identity crises.

In some cases, children who could behave 'normally' outside the home were unruly, combative, and verbally and physically abusive in the home. The parents sometimes allowed abuse toward them to escalate to dangerous levels as the children did not exhibit these behaviors outside the home and therapists mis-read the situation. Parents who endured abuse often under-reported or downplayed the severity of the events.

The need for trained professionals

The most important task for the provision of post-adoption services is the appropriate training of the professionals who will work with the children and their adoptive parents. There are few universities who offer course work on the unique dynamics of adoption. The abused child is being studied, but not how to treat the child in a permanent adoptive placement with a family system where the abuse is no longer occurring and healing needs to be addressed.

College course work is needed by physicians, social workers, counselors, clergy, psychologists, teachers, MRDD specialists, and for all others who may work with adoptive families.

Little has been written about training for counselors wishing to work with members of the adoption triad. In fact only a few articles have appeared in professional counseling journals to focus counselor interest in this field (Janus, 1997).

School personnel are often naive about adoption issues. Teachers routinely give assignments, such as the drawing of the family tree, which may prove complicated and upsetting for the adoptee. Counselors are needed to provide inservice training to teachers to enhance understanding of adopted children (Ng & Wood, 1993).

The good news is that more and more children's service agencies are realizing that the children in their care need to be placed in permanent homes quickly, minimizing the likelihood of multiple placements. They are also more aware that the emotional, behavioral, and educational history of the child or the past environmental impact will not just disappear at placement or at finalization.

The future of adoption

The new actions of the Congress and President intending to double the number of adoptions and greatly reduce the time children are in limbo is welcomed. However, agencies must not rush to meet "quotas" and lose sight of the fact that quality placements are more important than quantity. Much care and education is required to assure successful placements.

Agencies are now asking potential parents to take on the task of rearing children who bear the scars of past abuse and neglect. These children are often unable to trust the behaviors of the adults who offer them permanency.

It is the responsibility of placing agencies to establish and maintain realistic pre-adoptive training, and to provide ongoing support and education programs or contract for such services in each community. Adoption is a life-long process and adoptive families deserve public support in light of the formidable challenges and risks they accept. Failure to provide that needed support will be expensive both in financial and human terms.

A look at families at risk

A significant four-year study by Illinois State University (Howard & Smith, 1995) focused on adoptive families at risk of dissolution. Their findings emphasize that the serious problems of many special needs adoptees "endure long after adoptive placements become legal and despite traditional therapeutic efforts to ameliorate them. For many children, these problems escalate with age."

The report stresses the need for: "better preparation of adoptive families," "a broader effort to sensitize and educate the helping community to better meet the needs of adoptive families," and "long term support to adoptive families."

The subjects of their study were 401 families "at the far end of the continuum of all adoptions in relation to their level of problems and instability." Children in over half the families exhibited serious behavior problems such as lying or manipulation, verbal aggression, defiance, violation of family norms, tantrums, physical aggression and destruction of property. Support groups were reported by many parents as the most beneficial aspect of adoption preservation services. The overall findings mirror the experiences and state the same needs our support group parents have been reporting for ten years.

The study includes the following recommendations:

1. Thorough preparation of prospective adoptive parents. They need not only the child's history but ways in which that history may manifest itself over the course of the child's development.
2. Preventive services
3. Expansion of preservation services to provide easier access to families statewide
4. Increasing the number of adoption-knowledgeable professionals statewide
5. Development of respite care
6. Assistance with finding and paying for residential treatment

A mechanism is needed to find appropriate residential care for adoptees who need it without transfer of guardianship. *Families need to be able to arrange necessary treatment and receive assistance in paying for such treatment without being charged with neglect (as opposed to the current strategy which allows the department to pay but may cause trauma to the adoptive family).*

A later report, *An Analysis of Child Behavior Problems in Adoptions in Difficulty* (Smith and Howard, 1996), identified behaviors and problems that may lead to dissolution or placement and concluded that a continuum of services is essential. They state that many special needs adoptees have serious problems which endure long after placement. For many children, these problems escalate with age and parents exhaust their emotional and sometimes financial coping resources.

Dr. Denise Goodman, in *Here Today, Gone Tomorrow* (1990) said that some families in the post legalization period suffer problems which incapacitate their ability to function as a family unit. This dysfunction may result in the child being removed from the home permanently. Undocumented reports from residential treatment facilities state that up to 50% of their residents were adopted.

Goodman found that for many families, the only way to secure services for their child was to relinquish custody and place the child in residential care. Such a move is a giant step backward for the family that is struggling to develop attachment and a strong message to the child which confirms belief that adults can't be trusted and that he or she is unwanted and unlovable.

Dr. Goodman recommends educational opportunities that include behavior management and parenting techniques that enhance attachment and the long-term impact of abuse, neglect, and sexual victimization. Working with the adoptive family requires expertise in:

- attachment
- the impact of separation
- abuse and neglect
- sexuality
- family systems, and
- the interaction of all of the above

Disruption prevention

The University of Southern Maine studied 235 continuing and disrupted adoptions in 1986. Several common factors emerged as causes of disruption:

- Inadequate preparation prior to adoption
- Mismatch of child to family
- Lack of family supports and resources
- Lack of empathy and incomplete attachments
- Family system strain and overload
- Insurmountable obstacles
- Lack of post placement services (including post legal, i.e., post adoption, services)

Barth and Berry (1988), indicated that the provision

of post-placement as well as post-legal services are crucial to the success of an adoption, especially for special needs children whose adjustment will continue to evolve long after finalization. Thus, post-legal services serve three purposes:

1. Provision of ongoing support services after legalization to avoid crises.
2. Resolution of crises in adoptive families experiencing difficulties, with the preferred outcome of maintaining the child in the home.
3. Prevention of disruption, dissolution or displacement by helping adoptive families successfully cope with crisis situations.

Typical living costs, per child

The numbers below point to the astronomical expenses of maintaining a child out of the home.[†] Preventive services, specialized education, support programs, and financial assistance to adoptive families can be provided at a small percentage of the potential residential costs that can be incurred, a saving to taxpayers in the millions annually. *The figures also indicate that relatively inexpensive preservation services are indeed a bargain.*

Foster care $10,000
Transitional living $21,000
Shelter $30,000
Group home $40,000

Nearly all of the children of our support group parents have required residential care. Some were in substitute care for three or more years. The families exhausted all avenues of assistance prior to placement. Unfortunately, the choices available to them were inadequate for their needs. All the parents in our group have questioned the lack of preventive

---

[†] From IAMFC 1995 Winter Issue, Source: Child Welfare League of America, U.S. Dept. of Health and Human Services

and ongoing services that might have helped their children and reduced the need for placement. They told us that if they'd had the respite care and the support systems that are offered to foster care givers, they may have been able to retain their children at home.

Post-Adoptive Programming

Adoptive parents may feel uncomfortable returning to the placing agency when problems arise as they, sometimes rightfully, fear an unfounded accusation of being poor parents. If placing agencies provide appropriate pre-adoptive education, stressing that post-finalization issues are normal to the adoptive family, such fears would lessen or evaporate. It is not necessary that the service providers be the placing agency, but they have an ongoing responsibility for preserving the families they created. Some agencies contract for post-adoptive services such as support groups, respite care, mentors, retreat programming, and ongoing education.

Unfortunately, adoptive family preservation has not emerged as a service goal, even though the probabilities of growing numbers of disruptions and dissolutions will become more likely because of the increasing number of special needs placements.

Studies have proven that a disproportionate percentage of adoptees are in substitute care and residential care. Some of the children who are placed in substitute care have very involved families who reluctantly permitted such care for therapeutic reasons. Sadly, other adopted youth in substitute care have been abandoned by their adoptive families. Though there has not been a legal dissolution, the child feels that he has experienced an emotional divorce. This experience adds another loss to stimulate the grief process.

The Need for Education Programs

Pre-placement parent education programs

Most of the parents who attend our support group had no pre-placement education—even those who adopted older children through county children's services agencies. Those few who did attend education programs say they were perfunctory at best. Many of the pre-placement adoption programs were combined with foster care programs, and the majority of people who attended were in training for foster care. The pre-adoptive parents felt that the education did not really address their needs. They also felt that the agencies refrained from teaching about the negative aspects of adoptive parenting. They failed to inform them of the severity of behaviors or that the children might not improve. The probability of attachment disorder was not explored, nor were the dynamics of the grief process. They were not told that the children might need years of counseling and that the parents would need special kinds of parenting skills to do the best job of raising the children successfully.

The parents who did attend education classes admitted that they were not really paying attention when caseworkers spoke of possible problematic behaviors or a need for ongoing therapy. They all believed that they would shower the child with love and that the child would soon assimilate their values and goals. They wished that the agency had insisted on continuing education and had encouraged continued contact.

Most of our support group families said that they had done little reading about adoption. They assumed that their family would be "just like a biological family" after finalization. They admitted to thinking that they would not have any issues and that after a few months of family structure and affection any difficulties they did have would melt away. Most never thought their child would even think about the birth family.

The families who attended trainings felt that the classes answered few of their questions, although at the time, they wouldn't have known what questions to ask. Though agencies who seek homes for the special needs child are reluctant to be fully revealing about the levels of difficulties that may arise, today's pre-adoptive parents welcome trainings that educate them about the issues of the special-needs child they want to be able to provide superior care for. Parents eagerly pore over book reviews and newsletters with updated information on parenting techniques looking for better ways to be pro-active with their children.

Post-legal education and training

The task now is to encourage new families to become connected with support groups and seek further education for each developmental stage. They will also need information about methods of talking to their children about birth history and how to discuss and react to their child's later needs that may include locating biological family members.

The benefit of education is that it will empower the parents to handle problems themselves, help maintain their commitment to the child, and encourage realistic expectations. It helps them understand the child's identity issues and anger. Education and support for the child helps the adoptees understand that their feelings and questions are normal, and allows them to speak freely to other adoptees and adoption specialists who can allay their fears of rejection and further abandonment. The best features of the education and support of both the children and the parents are the increase of interactive, free flowing, less emotion-filled conversation, and enhanced communication about adoption and their relationships.

Roadblocks to obtaining services.

Many families with a latency age child are reluctant to accept the fact that their child is having difficulties. When they seek out therapists, they are seldom made aware of adoption issues. If they are mentioned, parents who fear the emotions of the child towards the birth family often shy away from admitting that the child may have any of these issues at all. The therapist may attempt to treat the many symptoms, but never reach the grief, loss, identity confusion, attachment and loyalty issues of the child. By the time the parents realize that adoption (loss and grief) issues may be at the core of the child's behaviors and feelings, the behaviors may be so extreme that the parents are detaching from the child.

This reluctance to seek assistance loses valuable time. The parent often contacts a therapist without knowing the importance of connecting with an adoption specialist. Therapists who are not trained in the field of adoption often waste time in unsuccessful treatment modalities. After these attempts, the child and the parents are no longer trusting of therapists and future treatment is far more difficult and less effective.

Parents who are just beginning to recognize that there are troubling behaviors and feelings in their child have come to the support group and heard other parents speak of years of therapy, years of problematic behaviors, and the feelings of hopelessness and helplessness. They become fearful that this may be their future or think, "My child's behaviors are not as severe as what I am hearing." They stop coming to support group meetings. Later, the behaviors worsen and they return, saying, "We wish we hadn't stopped coming. Maybe we could have prevented or averted some of what's happened."

The parents of our support and education groups have come to realize that love isn't enough. They also now believe that, although commitment is essential, commitment and love together are not enough. The parent must be educated about the possible issues, feelings, and behaviors in adoption, armed with resources, and have other essential qualities that can make the adoption of a special needs child successful.

The realization that adoption is a lifelong process, and the behavioral and emotional issues affecting many of the children who are in need of adoptive homes, has caused some child welfare agencies to look at the needs of adoptive families beyond legalization.

In conclusion, our recommendations are:

- The legal requirement that placing agencies obtain extensive birth family histories and provide these to the adoptive parents
- Pre-adoptive education requirements
- Post-placement and post-finalization continuing education requirements
- College education course work specific to adoption for teachers, social workers, counselors, psychologists, and others in the mental health field
- Adequate pre-adoptive preparation for the children
- Affordable treatment for adopted children and families at risk
- Required after-care and post-adoptive programming from the placement agency or referral and financial assistance for ongoing services

These and other suggested services are outlined in Chapter 2.

2

Types of Services and Support
for the Adoptive Family

In this chapter, we will speak both to adoptive parents and to those who work with adoptive families. Although the support group families who contributed most to this book are primarily interested in getting their message to other adoptive families, we also wish to inform professionals of the services adoptive families need and have requested.

Services for Pre-Adoptive Parents

Only two of our group member families had pre-placement classes. Most had no prior knowledge of adoption issues nor any idea that their children could face developmental delays, behavioral, or emotional crises.

None of the parents who wrote their stories entered adoption expecting the traumatic experiences that occurred. Most had adopted infants at a time when psychologists were promoting the idea that the environment was all-important. Genetics, they said, only contributed to physical traits. We now know that children do not come as an empty receptacle for us as parents to fill with all we deem important in education, values, and motivation to succeed. (One theory of that era that has proven true, however, is that the IQ could be raised in an environment of appropriate stimulation.)

The main purpose of this book is to help adoptive parents by stressing the ongoing need for education, a good support system, and appropriate expectations. Although the stories are of families who endured and are enduring tremendous stresses, they are not meant to discourage adoption. They are meant to relate the importance of preparation prior to adoption and the need to continue reading, networking, and recommitting to the child when times are the most difficult.

Telling these stories is all the more important now that children previously thought to be unadoptable are entering adoptive homes. A large number of children going to adoptive homes have attention deficit disorder, may be suffering from the effects of parental alcohol use during pregnancy, and abuse or neglect in the home of origin. These children have already paid a great price and adoptive parents are accepting the duty of healing their hurts and raising them to be functional and productive adults.

Adoption can be a daunting task, if the parents have no previous parenting experience and expect the child to adjust to a new family in a matter of weeks. Others mistakenly take for granted that the child will not grieve his former family, lost siblings, or have old behavioral problems recur.

So many parents call our "warmline" to seek help because they do not understand why their child is acting out or hurting himself or others when they have tried so hard to instill proper values and behaviors. Some adoptive mothers quit their jobs to home school. Most spend hours every week trying every avenue of available services looking for the "key" to their child's behaviors.

The following are categories of information that are required in a good pre-adoptive parent education program:

—

General subjects
1. Making a life-long commitment to the child
2. Sensitive adoption terminology
3. Genetics and the environment
4. Developmental stages of the adoptive child
5. Issues of loss, grief, separation, trust
6. How to talk with the child about adoption and the birth family
7. Lifebook preparation
8. Attachment Issues
9. Specialized parenting techniques (logical consequences, etc.)
10. Realistic expectations and encouraging the child's own talents
11. Searching and loyalty issues
12. Explanation of range of services to utilize and ways to access them

Subjects specific to those adopting older children and those with identified genetic, congenital, social, emotional, behavioral and scholastic issues include information about raising the child with:
• Attention deficit disorder
• Attention deficit hyperactivity disorder
• Fetal alcohol syndrome or fetal alcohol effect
• A different cultural or racial heritage
• Sexual abuse history and resultant behaviors
• Moderate to severe developmental, behavioral, emotional or mental handicaps
• Attachment disorder

Counseling for the pre-adoptive parent(s)
Counseling prior to adoption should cover the commitment that both of the partners need to have to ensure that later struggles do not place undo stress on the marriage. Some of our members found that raising children strength-

ened their relationships. A few others had great difficulties as they had different parenting philosophies or had neglected to nurture the marital relationship.

When infertility is an issue, the degree of acceptance is rarely the same for one partner as for the other. One person may be more accepting of their inability to create a biological family while the other is grieving deeply. The couple will need to be encouraged to talk out their feelings so the counselor can help them work through their grief. It is not likely that all issues will be resolved prior to beginning the adoption process.

The loss of either birth children during pregnancy or the dreamed-of fantasy child will cause issues of grief and frustration at varying stages in the life of the couple. Unrealistic expectations should be discussed as these grief and loss issues will be revisited as the adopted children grow. Many of our group members said they truly expected that they could mold the adopted child into the form of a biological child who would have all their values, interests, and ambitions. Their disappointment at the realization that the adopted child had other dreams, interests, and values led them to grieve the loss yet again.

The adoptive parent(s) may undergo a resurgence of the infertility issues when the adopted child or children do not meet the expectations they had for a birth child. Many adoptive parents are well educated with successful careers. They tend to expect that their adopted children will hold or adopt the same views of education and career. When they see a child with normal abilities fail or do poorly in school, they tend to spend great amounts of energy attempting to instill the same study habits they had. Such frustrations and misdirection may be avoided if the therapist can work with the prospective parents to accept the child that comes to their home, help that child find his or her innate talents, and celebrate the successes.

—

If a teenage daughter or son should encounter an untimely pregnancy, the experience could be traumatic for the infertile adoptive parent who must watch the pregnancy advance, as it is an experience they shall never have. One mother revealed her resurgence of grief as she sat with her pregnant daughter for each appointment in a medical office filled with other expectant mothers. She felt great anger and sadness. All of the feelings of great loss returned as strongly as when she first learned there would be no pregnancy for her.

Using an adoption consultant

There are many avenues to adoption. The prospective parent can discuss these with a knowledgeable therapist or adoption consultant.

Selecting a method of adoption and whether to adopt an infant, older child, child of another culture or race, or a special needs child, requires much research and discussion.

The single parent can also utilize objective input about specific parenting challenges. A couple often does not share the same level of commitment or expectations. The consultant may be helpful in sharing possible scenarios and encouraging the waiting parent to avoid the development of unrealistic expectations for behaviors, interests, achievements, and looks in the adopted child.

Those who feel they can only adopt an infant should educate themselves about genetic heritage. They need to locate an agency or attorney that will provide full information about the birth family history. The couple who begins the process believing they will only adopt a healthy child with no history of negative birth parent information, may find they are offered a child whose birth mother is mentally ill, uses drugs, or abused alcohol during the pregnancy.

Prospective parents may believe there is only one avenue to adoption (e.g., a private agency). An independent adoption consultant can explain all of the possible avenues to adoption, and help them sort through all of the methods and ease their way through the application process. If no independent consultant is available, they may be able to locate an adoption support group to help in this process.

Services for the Post-Adoptive Family

Selecting a therapist for your child and your family

Most of the families who contact us for services are veterans of negotiating the maze of therapists. They list counselors, social workers, psychologists and psychiatrists whose waiting rooms are familiar to them. However, many still feel they have yet to find the right therapist for their child and their family.

Seeking a therapist is not a sign of failure in adoption. Issues of loss, grief, control, and identity may surface again and again as the children mature and process the issues in more and more complex ways. An objective, well-trained and adoption-experienced therapist may be an invaluable resource for the child's understanding and coping strategies.

A family-oriented therapist is recommended, as the adoption affects all of the family members. The therapist will need to communicate with parents about behavior management techniques, how to manage their own anger and frustrations — and may need to work with siblings who also have concerns.

Before engaging the therapist:
- Ascertain the therapist's philosophy about working with adopted children.
- Ask what treatment techniques are used.
- Ask what are their values and beliefs about adoption.
- Ask if the therapist also works with parents and siblings.
- Ask about his or her philosophy about search and reunion.
- Ask if group therapy is available for the youth? (It can be

—

very helpful.)

- Ask about the therapist's diagnostic, clinical history and expertise in:

Fetal alcohol syndrome   Childhood depression
Substance abuse   Attachment disorder
Sexual abuse   Behavior management
Adoption issues   Acting out/violence in the home
Crisis situations   Attention deficit disorder
History of abuse, neglect, and/or multiple moves

Remember that you are the consumer. The therapist must be able to recognize the family/adoptive issues and treat them appropriately. Untrained therapists can be damaging as time may be spent pursuing therapeutic methods that do not address the causes and only skim over symptoms. When a young person is having emotional difficulties, the wrong therapist can create a lack of trust and an uncooperative attitude as well as feelings of hopelessness in the child. The right therapist may have to spend precious time repairing earlier damage before being able to make positive progress.

Child and adolescent therapists and family therapists

It is rare for a family to call the warmline for assistance and say that they are not in therapy. Most have seen several therapists. When we ask if the current therapist is familiar with adoption issues, the response is usually silence, then a hesitant, "I don't know." We then discover that adoption issues have never been discussed or the therapist has said progress has been negligible and suggests the family seek help elsewhere.

Frequently, adoption issues are ignored as irrelevant or go unrecognized by the therapist and the parents until a steady crisis state exists. It is time for therapists and families alike to be aware that the adoptive family is different and has unique family issues.

—

It is vital for the family to seek a therapist who is knowledgeable about adoptive issues such as grief and loss, attachment, loyalty issues, identity and the fact that parents revisit infertility issues and may need help with claiming, entitlement, commitment, and their own expectations.

Finding the appropriate therapist can be a daunting task for the family who has adopted a child with special needs. The therapist may need to be knowledgeable in such areas as sexual abuse, incest, attention deficit disorder, fetal alcohol syndrome, childhood depression and post traumatic stress syndrome.

It is likely that one therapist may not be versed in all of the issues facing a particular family. The parents will need assistance in selecting the most pressing issues and using that information to chose the best therapist.

One precaution we would like to offer is that the family may be over-treated. Some families tell us they have support group on Monday, child therapy on Tuesday, special tutor on Wednesday, family therapy on Thursday, etc. They have no time to just be a family as all of their time is taken up dealing with their "issues." The family may also need assistance in sorting out what they really need to address at any one time. Too much attention to therapy may leave the child thinking he or she is seriously troubled and can result in the child behaving as such.

The Counseling Process for Adoptive Families

The intake phase is an important aspect of the treatment process. Intake alone (learning the therapeutic needs of the family). may involve several visits as the usual family therapist contact has, in our experience, been precipitated by a crisis event. The family may need immediate attention to a crisis and information gathering may be spotty at first.

The adoptive family situation is often a complicated one due to the many dynamics involved. If the child was

in the birth home for a time, and experienced foster placements, this will have affected his or her behaviors and value
systems differently than the child placed just after birth.
If the parents are practiced, well grounded and have raised
other children, the dynamics will be different than for those
who have not parented before. The expectations of parents
whose birth children have had relatively few difficulties will
differ from parents who have raised other adoptive or foster
children.

The therapist must find a middle ground that does
not over emphasize adoption while leaving out other facets
and at the same time must not label all behaviors as adoption related. Tunnel vision that blames adoption for every
issue is as dangerous as ignoring adoption as a cause. In
truth, it rarely is adoption (i.e., joining or living in an adoptive family) that is at the root of a problem, but rather the
separation from birth family and the need to clarify and understand that leads to many adoption-related issues.

Therapy for the adopted child

The age of the child at the time of onset of therapy
as well as the age at time of adoption and prior history will
bear directly upon his or her issues and treatment needs. Is
the adoption open or closed? Are there known siblings? Did
the child live with the birth family? How different is the
culture of origin?

The child may not understand that he or she has any
adoption issues. (The term "adoption issues" is really a
mislabel as the issues really are of loss, separation, and grief.)
The therapist must allow time to establish trust. Let the
child know that the therapist is interested in the birth origins
and in talking about whatever the child may know. It may
take parental input to sort out fantasy from reality. Have
the child describe what adoption means to him or her.

Out of fears of disloyalty to adoptive parents, children

may be reluctant to talk openly about thoughts and feelings regarding adoption or the birth family. We have found that children as young as 6 have fully developed fantasies about the birth family (even to a complete description of the house in which they live). However, in their fantasies, children are rarely able to draw in facial features for the never-before-seen birth parent.

Bring the parents into the therapeutic process by explaining loyalty issues, e.g., "Can I love more than one mom?" Encourage the family to promote a positive feeling toward the birth family, even if the child lived with them for a time in very difficult circumstances. The therapist will need to find appropriate avenues to help to explore the stages of grief, separation, and loss.

The Parent/Therapist Relationship

Prior to seeking assistance from an adoption specialist, the family may have been confronted as "bad parents" by neighbors, extended family, school personnel and other professionals who are unaware of the family dynamics. The parents may be fearful of recrimination due to these past situations. They need to be assured that a therapist will be working in partnership with them to help the child and assist the parents in creating a calmer home atmosphere. The parents will need regular contact with the therapist to glean helpful suggestions for behavior management and ways to relate to the child that will enhance the attachment on both sides. Experience has shown that it is best to involve the parents in the therapeutic process from the beginning. This involvement eliminates the concept that the adoptive child is the problem. The therapist has the responsibility to illuminate the issues as family centered.

Parent support groups for adoptive families should be considered an integral part of the therapeutic process. If there are none available, start one. Or confer with other professionals and parents to form such a group. Support and/or therapy groups for teen adoptees have also proven most beneficial.

The parental relationships

The post-adoptive parents who seek counseling for themselves and/or their child should also be asked about their opportunities for recreation and respite away from the child. Mothers tend to neglect their personal emotional needs and health. The therapist needs to assist the parents to list past and present interests that may have been reduced or set aside due to family stresses. The parents need to be encouraged to intersperse personal time and relaxation even if it must be scheduled.

Discussions of parenting styles may determine whether there are conflicts in this area and whether the parents need assistance in gaining new techniques for behavior management.

Parents' Needs in Therapy

Too often the parents frantically search for answers for their children while ignoring their own emotional needs. The parent group describes a parent as having a "fuel tank" of coping skills and emotional strength. Crises and daily struggles drain the tank and leave the frustrated and exhausted parent stuck at the side of the road. The parent needs to get the tank refilled regularly, so that there is enough gas to get past the next set of struggles and crises, not run out in the middle.

How does the parent fill the tank and what are the ingredients?

1. One of the favorites is the weekend get-away. Try a bed and breakfast in the country or a state park lodge
2. Remember the friends you used to spend time with? Get out your calendar and schedule (in advance) one fun

evening per month with old friends.

3. Make a (regular) date with your significant other, spouse or best friend

4. Meet other adoptive families and switch off respite care days.

5. Remember the evenings of candle light, bubble bath, and music? Schedule one hour each week for this activity or other favorite.

6. Did you used to have a hobby? Make time for it or a new one.

7. Go regularly to an adoptive parent support group. Attend when things are going smoothly too. You can be a support and fill others' tanks.

8. Keep therapy appointments for yourself.

9. A therapeutic massage can do wonders.

10. Trade evenings off with your husband. One evening he handles the evening routine, the next night he's off duty.

11. Take a vacation without the child(ren). There are many inexpensive summer camps and there are adoption subsidies that may help with the cost. While the child is away, plan your vacation at the same time.

12. Laughter. Laughter. Laughter. Every parent needs a generous dose to refill that tank. Think what makes you laugh and do it.

13. Insert your own tank filling ideas.

14. And most important of all: Find or create your "Haven." The dictionary describes a haven as a place of shelter and refuge and safety, a comfortable retreat where one is protected from trouble. Your haven must be a place where no one may enter without your permission. It can be a chaise on the back porch, the bathroom, a rocker in your bedroom, a den in the basement, or a swing in the back yard. Each parent must establish a haven that all family members respect and honor. Stock it and furnish it with all your comfort needs. Knowing that it is there

can be relaxing in itself. Use this space when your tank is running low. It may take only half an hour for a fill-up.

After reading this list, a beleaguered parent may sneer, saying: "Yeah! Sure! How am I going to fit that in my schedule?" Our support group members stress that, "You just do it!" Write it on your calendar, but not just as a suggestion. Put in down and think of it as just as important as getting your children to all of their activities. Remember the tank must be full in order for you to function well.

Additional Therapy Concerns

The infant in transition

None of the families in our support group are in open adoptions, but they have great hope for the benefits of open adoptions. Discussions of ways the birth mother could assist in the transition and healthy adjustment of the child have often centered on the lack of information, and the parents often wished they could have a conversation with the birth mother to help understand the child better.

The group members stress that agencies and attorneys need to obtain as much information about the birth family as possible. The child will want to know about hobbies and interests, not just hair and eye color.

The following suggestions come out of the experiences of the group members:

The birth mother — a difficult decision

The birth mother makes the decision to make an adoption plan after she becomes aware that parenting is not an option. As the pregnancy progresses and later, after she has seen the child and relinquished custody, the birth mother will grieve the loss. In the past, many birth mothers were advised to forget and move on. We know now that no women really forget, and some are unable to move on. In cases where there were no other children the grief seems the most pronounced, but those who do parent other children may still deeply grieve the child who is not with them. The professional who works with birth mothers needs to ascertain if they have a support system, and encourage them to belong to a support group, and be prepared for periods of sadness on birthdays, holidays, etc.

Easing the trauma of the newborn in transition

We now understand that infants will have trauma from the loss of the feel, smell, sounds, and heartbeat of the birth mother. To ease the transition, encourage the birth mother to sleep with a small blanket or stuffed animal in the last months of the pregnancy, with the expectation that it will go with the child to his or her adoptive family. The infant who has been surrounded by the sound, smell, and feel of the mother for the first nine months needs to have a gradual transition to the adoptive parent. We also suggest that during the pregnancy the birth mother audio tape her voice singing soothing melodies and reading from childrens' books. The newly placed infant may be soothed by hearing the tapes. Make several copies as they do wear out.

Infants who are placed shortly after birth may then have a soft item to place close to them that had often been held by the birth mother. Some placement agencies are now asking the birth mother to present something of hers that the child may keep. However, they often suggest that the birth mother buy something for the child. Perhaps a wiser suggestion would be to give an item long in the possession of the mother that she had often held, such as a small pillow or blanket.

The children in our group treasured photographs of the birth parents as children and teens. They want to know what the interests and hobbies were when the birth parents were children and adolescents. Photographs or narratives of hobbies, sports, clubs, awards, and favorite possessions or pets are of great interest. When the children attend the series, they are encouraged to bring whatever they have from their birth family or pre-adoptive history. They share the items as though they are their greatest treasures. The others each show great appreciation and express how fortunate the owners are to have such photos or possessions.

Easing the transition for the older baby or toddler

The baby who has been in the care of a foster parent will need gradual introduction to the adoptive situation. Have the adoptive parents visit the child, increase time alone and begin to take over the role of caretaker gradually. Introduce the young child slowly to the new home and surroundings. On the day of placement, the foster parents should take the child to his or her new adoptive home. Foster parents must have an opportunity to say good-by. Encourage visits with the foster family after the move. The young child will feel less confusion and feelings of abandonment. The current system of moving young children with few or no visits causes great trauma that is only now being recognized by those in adoption work. The child must be allowed to grieve the loss of the foster family.

Take some of the suggestions from the infant transition. The foster mom can make a tape, hand down a blanket or stuffed animal. A letter would also be meaningful. Photos of the foster family and their home should be added to the lifebook.

Post-Adoptive Group Services

The adoptive parent support group

We include a description of how to form a support group with the hope that adoptive parents will come together where no services exist. Starting small is fine. Large groups may be helpful if speakers and an emphasis on education is the focus. But if the focus is open forum discussion, smaller is better.

There are many formats to choose from in selecting a support group. Support groups usually serve a particular phase in the stages of adoption. Some of the themes are:

- Groups for adults who are considering adoption and/or wish assistance in dealing with infertility issues
- Groups for adults who are seeking assistance to adopt in other countries
- Groups of parents with young children who want to address such subjects as how to talk to the child about adoption, creating lifebooks, sensitizing extended family and providing a social group experience for the children.
- Grass roots parent groups who meet socially and invite in speakers and present book reviews
- Groups involving parents and a therapist who meet to address issues that have arisen and to share ideas and parenting techniques.

> The service that is most praised for its effectiveness is the open discussion/education parent support group.

Forming an Adoptive Parent Support Group

Support groups may be formed when an agency assigns employees to create a formal entity, a therapist gathers several families who share like issues, or a few families meet around the dining room table and begin informal meetings. All of these methods serve the purpose of providing support.

Although we encourage adoption agencies to provide an array of post-adoption services, it may prove uncomfortable for parents to discuss their issues in the presence of a caseworker who may report the discussions to the family's own worker. Confidentiality and the fear of being labeled poor parents are two of the reasons that agencies should use contracted therapists and adoptive parents to facilitate groups. The therapist is a help when issues arise that need professional input. The members should, however, hold "ownership" of the group.

Agencies may be utilized to locate and inform potential members of the group. They may provide materials, the use of copy machines, inclusion in a newsletter, and help find volunteers to facilitate the groups. Support groups are the least costly and most effective aid to adoptive families and well worth the effort to create and maintain. The sponsorship of an agency or several agencies can keep a young group from faltering and help rejuvenate groups that begin to lose members as the children grow up.

Group formers will need to decide on the focus for their group. Examples include:

1. Open forum; no agenda or speakers. The parents gather to discuss issues and provide mutual support.
2. The formal meeting. Speakers are invited. Committees are formed. An agenda is planned and sent to each member.
3. A political group. The focus is to change laws and advocate for new policies
4. A group for new parents, parents of toddlers, parents of teens, parents and children
5. A group for transracial families, single parents, children with disabilities, etc.
6. A social group that meets to give the children opportunities to interact.

The group may be limited to a few friends or invite adoptive families from the community at large.

A successful group is one that provides education, shares information, identifies needs and adjusts the focus to meet these needs. The most important task is ensuring an influx of new members. Adoption agencies are the most valuable resource for referral of families. If the group becomes too large, a second can be formed.

If the families are willing, college students and social

work interns as well as professionals in training can gain tremendous insights about the needs and challenges of the adoptive family by attending several sessions.

Organizational suggestions:
1. Obtain a P.O. box or mailing address and telephone message line. Use the line to give details of meeting dates, times, and locations.
2. Create a membership list for mailings.
3. Begin a newsletter.
4. If dues or a membership fee is charged, careful record keeping will have to be established. The organization may need a bank account and a money management system.
5. Place regular notices in local and specialty papers. Notify pediatricians, family doctors, therapists, churches, schools etc.
6. Assign liaison persons to maintain contact with adoption agencies.
7. Create materials for hand outs that may be used by agencies.
8. Find a comfortable and convenient location with well lighted parking. Post signs to direct newcomers.
9. Assign book reviews, workshop attendance, and subscribe to adoption periodicals.
10. Design a mission statement to use as a guide.
11. Include an educational component as open discussion will not sufficiently hold a group together over time.

Support group for children (ages 6–11)
Children's interpretations of adoption change as they mature. The loving story of the "chosen" child sustains them and makes them feel special and even superior in the years before kindergarten. However, as the child enters the wider world and perceives society's view may be less positive and realizes he had to lose one family to gain his present family,

questions, fears, and confusion may arise. We find that a short education series followed by an ongoing support group can be beneficial.

When children can interact with other adoptees and talk openly about their concerns, the family dynamics are more healthy. Budding issues may be confronted and fears allayed. Questions may be answered in a manner that is pro-active rather than reactive. Children in such groups love to share lifebooks and birth family information, an activity their non-adopted friends would not understand. Addressing emotional and developmental tasks at this age can aid in decreasing problems in the more discordant teen years.

During this developmental stage, the normal grief response initiates. In most cases, unless the parent is aware of grief and how it may manifest itself in the adopted child, the behaviors go unrecognized. A child may feel anger or sadness but be unable to interpret the cause or articulate his or her feelings. Children need to be able to express their feelings and understand that sadness and anger over the loss is normal. We found that children are more open in group settings as they often may hesitate to speak of their feelings to parents to spare hurt feelings. At this age some children have unspoken fears that the birth parent may try to reclaim them. They don't fully understand the legal permanence of adoption. Many are concerned that their adoptive family may not be any more permanent than their foster placements.

It is also at this time that the child may experience the loss of a pet or move to a new neighborhood or see a friend move away. They can receive validation that such losses hurt other adoptees too. Sleep-overs, going away to stay with relatives, or going to camp may be a traumatic experience if the child fears abandonment, but such a group can pre-address the events and allay the trepidation.

A group of this type can be organized by an agency or

therapist to give structure and utilize the talents of adoption professionals who can manage the more emotional discussions and be able to identify children who need more in-depth attention. Parents may form social groups for the children to encourage interaction and discussion.

A children's group works best if composed of three parts fun to one part adoption related activities. Games, drawing, reading adoption related children's books, and sampling foods and activities from other cultures can make the groups enjoyable and non-threatening for the children.

The time-limited education series for parents and youth

Generally education series are limited to six to ten weeks. Each session focuses on a specific topic such as: how to talk with your child about adoption, coping with grief and loss, child development, search, anger, and parenting techniques for each stage.

Groups for parents and youth are held concurrently in different rooms. An early model for parents and teens was developed by Parenthesis Post-Adoption Program in Columbus, Ohio in 1986. That early series was updated to include the latency age children in 1996. (See reference listing for Charting the Course, A Therapeutic Manual for Post-Adoptive Families.) There are now education series for pre-adoptive families, parents with pre-school age children, and parallel series for parents and children ages six to ten.

The youth who attend our series learn that their emotions and thoughts are not unusual as the other group members validate their feelings about birth family and identity. The adoptive parent gains valuable information about the special challenges of adoptive parenting and benefits from the experiences and successes of the others. Guilt regarding parenting difficulties is alleviated through sharing with other parents. Parent participants are then invited to join an ongoing support group at the end of the series. Acquaintenships begun in these structured settings often change to long-lasting friendships among the families. They then proceed form a network that includes child visits, exchanged respite and on-going support for one another.

Although therapy is not the primary focus in the education series, it often occurs. Due to the sensitive and even crisis states of many of the families with adolescents when entering services, it is urged that one of the "leaders" for each group be a professional counselor or psychologist. Many youth have expressed suicidal ideation or experience extreme emotional upheaval as their feelings emerge and it is important that professional therapists be available to interact with families who experience heightened emotional times during the series.

Additional Post-Adoptive Services

The buddy or mentor families

Many times the above support groups and education groups naturally spawn matches of veteran parents with those needing a helping hand. Such buddy families may also be recruited from the ranks of "graduating" support group families, (parents whose children have reached adulthood). When the post-adoption specialists have an opportunity to select from a corps of volunteer parents, they look for parents who have stayed committed to the youth through the tough times and successfully negotiated through the maze of problem behaviors and available family services. Veteran parents can offer an effective parenting model, a shoulder in times of crisis and hope to the troubled family. Such links between mentor families and newly formed families can be both an inexpensive and successful resource for adoption agencies and children service agencies.

The "warmline"

Along with the support group and educational series that were offered by Parenthesis beginning in 1987 was the warmline. It was not called a hotline as it was only meant to be operated during office hours. However, the staff shared the responsibility and often monitored the line in the evenings as they rolled over the calls to home phones for the times the offices were closed.

This service is successful in slowing the process of degeneration and offering hope. It is often used by families who are in crisis or reaching a stress level that is unbearable. Each call is answered by a professional adoption specialist, not an answering machine or a receptionist. Ideally a warmline should be answered by another adoptive parent or post-adoption specialist. When a family calls they should be confident that someone knowledgeable about their issues will be answering the phone.

The warmline callers often mention or ask about one of several issues:

"I can't take it any more, where can I send this child?"

"We have been to several therapists and no one seems to understand or be able to help. What can we do?" "My child is violent to me, what can I do?"

"My child refuses to let me parent, we fight all the time."

"I did not realize it would be this hard. I thought if I just loved her enough · · · "

"My child has run away. He says we are not his real parents."

The first requirement in answering a warmline call is to display a non-blaming attitude. Parents have been told too often that they are at fault and are fearful of making the call as they believe they will once again be labeled as bad parents.

The specialist reviews the issues or presenting problem and offers information and assistance. We then inform them that such behaviors are not unusual in the families that call us. The parents are then invited to attend the support group, the education series, referred to other resources that can help, and invited to call whenever there is a need.

The warmline ranks as our third most valuable service, following the support group and the education series. One of our parents said, "Some mornings after an hour of chaos, I'd be dialing the number as my daughter climbed on the school bus."

Crisis counseling

It is not unusual for the adoptive family to experience several periods of crisis as the child grows and matures. The adoptive parent often has expectations that once the adjustment to the new placement is complete, there will be smooth sailing. However, the child may experience events that precipitate crises. The birthdays of siblings from whom he or she is separated may trigger upheavals. Mothers day, holidays, the anniversary of the day he or she was removed from the birth home are also triggers. Adopted children do not take moves well. Each move is a loss of friends and familiar places and as well as a reminder of earlier losses. The last year of high school and first year away from the family can also be traumatic.

When families are faced by a crisis, they can react in one of several ways. They may ignore it and hope it will be resolved without action. They may overreact and intensify the situation. Or they may seek help, but seek assistance in venues that cannot achieve the needed goals.

The families who have been educated prior to crises about when and where to find assistance will be better able to successfully manage crises when they occur. Specialized post-adoption counselors and support groups may provide the needed resources. Such counseling can help the family to normalize the situation, reframe it into understandable proportions, and lead the family toward appropriate steps for resolution. The same sources can assist the family in prevention techniques to avoid future occurrences.

Referral and information services

By the time most families call us, they have already sought out assistance from a variety of professionals and are skeptical about further referrals. Therefore it is the responsibility of the adoption specialist to become well acquainted with any provider before including them in the referral bank.

The adoption specialist can act as a referral clearing house for such information and services as:

- Available support groups
- Mental health professionals sensitive to adoption
- Subsidy and funding sources
- State and local self-help organizations
- Names of volunteer "buddy" families
- Dates and places for parent education programs and series
- Adoption books for parents and children; newsletters
- Available respite care and mentoring programs
- Summer camps and retreats for adoptive families

Respite care

Several years ago, foster parents set up a system whereby they could take a break from the parenting stresses and their foster children could spend time away in the safety of another experienced foster home. This system of respite has worked very well for foster parents who work with children who have troubled histories. Some of these same children have been placed in adoptive homes where their families have had no opportunity for such a break and are drained from the need for constant vigilance.

Adoption respite was intended for families with special needs children who need more skilled care than can be provided by a baby sitter, friend, or relative.

We initiated adoptive family respite several years ago

and it has been very successful. Foster care agencies ask for volunteers among their parents and allow our personnel to provide training in respite for the adoptive family. We then match the families to need and appropriate provider.

Respite is usually offered as an emergency assistance for up to 14 days or as a pre-planned weekend each month. The youth always goes to the same respite provider and the two families develop a trusting and open relationship over time.

The adoptive parent might be reluctant to initiate respite for several reasons:

- They feel guilty, as though they are abandoning their responsibility to their child
- They fear respite parents will do a better job
- They fear the child will feel abandoned or rejected

It is true that children seem to behave well in respite. The children tend to adjust well and enjoy the experience if the adoptive parents have presented the experience as a break rather than a punishment. The respite time gives all family members time to cool down. It provides an opportunity to assess the crisis situation calmly, as well as provide models and mentors for both the young person and the adoptive parents.

We suggest that parents who are feeling stressed arrange for periodic respite before crisis situations arise. Establishing the respite relationship during calm times will be much easier than first attempting to do so during a crisis, when respite might feel more like rejection.

Respite care should not stand alone as an intervention, but be accompanied by therapeutic and/or group services.

The adoptive family may chose several ways to attain respite:

- Arrange formal respite through an agency
- Trade services with another adoptive family
- Pre-arrange periodic visits with family or friends

—

Formal care agreements usually involve a set daily fee. Such services may be covered by adoption subsidy funds through childrens services agencies.

If the child goes to respite during crisis, a family conference should be arranged with an objective third party to determine goals to meet prior to reunification.

Respite care has proven to be an important service for families who are struggling to maintain their commitment and avert the need for residential care or longer terms out of the home.

Residential care

Residential care should only be utilized when all other forms of assistance are insufficient to serve the needs of the adoptive family. Residential care may be provided by foster care homes, hospitals, group homes or residential treatment centers. When an adolescent is placed in residential care, it has usually involved the intervention of the courts and a children's service agency.

Placement in such a setting seldom occurs unless the youth has been shown to be a danger to self or others. In some instances the need for intensive psychiatric care or drug/alcohol recovery services will necessitate placement. Placement out of the home for a child, especially one who was adopted as an older child, may be traumatic due to earlier losses and separations or fears of rejection/abandonment.

The parents should play an active role in selecting the appropriate placement. Parents who have researched the issues and the available providers can serve as advocates for their child to attain the best placement. Contact each facility and speak to the counselors, tour the facility, research the programming and services as well as available therapy and family input. Ask about the program's philosophy, recreation, educational services, medical services and policy for family and home visits.

—

At the time of placement, the family is often in turmoil and the parents and child may have great difficulty maintaining relationships. It is important that the family stay involved with the youth and the program. The child is quite vulnerable at the point of placement to feelings of having again lost the home and family. (One mother sent a card each week as a reminder of their love and commitment.) Residential care facilities and therapists who work daily with these youth must take an active role in encouraging visitation and involvement of the family.

Crisis presents opportunity. When family and youth behaviors reach crises, it also presents an opportunity to reframe the situation, heal the family system, and instill more successful coping skills. The youth may require long term residential care, but the family can be encouraged to maintain its bonds. One of the most important lessons that veteran parents tell newcomers is that adoption is a life-long commitment. The family should be reminded that a youth has about a fifty-year relationship with his parents. It is quite likely that there were many good times in the years before the crises and problematic behaviors and there will be many such years after the crises are long forgotten. A child/youth/adult never really reaches a time in life when there is no need for family.

Many of our support group members have experienced of out-of-home placement. Most of those who stood by their children and maintained the connection found that the family could eventually heal and re-attach. Many families are healthy again in the adult years of their child.

Parents

I know not where they are. Why they are or why they left me.
Agencies take good care, but I am lonely by myself!
Not knowing where or why.
What did they do? Why did they do it?
It is a mystery. Why did they go?
          AND LEAVE ME?!!
A first it was confusing getting passed around.
From family to family, from town to town.
I don't know why I'm put with two boys plus one little girl.
And a kitty cat, and a garage.
Why the first two rejected me to get a couple more.
Why did they leave me and shove me out the door?
Was it for my own good, or was it just me?
They set me on the doorstep of that big agency.
They gave me a new family with a lot of kids.
The family called me John.
And said they loved me.
          Then passed me on again.
Not long ago I got pictures of that big family.
And saw all of the writings that say "We love you John".
And yet I still wonder why they passed me on?

                                        Brian, age 14

PART TWO

SUPPORT GROUPS
AND
EDUCATIONAL GROUPS

I'll Hold My Own

I have people constantly looking
*   over my shoulder.*
I have teachers who never let me be.
I have parents who sometimes yell at
*   me.*
I have birth parents whom I never
*   see.*
I have peers who tell me drinking,
*   sex, and getting high*
*   are my kind of fun.*
I can't please everyone.
So I search to find what is right for
*   me.*
Yet in spite of this personal tug of
*   war,*
I hold my own.

3

Our Long-Term Parent Support Group

This chapter provides a general overview of the families who attended our support groups over the years. It also includes topics discussed in group meetings and offers guidance gained from experiences as adoptive families.

Describing Our Support Group

This composite of discussions comes out of the years that have been devoted to aiding that portion of the adoptive population that has struggled with children who have had an especially difficult time in their adolescent years. It tells, through the voices of the parents, of the unexpected twists and turns, tragedies and achievements. In sharing their thoughts and ideas, the support group parents hope to help other adoptive families as well as the professionals who work with them. Their words offer insights as to the needs of some specially challenged adoptive families. It points out the priceless benefits of support groups in preserving adoptive families and helping to achieve optimal family health.

We have discovered that the topics of discussion change with each developmental stage of the child. Early

examples of discussion topics include:
- How to tell the child about adoption, and how to approach ambivalent extended family
- Attention deficit, attachment issues, and temper tantrums
- "Why weren't we told that parenting our child would be this difficult?"

As the child matures the parents move on to:
- How to find a knowledgeable counselor and other services
- Dealing with the sexually active 13-year-old
- Defiance "My child won't follow house rules anymore"
- Running away
- Struggling with the decision to seek out-of-home placement

Then the final phase includes:
- Poor academic work in high school – truancy
- Teen pregnancy
- "How can we let him drive when he is so irresponsible?"
- Involvement with the juvenile justice system.
- The older teen's inability to manage the breaking-away process of emancipation and independent living

The group has taught those of us who work in post-adoption that families who are having severe difficulties are more likely to stay committed when they have a strong support system. Parents who understand the behaviors, the anger and grief, and the search for identity, are more likely to "wait out" the tough times. Even children who have extreme diagnoses seem to function better after the teen years have passed if the parents were able to maintain a steady state.

Adoptive parents seem, from the make-up of our groups, to consist of adults in strong, committed relationships. Divorce is rare in adoptive families, 11% as compared to nearly half of the general population. (Search Inst. Report 1993)

The couples usually attend together and tend to agree on parenting style and discipline methods. Dad is very involved. They do not always feel the same commitment or emotion at the same time. When one is angry and ready to give up, the other is wanting to try "one more" method, or counselor, or tutor, or medication. In other words, when one parent is spent, the other carries the load. It has been said that the grieving or angry adopted child will direct his emotion more toward the adoptive mother. This has certainly been true in our group members' homes. The father who is sensitized to this tendency can be the mediator, disciplinarian, and teacher to the child at times when the mother/child relationship is under strain. The couples support each other in sessions and at home. They learn to present a united front at home to the children.

The parents in the group are taught to take breaks together and be a couple again. There is one bed and breakfast several miles north of our town that gets a sizable weekend business from our groups' couples.

But our group has single parents too. Some of them have well-designed support systems, regular respite care, and an opposite gender role model for the children. Others lack a sufficient support system but have been able to turn to other singles and couples when they need to compose a new plan of action, or need time to rethink a problem or find a sitter for a business trip. They watch each others' children for short periods of respite. Single gay parents also have a struggle in forming and maintaining an adequate support system. Those who have partners and are in long-term committed relationships, however, have been able to achieve a shared parenting and successful support system.

The parents have read most parenting and adoption books. Most have taken parenting classes, been to many counselors and psychologists, and sought assistance for academic issues and problems. Many parents are professionals.

Some are teachers and social workers. Many of them adopted infants, believing that they could mold the child in the direction he would then go. Few had any pre-adoptive education courses. Most reached us after traveling through a maze of agencies, doctors, and other helping professionals who tried to help but were not versed in adoption issues.

Nearly all had been told by professionals that their children's problems stemmed from bad parenting. They came to us expecting to be blamed for their child's behaviors. Many told us in their first call that they were ready to give up and wanted to know how to end the adoption. They had tried everything and had no energy left and no longer felt a commitment to their child. We found that the education series helped recommit the parent to the child. *The child may not have improved his behaviors appreciably after the series, but the parents understood the feelings and actions that caused the behaviors and were better able to react in positive ways.*

The subsequent support group allowed the parents to vent their frustrations in a non-judgmental atmosphere. They came back month after month and year after year. Many now come to help others. Their children are grown and they still come to listen and offer advice to the new families. The group members often talk now of their sandwich positions. Many of the parents are still assisting their struggling young adult adopted children and also caring for aging and ill parents. Four of our parents lost mothers in one year.

Our group's adoptive parents tend to be older and try to parent using logical consequences. They introduce their children to many activities in order to nurture any talents the child possesses. The adoptive parents want to be like any other biological family. Most were told they could be when they adopted. Our staff teach them that the adoptive family is different and that they must let go of the expectations they had and raise the child they have. It is hard for them to let go of their fantasy child, the one they hoped would have musical talent or sports ability, or be an A$^+$ student. Most parents had been taught that environment is everything, and daily doses of love and affection could heal all wounds. We teach them that they must accept the genetic history of their child, and the fact that the children will grieve for parents they have never seen even though you are near and offering love. Parents struggle to understand that they must be open and accepting of the birth family, even one that caused the hurts that survive many years later. We teach adoptive parents that to belittle the birth family, belittles their child.

It is not easy for the adoptive family who dreamed of going camping, to ball games, scouting or top academic achievement, to accept and nurture interests and talents they have not previously valued. It is not easy for two parents with master's degrees to accept that their child has no interest in education, and even throws away his homework on the way to school after they have spent four hours the night before coaching their reluctant and angry youth.

But those who come to group and keep educating themselves during all the developmental stages of their child's life, find they can get through the difficult years. They will have a young adult that comes back years later to say "thanks for hanging in there with me all that time I was messing up." The families we work with are those with the most severe problems. They all wish they had known more, had been given better support and resources for their children.

For the majority of members, their children's path to maturity has been very difficult. However, most say that they deeply love their now-adult children and remain committed to them. Some still struggling with adult adoptees who have been unable to make the adjustment to adulthood take solace in the knowledge that their young person is still in a better place than he or she would have been without the long-standing efforts of a committed adoptive home.

Our parents know they made the right decision to keep the adoption in place, even though most of the children had to spend some months or even years in substitute care. Those parents who have experienced the loss of their own parents have realized that a "child" still needs parents long after they reach 18. It would have been easier for many of the families to send the child away during the years of acting out, and say they made a mistake, that adoption didn't work for them. But with the help of education and support from others, most families maintained the fragile and fractured relationships until the child could mature, and realize that he did need his family. The lesson they teach is that once a commitment is made to a child, it cannot be broken by the parent. There have been exceptions where dissolution became necessary when a child was unable to adjust to living in a family after years of pre-adoptive institutional care or when a child became so dangerous that the safety of other family members was compromised and resolution was not possible.

When an adopted child is struggling with identity issues, control, trust, and their feelings about birth family, they also must deal with the fact that they are supposed to be slowly moving away from a family as they mature. Some are unable feel attached to the family, are uncertain about education, and/or enter into poor peer relationships. An adopted youth may consider that adoption ends at age 18, may fear going away to college though he tells the parent he can't wait to get out of the house. Therefore, it is the job of the parent to maintain the commitment the child is unable to make, until the child reaches a maturity level sufficient to have worked out his issues and be ready to "rejoin" the family.

Those parents who have been with us long enough for the children to reach adulthood have had the widest range

—

of experiences. The question is often asked at workshop trainings, "What happens to the children later?" Well, most of them do fine. It does seem to take a while longer for independence and maturity. Some are in college, some are married and parenting children. Some are still at home, working at fast food restaurants. Some have had babies as teens. They are pretty much like youth raised in other settings.

What to Consider Prior to Adoption

Only two sets of the parents in the support group had any pre-placement education. Few others read about adoption prior to or in the early years after adoption. Those who adopted older children found little or nothing in the library to help them understand what to expect or how to parent. Adoption agencies and new parents were still operating under the old belief system of "take the child home and raise it as your own."

Group discussions often centered around the parents' frustrations that they were inadequately prepared for adoption and that they see too few changes in today's pre-adoptive preparation. We have therefore included their thoughts and suggestions for those preparing to adopt.

"What I wish I had known"
For instance:

"I wish I had known how important searching was going to be."

"I wish I had understood that a child may grieve for someone he or she has never met."

"I wish I had understood how a child feels about being given up by a birth parent."

"I wish I had known that there were adoption issues"

"I wish I had known how powerful genetics are. — We were told that the baby came to us as an empty slate on

—

which we would write his future."

In preparing to adopt, they suggest extensive reading, talking to families who have adopted, attending a post-adoptive support group to learn of possible issues and challenges, education classes, and consulting a counselor to work through issues and learn of their adoptive choices.

Reported reasons for adoption

Most decisions to adopt come about after much pain and acceptance of loss, but not all. Reasons include infertility, altruism, health issues that make a pregnancy unwise, or desire for a larger family.

When we look at the persons in our support group, we find many reasons that they chose to build their families through adoption. The most frequent reason was infertility. Some families had birth children before and some after. A few were aware of the need for homes of children from depressed countries, children of other races, and older children who were categorized as special needs. Few had any prior experience with adoption or even knew anyone who was adopted.

Some of the parents who attend group raised birth children and decided they would like to raise a second family. Some of them chose to adopt sibling groups. These veteran parents were successful with their birth children and although they knew they were taking children who had difficult histories, they did not expect the depth of the challenges they are encountered. However, their past successes bolstered their belief that they are good at parenting and their prior experiences made them excellent choices for the older special needs children.

Relationship of the couple and readiness for adoption

Typically one partner is more enthusiastic about building a family through adoption than the other. If the couple should adopt and the child has many difficulties, this gap can create relationship problems The reluctant partner may blame the other for the situation. Unresolved reservations about adoption may also lead the reluctant partner to detach from the child when problems occur which can lead the other parent to cling to the child and move away from the marital relationship.

A reluctant, uncommitted parent may also resent the time the partner invests in the child. Although, as a rule, adoptive parents have a smaller percentage of divorce, the stresses and strains may be inordinate when the child has recalcitrant behaviors.

All of the parents who joined the group as married couples are still enjoying healthy, enduring relationships. They say they endured because they made sure to nurture the relationship and to agree on parenting styles and work as a team.

Pre-adoptive counseling can help with decision making

An objective counselor can help potential adopters learn about the options open to them. They can learn of the types of agencies available to them. They can explore domestic versus international adoption. The couple (or single parent) can learn about the issues involved in adopting an older child a child of another race or culture. They can look at their relationship, readiness and the expectations they hold for an adoptive family. The counselor should have an extensive knowledge of post adoptive issues.

The single adoptive parent

The single parents in our groups experienced high stress levels and had a more frequent need for respite care. It was also more difficult for them to attend group as we could not provide child care. They seemed to need more encouragement and reassurance that they were providing well for the child's needs.

The single person who is considering adoption needs

an assured support system, and friends and family who can provide regular respite care. Many of the single parents we have served adopted older, special needs children. They are often selected to adopt children who have early histories of abuse which lead the child's caseworker to believe that the child would adjust better with a single parent.

While the child's history and psychological profile may be carefully considered, the single parent's ability to manage acting-out behaviors and difficult adjustments are often overlooked. It is crucial for the placing agency to assure that support systems and ongoing care is in place for the family to succeed.

When there is only one parent in the household, he or she may find that it is a challenge to arrange summer schedules, take time off from work for the child's appointments, after school activities, and meetings with school personnel.

Transcultural adoption

Most of our parents were sensitive to the cultural needs of their children, however many feel they were not aware of the degree of "differentness" that all adopted children feel. They found that children had less issues with racial differentness than with adoptive differentness.

They feel it is important to observe holidays and customs of all the family members, not just the adopted child. Failure to observe the ethnic and cultural customs of other family members can actually add to the child's feelings of differentness.

Caucasion parents who adopt a child of a different race or culture, are no longer a Caucasion family, they are a multicultural family. Potential parents should discuss how they would feel if their teen dates or marries a non-Caucasion. It is possible that your grandchildren will be a different culture and race and parents need to work through their feelings about the possibility before adopting a child of another race.

—

One mother of a three year old Asian boy said she lived in a Caucasion neighborhood. She wanted to know what she should do about finding an Asian wife for her son. We explained that she should be arranging for the child to interact more with other children of his culture. We also explained that he will select his own life partner, and his choice may not be someone from the country of his birth.

Adoptive families are different

All of the parents were perplexed, confused, and exasperated by extreme behaviors not exhibited by children of friends or family. Each remembers finally seeking professional assistance. The (first, second and sometimes third), psychologist or counselor did not mention adoption issues. Few professionals or parents seem to know about the specialized counseling needs of adopted children, even today. Most families who sought counseling said the subject of adoption was never brought up.

Most members feel that prospective adoptive parents are woefully unprepared and uneducated about caring for a special needs adopted child. Most counselors and social workers have limited education or understanding about adoption issues or the cares and concerns of children that must grow up without their primary families. The children who are adopted after removal from birth families are not adequately prepared for adjustment in an adoptive home. Sadly, adoptive parents are blamed by almost everyone when the children have behavioral problems. Most adoption agencies abandon the families at finalization as though the adoption were over, not just beginning.

It is important for the reader to understand that families grappling with the behaviors and emotions of troubled adoptees need to know they are not alone. Families can and should receive assistance when and if the child has emotional, social, educational or behavioral problems that are beyond any normal family's ability to manage.

Advice from the group in times of struggle

Group members suggest taking time to reflect on the reasons for choosing to adopt. Remember all of the experiences of parenting your young child that would have been denied to you if you had not adopted. Remember that you are really the only forever family the child has. Maybe the tiny loving child you brought home has become troubled in the adolescent years due to issues of loss and grief. The child will mature and will become an adult who understands that you hung on in the tough times.

There will be good times again. There will be peaceful family gatherings again. There will be grandchildren. There can be a return of your dreams.

Discussed Issues and Behaviors

Five issues are highlighted in this segment as they were often the cause of discussion in our group sessions. Those issues include:
• Birth family history
• Talking to the child/ teen about adoption
• Search or reunion issues
• Separated siblings
• Residential Care and respite care

Birth family history

Most adopting parents are not cognizant of the degree of importance that birth family information will hold for their child. After waiting for that long uncertain period to finally have a child, it is often not among the top priorities to glean masses of information about the birth family. However, we have learned that is indeed the time to gather all you can as the trail may quickly grow cold. This task is especially important where information may also be the most elusive: the out-of-country adoption. These beautiful children brought to live in loving American homes have lost so much that parents must relentlessly pursue birth family information at the time they are processing the adoption. In some countries, relinquished children must be considered abandoned in order to be sheltered and eligible for adoption. The agency personnel can provide details that can assist the youth in searching years later. Many young adoptees express feelings of hopelessness when talking of a search. However, though they may not find the birth parents, they may learn of the community where they were born and the culture and customs of the people.

American children want to know many things about their birth family. The birth mother is, of course, of primary interest. They want to know more, however than her hair color and age at the time of the birth. They want to know what her interests were. Did she have activities where she excelled? Did she or the birth father have a favorite pet, hobby, sport, school subject, etc.?

Adopted youth who have possessions that have been passed on from the birth mother feel fortunate and hold them as their most precious possessions. The same is the case for letters written and held for the child. We have urged local adoption agencies to ask birth mothers who are making an adoption plan to do the following.

1. Look through their possessions and find an item or two that can be given to the child. The items should not be new. We suggest old stuffed animals.
2. Locate a few photographs of the birth mother, pets, favorite activities, favorite places, childhood pictures of her and siblings. Photos from the birth father are also appreciated. If this is a closed adoption, photos can be chosen that will not compromise this privacy of the birth family.
3. We now know that even newborns can be traumatized by the loss of the familiar voice, sounds, and other environmental markers when transferred to the adoptive parents.

—

We suggest that the birth mother audiotape her voice singing children's songs, reading from children's books, or reciting poetry for children. These soothing sounds may serve to quiet and relax the infant. It will also become a precious possession as the child grows. So make several copies, as they do wear out. (The tape recorder can be supplied by the agency.)

4. Ask the birth mother to obtain (or the agency can provide for her) a small blanket. Ask her to hold it and sleep with it, allowing the item to absorb her scent. Place this blanket around or next to the infant as a comfort.

5. Ask the birth mother to write about herself and her family, and the birth father. The adopted child wants to know what the birth mother was like as a child. Was she shy, or a tomboy? Describe any pets. Talk about favorite places and school subjects. This should be a positive piece, not sad or talking about why she could not parent. The idea is a fun biography. Ask for one from the birth father also or ask the birth mother for her memories of his interests.

There are other ideas for making the transition of the infant or child less traumatic. Post-adoption support groups are a good resource for agencies and attorneys who offer adoption services. Children who have these possessions also seem to have a better sense of self worth and fewer identity issues in adolescence.

Families who have little obtained information

We advise parents to return to the agency or attorney and request all non-identifying information. The child will be grateful for the efforts made on their behalf. It is important to make this effort whether the child is five or fifteen.

Talking to your child about birth history

Children do not have to be told every piece of information as written in a business-like report, but may be given more complex information as they mature. The first of two guidelines we offer is; tell the child he or she is adopted in their toddler years. They accept it well. They will not understand the concept, but do become familiar with the terms. The second guideline is tell them everything, over time, before age twelve. Youth may not process negative information about the birth family well in the teen years. This is, after all, the time they are determining their identities.

Searching for birth family information

Most of the parents in our group assumed early on that they should do as advised by the agencies and "take the child home and raise it as your own." They never imagined that the child would have a later interest in the birth family and barely listened to the limited information offered by the adoption agency. Years later, the children began to ask questions the parents could not answer. The children resented the lack of information, assumed the parents knew and were hiding negative information, and pressed to know more. The parents often felt threatened by the discussions and questions. Did this quest mean that the child would return to the birth family some day and the adoptive parents would face the loss of their child? One of our families who wrote their biography did have a tragic experience when their teen son located the birth family. No other family in our group has had a negative experience when helping with a search or to locate more information.

For most of the families, the child's birth family concerns and identity issues melded and reached a crescendo in the early to mid-teen years. The parents faced more rebellion, and more confrontations about their authority to parent and to set limits. They were perplexed when a formerly complacent child suddenly began wearing all black, had body parts pierced, and began trying on personalities and identities like others would try on coats in a store.

The families that resisted their children's experimentation most also endured the most radical changes in lifestyle. It seemed that the teens weren't sure who they wanted to pattern themselves after but were quite sure it was not their adoptive family. Many youth who did not know their birth family began to emulate their idea of the fantasy birth parent. If the mother had been a teen at the time of the birth, the teen wanted to be sexually active at that age. If the teen imagined the parents were poor students or drop-outs, their grades would slip dramatically. Many of the youth left school prior to graduation or barely slipped through when parental efforts and the school personnel's tenacity prevailed.

Few of our group's children actually entered into a search for birth family, although nearly all of the youth who attended the group series stated they would do so some day when they were prepared for the outcome.

Searching during childhood and adolescence

Few young adoptees are prepared for search outcomes. Children who have been placed in closed adoptions after involuntary surrender by parents who have neglected or abused them, can be especially traumatized and regress when reunited with immature or poorly functioning birth families.

One of our support group families, who has 14 and 9 year old siblings, was located by the birth mother who is a substance abuser and her behavior has become a serious problem for the adoptive family. Fortunately this is only one case in the hundreds of families who have sought our services.

Many children who have lived with their birth family miss them and grieve for them, even if the conditions there were chaotic and unsafe. Children adopted at school age or in early adolescence often have clear memories of the birth family and may try to sabotage the placement in the hope of returning to their familiar surroundings and family. Children who have lived in chaos appear to find comfort in such an environment and will attempt to recreate a chaotic environment in the adoptive home.

The separated sibling

The hardest losses, however, are siblings who experience separation and the reticence of adoptive parents to help them regain and maintain contact with each other. The adoptive parents, trying to erase any trace of the chaotic past, may mistakenly refuse to allow ongoing relationships between children who have been very close and often depended on each other for safety and support. There may also be extended members of the birth family who were loving and supportive who could help the children adjust to the loss of the birth parents if all of the birth family were not lost to them. Often children find themselves separated and living in different adoptive homes. It can be a real benefit to all involved if the children have regular contact.

Children's service agencies who routinely separated children in the past now realize the importance of keeping them together. Adoptive parents who accept the responsibility of sibling groups face special challenges parenting children who have experienced troubled pasts. However, the benefits to the children over time is immense. Such prospective parents will require extended training and support all through the children's growing years. They will need respite care, counseling, and financial assistance for the expenses incurred in rearing the children. The children will need sensitive and prolonged preparation to help them adapt to the adoptive home.

There are two conditions, however, in which we cannot recommend maintaining the children in the same placement. When one child victimizes another, emotionally, physically, or sexually, they should be placed separately but with regular, monitored, contact maintained. If they can receive successful counseling to end the victimization, placement together could again be considered. The second condition is when the children have experienced long-term separate, stable placements. Moving them back together could be detrimental to their developmental and emotional needs.

According to the youth in our Charting the Course groups, separation of siblings is one of the most painful experiences to endure. Often the adoptive parents do not know what has happened to the siblings. The youth worry a great deal about the safety of siblings whose whereabouts are unknown or where contact is forbidden. One of the main reasons for the desire to search is to assure themselves that their brothers and sisters are well and safe.

Adolescents in closed adoptions who were adopted as infants wonder if they have siblings who are unaware of their existence. When searches result in meetings with a birth mother, one of the first questions is "Do you have other children?" It is very painful for the adoptee when a newly found birth parent refuses contact and does not tell other children of the adoptee's existence. Though the adoptees sincerely want to contact siblings, most do not want to contact them over the objections of the birth mother.

Respite care and residential care

Parents and youth who found themselves in a daily battle zone, related that confrontations became more frequent and more volatile over time. However when group leaders would first suggest respite care, parents were very reluctant to use the service. There were several reasons. They feared the child would feel rejected. They worried that the child would like the respite care home better and the problems would get worse. They were concerned about the different parenting styles and rules in the respite care home.

It was explained that the respite should be presented to the child as a taking a break from the tension in the home and not as a punishment. The children often like the respite care home and that is preferred over viewing it as a punitive experience. Our foster care providers have been fully trained regarding adoption issues, and work with the parents in a team effort to assist in working through the families' issues.

Those families who then utilized the service were pleased about the results. Many of our past and current support group families scheduled weekend respite once per month. Once a respite care relationship was established between parents and providers, it facilitated the ease of scheduling and emergency respite could be arranged when the family was in distress or crisis.

Our parents suggest that families who would like to utilize respite care should seek out agencies who have personnel trained in, and sensitive to, adoption issues.

Residential care was needed by most of the children of our group members at some time during the adolescent years. When our families made the difficult decision to seek residential care, they had exhausted all other avenues of assistance for their child. Often there had been a psychological assessment, and perhaps hospitalization before the decision was reached to seek residential or institutional care. Due to the limitations of insurance coverage, few families can access such care privately. Most are forced to go to the court system or children's services to request help for their child. In our area the only current way to access such placement through Children's Services is for the agency to take temporary custody of the child. In our experience, by the time the parent seeks such help the family situation is in crisis, and there is an urgency for placement to insure the safety of the child or other family members. Most of our families reached this decision after the child had attempted suicide more than once, physically attacked another family member, became unmanageable even with medication, or refused to take medication.

Ideally, any residential care facility or agency will seek an accurate assessment of the situation and the needs of the child, and initiate appropriate treatment. Only after the child is stable should he or she be released or moved to a different care level. Our support group parents have discovered that they must be pro-active in seeking out the best placement and convincing the courts and children's services to select their placement of choice.

The children's behaviors have often been so severe for such a long time that it is difficult for the exhausted parent to advocate well for the best placement. We have often suggested that parents acquire legal council to help them clarify and work through the legal and bureaucratic requirements. There have been cases where Children's Services caseworkers have treated the parents as abusers (because they are not accustomed to working with parents who are working so hard for their children) or have suggested that they are overreacting to the problem and that they need to try harder or take parenting classes. Those who took parenting classes found that they were not appropriate to their needs.

Some children have experienced many placements outside of the home as professionals tried program after program. A few of these programs were successful, but many were not. When the child is determined not to accept assistance, it cannot work.

We did find that those children who had treatment foster care placements or group home placements, did stabilize for the most part. The most successful cases involved parents who were very active in every aspect of the treatment, and maintained their commitment to the child.

The decision to turn over temporary custody and lose parental authority is a terrible one. However there are situations that require such action. When the juvenile courts, children's services, and the parents work as a team, the outcome has the best chance of success.

Children's Behaviors Discussed

Several behavioral problems were discussed again and again as new parents joined the group or as children manifested new behaviors. Many of the following behaviors will also be discussed in other segments of the book, however, our parents chose to address some of the issues that are most distressing. Many of the behaviors resulted from the previously listed Issues. The following segments will illustrate their views on selected subjects from the following list.

Running away   Refusal to do chores
Stealing   Choosing unsavory companions
Lying   Jekyll and Hyde problems at home
Physical violence   Refusal to follow house rules
Verbal attacks   Poor school performance
Anger/Tantrums   False accusations of abuse
Sexual acting out   Pregnancy in the teen years

Running away

Some of the youth have threatened to run away, some have run once or twice, others have a pattern of run-away behaviors, Reasons for running:

• to find the birth family
• to be with others they think are like the birth family
• to object to rules and structure
• to act on a moment of anger
• to punish Mom and Dad
• to press the parents for a commitment (do you love me?)

Youth usually run in anger, without pre-planning. They may pack all their belongings or just walk out. Few have any cognizant awareness of a reason other than the event that made them angry at that moment.

Parents report panic at the thought of their child out

—

in a world they are not prepared to face. The children are only aware of their own anger. They usually regret the run as soon as the sun goes down or as soon as their companions go home. Unfortunately the children are often able to find people who will take them in. The younger children may use the guise of "Can Jimmy stay over tonight, his parents are away?" This may work on a weekend but rarely on a school night. The young child may become frightened, and return home a few hours later stating that he only came back for a place to "crash" and has no intention of staying. Older youth often know of places where they can stay with no questions asked. People who harbor runaways permit the teen to use either the threat or real act as a tool to manipulate the family.

Runaway behavior needs to be investigated for several reasons. Parents from our group suggest from their experiences: possible substance abuse, sexual activity, or the possibility the youth is having identity confusion concerned with the adoption and may be questioning the depth of his parent's commitment. Counseling and striving toward improved communication is primary. Our group members suggest that parents who are concerned about such issues: talk to teachers, the child's friends, and adoption support group leaders and members to gain insights about the particular situation. Anger will not help and can exacerbate the situation. If the parent cannot talk with the child without anger, a family member or friend whom the child trusts may be called in to mediate.

Support group advice about running away

Tips for the parents of a child who is threatening to run away. Do the following calmly. Speak in a quiet voice.
1. Do not say "There's the door," or otherwise give permission.
2. Do not help them pack

—

3. Do tell the child he or she does not have permission and leaving the house will result in consequences. Make sure the child knows there will be consequences and that you will follow through.
4. Do tell the child that you love him or her, that this is home and it is where he or she belongs.
5. Do be firm but do not get into a physical struggle.
6. Do engage the youth in conversation about what is upsetting him or her.
   - Refrain from responding defensively or in anger.
   - Let the child vent as long as there is no violence.
   - Agree that life can be frustrating, empathize.
   - Again, if you are too angry, call in an objective party to help calm the situation.
   - Ask for alternative solutions from the child or offer alternatives.
7. Remember, it is more important to keep the child safe for the moment than to confront them about their shortcomings, mistakes, and behaviors.
8. After the situation is under control, go to your "safe place," turn on some soothing music, and take a nice long bath. Tomorrow is another day.

Poor school performance

The majority of children of parents in our support group had great challenges with their children when they were in school. Few of the children were motivated to do school assignments. The following scenario was reported time after time as new parents joined the group: The parents would be contacted within a few days of the beginning of the school year to be told that the child was disrupting classes, refusing to sit at the desk, and that little, if any, assignments were being turned in. The teacher would then inform the parents that it was their responsibility to make the child do the assignments. The parents would begin a pattern of asking the child what assignments were due and the child would say there was none or that the work was completed at school. The parents would then set up a system to have school personnel write down the assignments. The child countered by forgetting the needed books or leaving the assignment sheet at school. Sometimes the parent would take the child back to school to retrieve the required items.

The parent and child would retire to the "homework area" and begin work. The child then whines, argues, breaks pencils, tears paper, and turns a 30-minute session into a three hour battle. At 9 p.m. or later all participants go to bed exhausted. The next morning the child throws the homework in the trash before class, or "loses" it.

The teacher reports that assignments are still not done. It takes a while for the parent to discover what has happened to the homework. The nightly battles may go on for years as the parent tries to satisfy the demands of the school personnel and tries to force the child to cooperate. The result is that the school personnel don't believe the parent is trying. The child/parent relationship is in chaos. The average IQ student whom you know is capable of completing the work brings home failing grades each term.

There are ways to break this pattern and receive assistance for school performance. The parent needs to request an evaluation to determine if the child qualifies as learning disabled. See the chapter on obtaining school related services for children. Severe behavioral problems is a qualifier. The child may need psychological testing that can be provided through the school. Check for hearing or vision difficulties. If a determination is made that the child needs an Individual Education Plan, many services are available. Use them. If the child does not qualify and no reasons may be found for the school difficulties, other approaches may be tried.

Our group parents realized that the constant battles

over school interfered with other parenting tasks that were essential in the development of their children. Most of them gave responsibility for school work over to the child. They would show an interest, but did not nag or participate in homework. The parents discovered that most of the children did not do worse. Some didn't do any better, but the parents were learning to choose their battles and realized they were losing the school wars.

Tantrums and acting out in anger

One of the most discussed topics in group meetings is anger in the child. The parents tell of children who become angry quickly and act out violently. The children's behaviors include shouting, breaking their possessions, knocking holes in walls, breaking down doors and hurting themselves. The parents are perplexed at the sudden onset and their inability to stop the angry outbursts. We have found that the best way to manage such anger in a young child is to, first, make sure the child is safe from self harm, then ignore the behavior. Turn on the vacuum cleaner, put on a set of earphones and turn up the volume, or leave the area. We do not recommend sending the child to his or her bedroom. This indicates rejection and the room becomes a place of punishment rather than a place of comfort. The child who tries to hurt himself or herself may need to be restrained. If the parent feels restraint is necessary, it is important to soothe the child, rather than to exhibit anger of one's own. Responding to angry outbursts and tantrums with anger is rarely successful.

Let the child know in quiet times that there is a consequence to angry outbursts — and then follow through. The use of logical consequences has been the most successful discipline technique. Many of the children in our groups have multiple problems that make self control difficult. A combination of ADD, fetal alcohol effect, and inability to fully attach to the family may lead to increased impulsivity and inability to control anger. The parent who realizes the limitations of the child and reacts quietly and without anger, will better manage the tantrums.

Angry teenagers would provoke family arguments by refusal to do household chores, clean their room, or by "borrowing" other family member's possessions. Some would break curfew, or openly refuse to follow parental rules. Veteran parents advise others to carefully pick battles. Let the room be a mess, make school work the responsibility of the youth, and refuse to let the teen make you respond in anger. Set consequences for infractions and then quietly and calmly follow through. The parent who threatens a consequence and fails to impose it will find the child becomes more blatant about breaking rules.

Physical and/or verbal abuse from the child

A few parents reported verbal and physical abuse toward siblings, but the majority of the aggression was directed toward the adoptive mother.

When there was physical abuse toward a sibling, it was often managed by keeping the children separated as much as possible and giving individual attention to each child. There was only one family that had to request alternate care as one child was endangering her younger sister.

Verbal abuse usually begins just prior to the teen years and may escalate as the youth struggles with identity and the issue of independence as opposed to need for security. The young child who fears he will be rejected by the adoptive parent as he imagines he was by the birth parent, may use verbal abuse as a test or an attempt to reject before he can be rejected.

Several parents reported that their children began by defying rules and shouting, "You have no right to tell me what to do." The mother's possessions may be taken or broken. Arguments became face to face confrontations from which the child would not let the parent disengage, i.e., the child follows the parent from room to room, continuing to shout long after the parent has said the discussion was over. The child follows the parent to the bedroom and screams through the door or beats on the door.

Verbal abuse does not always lead to physical abuse. Reports of physical abuse include putting a knife to the mother's head, and striking and knocking a mother to the ground. One had many instances of pummeling the mother when angry. Few of the mothers reported significant physical injury, but they became fearful. The other parents in the group would react by wanting to know why the parent allowed such behaviors. They would listen and offer advice that the parent call the authorities if it happened again. It surprised some members that many of the parents endured repeated episodes before taking action. The mothers had refused to call the police because they feared that once the authorities were involved, the parents would lose control to the courts and the child would further reject them and their efforts to parent.

Eventually each family did ask for help through children's services or the courts. Typically, the youth would return to less aggressive behaviors for a time. Some refrained from escalating the aggressive actions, but others had to be moved to alternate care or residential housing. None of them were in juvenile detention facilities for more than a few weeks.

In most families, the dangerous behaviors abated as the child reached maturity. None of the youth retained anger at the parent for involving the authorities. The behaviors did seem to improve once the youth understood that the parent had limits that could not be exceeded without consequences. The parents who imposed consistent consequences were the most successful at reducing the frequency and severity of the abuse.

Allegations of sexual abuse

When parents first attend the group they are reluctant to relate that an adoptive father had been accused of sexual abuse. It is inevitable that the subject comes up at group meetings on occasion and a large percentage of our fathers have related the humiliation that they endured when their adopted daughters made the allegations. The allegations usually occurred after the parent and child had been engaged in power struggles for a significant period of time. The daughter would usually tell her parents that she no longer wanted to live in the home and under their rules. When other manipulative behaviors did not succeed in a desired reduction of parental authority, the teen girls made the allegations in an effort to be removed from the home.

When the father took an active role in rearing the child, he became a target when the teenage girl felt the restrictions were extreme. Most of the youth were ignoring curfew, some were sexually acting out, school work was poor, and they were generally oppositional in behavior. When the parents refused to back down on restrictions on activities, car use, or dating, the sexual abuse allegations followed. None of the allegations toward any of the fathers were substantiated, but nearly all resulted in the child leaving the home. The parents would resist the return of the child to the home long after the allegations were put to rest. The formerly affectionate fathers no longer felt they could trust their daughters and did not want to be alone with them at any time. It takes a very long time for the relationship to heal once such an allegation has been made.

Sexual promiscuity and pregnancy in the teen years

Most of our families reported that their teens began sexual activity in early to mid teens. Two teen boys fathered children. Several teen girls became pregnant. None of the parents had expected, at the time of adoption, that they would be helping to parent an infant grandchild when their child was still a teen.

Adopted teen girls rarely make an adoption plan for their babies. Most decide to parent, in part to keep their infant from experiencing the losses they had, and in part to show the birth mother they can parent. Many of the teen girls who were adopted at an older age after experiencing abuse or neglect in the birth family, have social developmental delays. Some have attachment issues, care little about school work, and choose companions that are reminiscent of their fantasy or real birth family. One teen (who lived with her birth family till she was six) told her adoptive parents, "I came from poverty and ignorance and that's who I am. I hang out with guys who are trouble makers because I feel more comfortable with them." She often chose to have relationships with boys who were physically abusive toward her.

The parents are greatly distressed when a pregnancy occurs. They feel the child they have worked so diligently with, has rejected their efforts and has sabotaged her chances for education and career. The adoptive mother who has had to deal with infertility, must take her teen daughter to the obstetrician and often relives the pain of her infertility. Some of the teen girls have parented well, returned to school and are functioning well as single parents. Other teen girls have abandoned their infants to the care of the grandparents and a few have had multiple pregnancies.

One teen who was adopted as an infant became pregnant at age 19. She had been a good student and typical child till age 13. She then became involved in alcohol and drug abuse. The parents feared for her life. When the girl realized she was pregnant, she stopped all drug and alcohol use. She slowly changed her life. By the time the child was two she had gained an education and was fully employed and supporting them both. The adoptive parents provided emotional support, financed her schooling, and helped care for the child while she worked toward independence. She is doing well and the little boy is healthy, physically and emotionally.

All of the birth control methods have been discussed in group. Some of the teens will willingly use the depo-provera shot. Few other methods have been successful as many of the teens refuse to use them. One thirteen year old girl told her mother, "I want a baby as soon as possible." The parents tried to make sure the girl had no opportunities to be alone with a boy. They discovered that she was going to boy's homes over the school lunch hour. They convinced the school counselor to order her to remain in the school building for lunch. She then began meeting boys after school. The mother started driving to school to pick her up as soon as the final bell rang. She had to also drive her to school, only dropping her off five minutes before the morning bell. The parents' lives were reduced to accompanying this girl all her waking hours. She graduated high school without becoming pregnant. She is now 20 years old and every three months announces that she is pregnant. She has not been able to conceive, though she has used no birth control for two years.

Another teen girl, adopted at age six, became pregnant at age 16 after meeting a boy at his home after school. The girl had a history of physical abuse toward the adoptive mother. This young mother becomes angry and frustrated when the baby cries. She once left him at a mall with strangers who brought him back many hours later. She takes him out without telling the adoptive mother where she is going and often fails to take food or adequate clothing. The parents fear for the safety of the baby. They have acquired legal guardianship of the baby and now have just learned there will be another baby. (Their daughter went to visit a boy who lives across the street. His family has not acknowledged that the baby is his, nor did the first baby's father.) The girl is now 18 and a senior in high school. They fear for the future of this new baby as the daughter says she will not allow them to have guardianship. This couple, at age 50, is not prepared to raise their daughter's children. They fear that she will continue having pregnancy after pregnancy.

Poor school performance, lying, and stealing are discussed in the chapters on scholastic interventions and therapeutic interventions.

Surviving the Teen Years

A panel of several of our group members shared their thoughts and feelings on "surviving the teen years" at an adoption retreat. The following are excerpts from their presentation and the audience discussion.

Humor "You have to find humor in any difficult situation. Humor keeps you healthy. Example: When one of our group reported that her child had run away again, someone offered, 'Maybe she's preparing for a career in the travel industry!' Parents who can find humor in situations that would bring others to their knees, have found a useful survival skill."

Prayer "Trust that a higher power meant you to raise your child, whether it's what the child thinks he wants or not. There have been times with all of our children when we had no idea where they were or what was happening to them. The only thing we could do was ask God to protect them. And He did."

Adoptive parents group

"No parent is perfect, and we all do things we wish we hadn't. We lose our tempers, saying things that cause hurt. I started to believe that if only I were more easy-going, a different kind of mother, my child would behave differently. When I joined an adoptive parent support group, for the first time I found myself among people who understood the level of dysfunction and defiance going on in our home; and none of those people blamed my parenting skills for the problems. I discovered that:

"We all came from different religious and financial backgrounds. We all had different temperaments. We all had different parenting styles. Our children had different life experiences and different birth family backgrounds. Our children were adopted at different ages, from two days old to 12 years. *But they were all exhibiting the same behaviors! You'd think the same child was going from house to house!*"

What behaviors were we living with?

Lying, stealing   Abusing drugs and/or alcohol
Running away   Sexual promiscuity
Defiant behavior   Contacts with deviant peers
Fighting in school   Devil worship
Truancy
Getting terrible grades and refusing school assignments
Anger and sometimes violence to mother
Refusing to respect parental authority or values

How did we regain our energy?

1. Parental respite —"Many of us like a certain bed and breakfast in the country for a weekend get-a-way."
2. Youth respite —"Our children responded well to summer camps, trading off with a buddy families, and monthly weekend respite care."
3. Adoptive parent support group —"Go all the time, not just when you are in crisis. You can be a support for others."
4. Counseling —"Make sure your counselor is specially trained in adoption issues. Your counselor can be a great help to you as the parent. When many of us found ourselves involved with the courts due to unruly behavior and defiance of our children. Our counselor was able to testify that the problems were caused by the child's rage,

not by our parenting."

The only counseling that seemed to help the children came from the education and support series that allowed them to talk in a safe place with other youth who shared the same confusion, rage, and poor self-image. The education series helped the children cope with loss and adoption.

When our child went from our home to alternative care

"Our daughter's behavior got to a point where, for the safety of all of us, she had to leave our home. She refused to talk to us on the phone, and refused my visits. So, during the time she was away, I sent her a card every few days reminding her that we thought of her every day, that we loved her, and that we were a constant in her life. She never acknowledged the cards, but I learned several years later that she saved those cards and still has them."

External detriments to a healthy adoptive experience

The county children's services. "When we went to them for help, they insisted that all our problems were due to poor parenting skills. They required attendance at basic parenting classes that talked about using "time out" and giving gold stars for good behavior. We had tried these techniques years earlier only to discover that regular parenting techniques didn't work for the problems we faced with our children. Adoptive parents need specialized skills taught by adoption specialists."

Dishonesty from the adoption agency. "Many of us were told blatant untruths or discovered later that much information about the child and his or her history had been withheld. They told us the birth mother did not use alcohol or have psychiatric problems. We were left handicapped—with important pieces missing. We would have parented differently had we had all the information."

—

The juvenile courts. "The courts are so inundated with children who come from abusive and neglectful situations that we too, were assumed to have caused the child's behaviors. We were neither abusive or neglectful, but were often treated as though we were." The courts are used to handling abusive or neglectful parents. When confronted with loving parents of an out of control child, they didn't seem to know how to handle such cases and assumed the parents must be the problem.

Some parents have found the judges and referees were sympathetic and understanding to the their family situation and the needs of the child but were constrained by legal and financial limitations when ordering treatment programs or alternative care. Some parents find that legal representation is required in order for the court to gain full information of the issues involving the family and the child.

Parenting techniques we found effective

A united parenting team. "Parents must stay in tune with each other and communicate regularly, in order to share the same understanding about what is going on in the home." Example: The child may have been doing everything he can to push mom's buttons all day. By the time dad comes home mom has reached the end of her endurance and is shouting at the child. Dad assumes her temper is causing the problem and that she needs to be more reasonable with the child. When he accuses her, an argument ensues and he feels justified in his accusations. If the father had been fully informed of the behaviors and the escalating situation, he could be more supportive of her. The child may use this miscommunication as a way to manipulate the parents."

Pick your battles. "Forget neat rooms, bizarre makeup, and homework marathons, and concentrate on battles that involve child or parent safety."

—

<u>Realistic expectations</u>. "Adopting a child will not give you the family you would have had with birth children. The child comes to you with his or her own genetic code and history. Accept that child and seek out his or her talents and abilities. Do not try to force a child to like baseball because you do. Take every opportunity to try out new activities and learning opportunities, until you discover the child's interests. Nurture them."

<u>When the situation becomes unbearable</u>. "It may help to borrow a leaf from the pages of Alcoholics Anonymous. Realize that you are powerless over your children's behaviors; that your lives have become unmanageable. With that admission, realize also that you cannot allow yourselves to become paralyzed. Learn to take control of your lives, including making the hard decisions. Sometimes the hard decision is filing unruly charges or having the child removed from the home. Sometimes the hard decision is bringing the child back home."

Action recommended for the family in crisis

"Join a support group. Find others like yourselves."

"Take inventory of your problems and their cause."

"Research your child's birth family history."

"Educate yourselves about adoption, loss, and grief issues."

"Accept the child you have, let go of the fantasy."

"Stay committed to your child."

"Keep attending the support group to help others even after your crisis has abated."

One family proposed that the following prayer can apply to adoptive families. It was borrowed from Alcoholic's Anonymous:

God grant me the Serenity to accept the things I cannot change,
Courage to change the things I can,
and Wisdom to know the difference. Amen.

—

What should you avoid that could hurt your child?

<u>Secrecy</u>. "It is a mistake not to tell a child that he is adopted as soon as possible. If he has thought for years that you are his birth parents, his life may implode when he finds he's adopted. Everything he believed about himself was a lie. How can he trust you not to have lied about everything else?"

"We cannot protect our children from the pain of the loss of the birth family. As soon as he knows he's adopted and understands the implications, adoption/grief issues will surface. Delay in telling the child will only result in greater emotional upheaval later."

<u>Speaking negatively of the birth parent</u>. "No matter the history of your child or the amount of ill treatment he may have received, you cannot be negative in the things you say about the birth parent(s) to the child or others. He knows they provided his genetic background. If you make them sound terrible, what does that make him? You will place him or her in a position of having to deal with divided loyalties. The adoptive parent who has empathy for the birth parent will help the child to have a better feeling of self-worth."

<u>Threatening to remove the child from your home</u>. "Threats can prove a self-fulfilling prophesy. If you threaten to do it, the child thinks, 'Why have it hanging over my head? If I have to leave, I'll just get it over with.'" *Children who have suffered losses may fear rejection by the adoptive parents. The adopted child may test the parent many times as he or she is growing up. Threatening the child only proves to them that you may abandon them.*

<u>The adopted child and birth siblings</u>. "Your adopted child has a great need to remain in contact with siblings, and it is very important to foster that relationship. The child may feel more grief for a lost brother or sister than a birth parent.

—

Often children are separated in adoption and adopted by different families. Some mistakenly feel that the children are better off to sever those ties. They will actually attach better to the adoptive family, and trust will grow, if they can have contact with siblings. Some separated siblings spend years wondering if their brothers and sisters are safe or alive. It is often of primary importance for the separated adoptees to know the whereabouts of siblings."

4

The youth groups

This chapter explains our youth educational programming and re-lates its effects on the youth who participate. The 10-week parallel education series for adoptive parents and youth is the oldest and best known of our services.

Our most intensive interaction with children and ado-lescents has been through the youth sessions of our Charting the Course psychoeducational series. The group sessions enabled us to familiarize ourselves with the feelings and thoughts of adoptees who were struggling with their identity, grief, and birth parent and adoptive family issues. All facets of their lives were affected by their losses and their adoptive status. It is a common belief that children adopted in infancy do not develop adoption issues. Children who have endured maltreatment in their birth homes are ex-pected to have more difficulty adjusting and suffer more from the issues of loss and abandonment. However, many of the families who have attended our support groups adopted sup-posedly healthy infants, but experience the same dysfunc-tional behaviors with their children as those who adopted older children who had undergone great trauma.

In the beginning, the series only included programming for parents and teens as the families who came to us usually had children over the age of 13. A few years later we noticed an increase in calls from parents with younger children. They were having temper tantrums and saying "You can't tell me what to do. You're not my real mom." Families came to us with children who were angry, oppositional, and exhibiting behaviors the parents could not understand. As a response to the need to assist the younger children, we created programming specific to the children aged 8 to 12.

The integration of an intake session

The series consisted of several components we used to create an atmosphere of openness and trust, so the youth would be able to talk of their feelings in an accepting atmosphere. The first phase was an informal intake session.

In the years before we added an intake session, teen groups related awkwardly the first night as a group of strangers got together for the first time. We decided to give the series a jump-start by adding an interview process. We hold screenings in a home of one of the facilitators. Appointments are scheduled for every 45 minutes. While the parents in one family are with the counselor in one room and the parents of a second family were filing out paperwork with a coordinator in a second room, the youth are invited into a comfortable room with the persons who will be their group leaders. The youth have an opportunity to meet others who will be in their class and get acquainted with group leaders in a non-threatening setting. The youth are asked if they know the purpose of the series they will be attending. They usually respond that they know nothing. We then assure them that there will be no formal counseling, and they all relax, losing their apprehension that the series would be just a trick to get them more counseling that they do not want.

After an explanation of topics the Charting the Course sessions will include, conversation often turns to issues they

—

would like to bring up during the series. As a result, the youth come to the first session already acquainted with others in the group and retaining few "first night" reservations. We get right into fun activities such as trust walks and games. Even the most reluctant participant wants to come after the second session.

We have even had court-ordered attendance for several youth and one teen girl was brought to the first session by the police. (This incident occurred prior to initiating the intake interview.) She had dressed in pajamas and a robe, to avoid coming, but was brought in that attire. She attended the rest of the sessions voluntarily and became one of the best contributors in the group.

One 15 year old was brought by his parents to the intake interview and refused to get out of the car. He pretended to be asleep in the locked car when the group facilitator went out to try to coax him in. He came to the building the first night of the series, but sat on the stairs and told a group leader, "I'm not coming in that room with those others and you can't make me." The group leader agreed to this and then went in to start the group. As the other group members were laughing, talking, and moving around in the activities, one of the group leaders noticed the reluctant youth looking in the window. The next week, that youth was the first to arrive and sat excitedly awaiting the beginning of group. He participated fully and appropriately the rest of the nine weeks.

What do young adoptees want to know?

Some people suggest that there is information that a child should never be told about his birth history, such as a conception resulting from rape or incest. Some tell us how difficult it is to relate information that birth parents are mentally ill or incarcerated. Others say, "Tell them everything yourself, or someone else will." Some experts advise telling them everything before the age of 12 as they are best able to handle the information before adolescence.

During the series we ask the youth what they think they should be told about adoption, their histories, and at what age. We began surveying the teen groups and later surveyed the latency groups (children ages 8-12) regarding their thoughts about what they should know, and when they should know it.

The first question we asked the group members was when should a child be told that he or she is adopted. All agreed that every child should be told when they are very young (toddler age). The ones who felt best about adoption said they couldn't remember a time when they didn't know. "It's like I always knew," they say.

To stress the importance of "always knowing": A 16 year old told us about when she was seven, playing in the neighbors yard with another seven-year old. They began to argue and the neighbor girl said "What do you know about anything? You're adopted." She had never heard the word before and went running home to ask her mother what it meant. "I have never felt the same since," she told us. It shook her world to hear she was not "who I thought I was."

Another 17 year old teen joined our series after learning six months earlier that he was adopted. He had been adopted as an infant by a couple who divorced when he was quite young. A few months earlier, after an absence of many years the man who had divorced his mother, came to visit. As they sat talking in the park, the teen mentioned something about a genetic inheritance, to which the older man replied, "You know that isn't possible. You're adopted."

After confronting his mother, the boy was told that they had informed him as a very young child and he must have forgotten. He had no memory of being told and chose to believe they had deceived him. He said he had to go out and find out who he was as he had been living a lie for 17 years. At the time he began our

—

series, he had not spoken to his mother or step-father for several months, and could not find peace. He ran away before our series concluded. He found a birth brother who was adopted by another family. The runaway pattern continued. At this writing, we do not know if he has been able to resolve his painful issues.

As we continued surveying the youth group members, they relayed that they can handle at a very young age, if told that the birth mother was too young to parent and had made an adoption plan. They felt that information that a parent has a mental illness or retardation is not difficult to bear. They felt strongly that no child or teen needs to be told that the mother was promiscuous or a prostitute.

Several youth believed that it is more difficult to learn that a married couple made an adoption plan, especially if they were already parenting older children. The loss of the siblings and being raised without them was stressed as especially painful to them. One 15 year old boy asked, "Why did they keep the other kids and not me?"

When we discussed rape, the responses were mixed. Many of the girls said that they could understand the placement better in rape situations. One teen who had experienced a date rape, was told later by her adoptive parents that her birth mother was raped. The teen said that her experience made her feel very close to the birth mother.

All of the members felt that young children should not know about rape, or incest, but maintained that their birth history was, after all, their birth history and felt they had the right (at the proper age) to know everything involved.

The only information about the birth family they all agreed they did not want to know was if one birth parent had purposely caused the death of the other.

Discussions about information and closed adoption were always the most lively and each had strong opinions.

—

What about the birth father?

When the discussion turned to the birth father, there was not as much interest in ever meeting him. Boys were interested in whether he played a sport well, or if he was tall. Most wanted to meet the birth mother someday, but as one teen put it, "I would like my birth father to stand in the daylight at the town square so I could drive by real slow and look at him." No contact was wanted. This attitude seems to be shared by many of the youth. It appears that a majority of them blame the birth father for their need for placement. They often express frustration stating that if the birth father had only been responsible, they could have remained with their birth family.

Talking of search

All of the youth are ready to talk about search and are surprisingly open about their hopes and fears. The latency age children who were adopted as infants all have a great curiosity about their birth family and openly express their desire to meet them.

The children who remember their birth family and the problems that they experienced with them, tend to be angry and uninterested in a reunion. They do mourn deeply for siblings that they no longer see. Some mention a pet or an aunt or cousin they miss.

The teens are split in their feelings about a meeting. Many want to meet just long enough to see if they bear any resemblance, and to ask "why." A few who are angry about the rules and expectations in their adoptive family have a picture of a permissive birth parent who would accept them as they are and offer a less restrictive "free-wheeling" parenting style.

One of the sessions addresses anger

On the night we talk about anger, all of the youth relate feeling out of control from time to time and not understanding why or how it happens. They say they are angry with their adoptive parents, or kids at school. They seem to be grateful for our suggestions and ways of practicing alternative methods to manage anger. We, of course, talk about hitting pillows and kicking boxes and all of the usual diffusers. The two they like best are running outside around the house and the empty chair exercise.

They like our suggestion of going outside and running around the house until the anger leaves them. But the most powerful exercise of the night is when we pull an empty chair to the center of the room and allow one of them to volunteer to speak to the "person" in the chair who has angered them the most. We instruct the youth that he cannot strike the "person" but must tell him or her why the anger is there, what the person did to cause it, and what is needed to diffuse it. Most participants select a person they know from school who has angered them. Some have chosen a birth parent from which he or she had experienced abuse or neglect. One of the group leaders stands behind the youth to assist. The first volunteer always begins very quietly, and awkwardly. Then, as he or she realizes others actually understand and are not going to scoff he or she begins to really tell the "person" how they were hurt. The anger rises and the youth tells what was done and how he wanted to retaliate. He is then encouraged to tell the "person" what he needs from them. The message we all hear from the anger is the deep hurt behind it.

We are then able to explain to all the youth that anger is often masking pain. They are very open about what angers them and for the rest of the series are able to talk about hurting too.

The birth family fantasy

We invite an experienced speaker on the sixth evening who is a birth mother who made an adoption plan for her infant at birth. In preparation for that night, we do an exercise the week before that asks the youth to think about and talk about their fantasies about the birth family, if they have not met, or their memories of the birth family, if adopted at an older age.

The fantasies and impressions change as the children age. Younger children often fantasize that they were kidnapped and given to unsuspecting adoptive parents. They don't seem to fantasize their adoptive parents as being the kidnappers. They also see the birth family as intact and searching frantically for them. When the young children picture the house, it is always in a neighborhood much like the one they live in or in some cases like a movie star home or a king's palace. The boys visualize dream sports cars in the driveway. You see, some of them imagine they are the children of royalty, a star, or a sports hero. They look inside and can describe furniture, and all of the features of the people inside except for the faces. The faces are blank.

The exception is the child who was born in Asia or South America. They tend to see poverty and hunger in their visualizations, which do not change as they age.

However, when this exercise is done with teens, their fantasies are quite different. The homes are often described as small, inner-city, dirty, with junk cars in the front yard. The people inside are unkempt and may be consuming drugs or alcohol. Thus, the picture presented by the teen is of people who are not functioning well, even years later. It is at this time that the teens are searching for their identities and sometimes trying on the imagined negative identity of the birth parent.

The night the birth mother comes to visit

On night six we invite a specially trained birth mother to speak to the combined children's groups. Another birth mother comes to speak to the parent group. The children are told at the very beginning of the series which night the birth mother is to speak. Each subsequent evening at least one child asks to be reassured which night she is coming. Some ask if it could be their own birth mother.

The children are nervous that night, as many are in closed adoptions and were placed as infants or so young that they have no memory of their birth family. However, our birth mother is able to relate to children who were involuntarily placed out of their homes by reassuring those children that their mothers cared for and loved them no less. The children we wish we could bring someone for are those from Asia or South America or other countries of origin.

When our birth mother begins to speak, we never have to ask the children to be quiet. Their eyes are glued to her face and their ears to her every word. She speaks for about 45 minutes, telling her personal story of the events leading up to the pregnancy, how she felt when she learned of the pregnancy, how she came to the decision about an adoption plan, and what has happened since in her life. She speaks in language a child can understand and shows photographs of the infant she has not seen for 14 years. She tells of buying a Christmas ornament for each of her three children as well as the child in the photo. Each year she puts the ornaments in a box she is saving for the girl.

At the end of her story she asks each child in turn what they know of their birth family and if they have anything to ask her or say to her. Some are shy, others are bubbling with questions. A few show their anger, hidden until now, toward the decision made by their own birth mother for placing them. When she asks them what question would they ask their birth mother if given the opportunity. Almost every one says, "Why?" "I want to know why."

We find that even children who have been reluctant to share their feelings, open up to her. And for the rest of the series they remain open and willing to share.

One bi-racial teen leaned forward in her chair nose-to-nose with the birth mother after one very emotional session. The girl knew the child that the birth mother had placed was bi-racial and wanted so much for them to be a match. It was obvious, that just for a moment, it was.

This assignment is a very taxing one for this birth mother, but she sees the good it does to give the children an opportunity to listen to her story and talk to her. They all accept her answers. They all leave very quietly, deep in thought.

In session seven, we ask to hear the feelings and thoughts about the birth mother's visit. Almost all are glad she came. It makes their birth mother a real person for them,demystifying her and deflating some of the fantasies. She is someone with feelings and represents a birthmother who still loves them. It gives them deeper feelings of self worth.

Emancipation v. separation and loss

Many of the teens in our education series have three main issues: Self-identity (who am I), anger at their adoptive status, and an unrecognized fear of losing the adoptive family (through emancipation) when they leave home.

These are the teens whose grades plummet as they approach their senior year. They sabotage opportunities for jobs, college, and independence. The behaviors vary but all mean the same thing. "Will I have a family and will I be safe after age 18 and graduation?" Some who seemed to excel in a sport or talent, begin to lose interest. They may neglect former friends and regress socially and emotionally.

Of course, most of the parents feel defeated and angry at the lost opportunities. Many of their children barely graduate, drop out in the senior year, or have so many infractions and truancies that they are expelled.

Many adoptees may purposely provoke rejection and

emotional abandonment by the parents as they feel that they are supposed to be moving on. They really want reassurance and to hold on, but they rebel and force separation. This is not something they've thought about or planned. They are only acting on feelings they can neither understand nor control.

The youth often express their feelings in anger and confusion. They no longer want to communicate with the parent and create chaos where they can. We tell them several things:

1. Adoption is forever. It does not end at age 18 or graduation.
2. Their parents made a lifetime commitment to them when they were very small and unable to make such a similar commitment. They are now old enough and mature enough to make the commitment to really be a member of their family.
3. Their parents may dislike their actions and may be placing restrictions they rebel against now. We tell them to try to remember the early years and how they felt in their families then. (We then discuss earlier good times) We tell them that after the tough teen years are over, they will feel that way again.

In response to the above information, many of the teens groan, hoot, or loudly deny that they will ever want a relationship with the adoptive family. But as weeks progress, the parents report a positive difference in communication and demeanor, and the leaders notice a softening of the anger and resistance.

As the feelings and behaviors are covered in the youth groups, the parent group leaders address the same situations and give tips on how to respond positively and regain communication.

Parents have reported that the drive to and from group sessions becomes part of the process, and often children initiate talks about other members of the group as a way of discussing their own feelings, thoughts, and issues.

The anger, confusion, and fears may be far less when the youth is:
- Free to express his/her frustrations and fears about adoption
- Given permission to love the birth family too
- Given all the birth history information in a nonjudgemental way
- Free to explore innate talents and supported in later search efforts.

As the teen series comes to a close

It is wonderful to watch the metamorphosis of each angry distrustful teen to youth who are eager to speak openly. As they are able to discuss their pain and fears, we can see the pain lift from their faces. It usually only takes one or two sessions for the teens to engage, but there was one holdout who remained angry and closed through nine sessions. Each evening as the group leaders met to share our sessions, the teen leaders would despair of ever reaching this angry 16 year old girl. She wore black clothes, black fingernail polish, and black lipstick. We sadly admitted that she would be the one case to point to where we had failed to break through the armor. But on the last night, we saw a different girl. She wore colors and her beautiful face was make-up free. She was relaxed, and open for the first time. She cried about leaving the newly discovered friends and hugged us and said thank you. There wasn't a dry eye that night as we relayed her responses in staffing. Her parents let us know she was now less angry at home too. We wished we could do another 10 weeks just for her.

On the last night, we always give the members little "autograph" booklets we prepare. The youth pass them around the room for each member to write positive comments to one another. Despite any rivalry, teasing, or personality conflicts during the series, we have never seen a negative statement in one of those booklets. Most of the youth trade phone numbers and some even do over-nights and maintain contact long after the series has ended.

A few youngsters come through the series more than once. One of the families came through three times. Each time the girl, at a different stage in development, said she learned something new.

Unconditional acceptance is our rule. The leaders do set group rules. The most important is no put-downs. The teens slip from time to time as the sessions evoke more emotion. Each slip has always been followed by a sincere apology. We treat the youth with respect and take them seriously from the first meeting and they reward us with their trust and affection. When we report the children's openness and affection as well as appropriate behaviors to the parents, they often ask if we are really talking about their child.

We must admit that it is relatively easy for us to achieve this because we are not the parent who has to manage the upheavals in their day-to-day lives. We are not miracle workers, but the parents do take note of the success we achieve and are willing to try more of the tips and parenting approaches they are being taught in their parallel class.

Teen group series scenarios

Nicholas — We met Nick when he was 14. He had been adopted at the age of nine along with a birth sister who is three years younger. He had a history of runaways, verbal defiance, and school failure. He had physical fights at school, made suicidal threats, and had broken into homes to commit thefts. His birth mother had a history of drug and alcohol abuse.

In group he spoke openly about his inability to commit to his adoptive family. He was very worried about the health and well being of his birth mother, fearing she may have died. He missed his other siblings. He was quiet and respectful in group, but spoke truthfully about his feelings. He said he loved and respected his adoptive father but fears his behavior has caused him to give up on him. Nick does not understand why he behaves as he does and is perplexed by his actions. This young man was in residential care for a time following group, but his father remained committed to the adoption and to Nick.

Greg — Greg's parents contacted us because he was expressing anger toward the birth family and was rebellious in the adoptive home. He had been diagnosed with ADHD and was taking medication for depression. This 17 year old had been adopted as an infant.

In group, Greg expressed gratitude for his adoptive family and their willingness to let him be himself. He brought artwork to share. He was concerned about his temper, relating that he had broken the hand of a 10 year old who had hurt his younger sister. He wanted to talk to his adoptive parents about searching, but feared mentioning it to his parents. He worried that his birth mother might not be alive. He expressed a desire to be closer to his adoptive family but does not know if it was possible as he had hurt them so much. This very bright young man had always sabotaged any chance at success. His parents remain committed but he established a distance that they cannot span.

Cathy — This very angry 13 year old had been acting out, physically attacked her mother, took pills in spur-of-the-moment suicide attempts and ran away. She had been adopted in infancy after an adoption plan was made by her 16 year old birth mother. She had had psychiatric care from the 2nd grade due to her many suicide attempts. From the age of six, she expressed a desire to know her birth mother. She imagined she was a princess in the early years but had recently begun fantasizing that the birth mother is a prostitute.

She was angry about the restrictions placed on her by probation and her parents. She felt no commitment to her family. It took her a long time to trust in the group, but she did so once she was sure there would be no repercussions and we would maintain confidentiality (an important issue with many of the teens). The anger was masking great pain in this young girl. She allowed us to see the pain and tried the anger management techniques. Her mother gained much from the group in communication skills. She was still maintained at home two years after the series.

Allison — This sixteen year old was adopted at three weeks. She was told by a friend when she was eight that she was adopted. She seemed to recover from the shock but began acting out at 13, when she was given information on birth family history. She has been very angry at the adoptive mother, is truant and failing. Allison came to group very angry at her adoptive family. She admitted that she was drinking and sneaking out at night with friends. The night of the birth mother visit in group she angrily accused her of placing the child out of selfishness. She then said that her birth mother had placed her so that she could study medicine. She thought that the poorest of reasons for a child to lose her birth family and heritage. She said she didn't want to get good grades because she knew her birth mom was a good student and wanted to be nothing like her. After the series she realized that the anger she had been exhibiting to her adoptive mother was really not meant for her. She raised her grades and the mother-daughter relationship is now close and caring.

Issues in the Latency Group Series (Ages 8-12)

The children who attend between the ages of eight and

twelve share some issues with the teens but they are less able to understand their budding discomfort with adoption and their losses.

The children are, of course, more willing to attend the classes than the reluctant teens. However, they have been attending classes all day and do not care to be, once again, in a school-like setting. Many have been diagnosed with attention deficit disorder, and most of those with hyperactivity.

They test the group leaders to the limits of patience with their desires to run, jump, and generally ignore the structured activities. They may become even more disruptive after realizing that some of the discussions involve uncomfortable topics. They are told that the sessions are about adoption, that they can ask anything they want—and they do.

They love the trust activities and begin to ask each other about their own adoptive experience. They openly declare love and affection for their adoptive families, but express surprise when told they may love both their biological parents and their adoptive parents. They ask if it is really OK as they thought they had to choose.

We explain to the parent group that giving permission for your child to express love for the birth family frees them to express love for the adoptive family too.

Learning difficult information

Many children have quietly said they know little about their birth family but are sure the adoptive parents are keeping something from them. In each instance, when we asked the parent if there was information they were withholding, they said there was.

One bi-racial child had never been told that her biological mother was Caucasian. The African American adoptive mother feared the information could cause identity confusion. She felt the daughter was comfortable believing all of her heritage was black. During the series the 12 year old girl shared feelings that her birth mother was Caucasian but had never brought it up to her adoptive mother because she did not want to upset her. We advised the mother to have an open discussion with their daughter, which has resulted in a closer, more trusting relationship.

In another instance the birth mother of a sibling group of four had recently died. The two teen boys attended the funeral services but the very sensitive 7 and 8 year old siblings had not been told. The older teens had been placed in a position of keeping information from the younger children. We advised the parents to tell the younger children during the 10-week series so that our staff and the other group members could help them process the loss. The children did well with the information, planning a special grave-side service. The young daughter even wrote a poem. Had the children not been told by their parents, they would have found out eventually, and in a manner that could be traumatic and lead to loss of trust for the adoptive parents. This could have caused them to distrust both their parents and the older siblings.

The birth family fantasy

In the fifth session the children are taken on a fantasy walk and helped to discuss how they picture their birth families. Most have little or no memory of them as they are in closed adoptions. Their responses differ greatly from the teens. In the children's fantasies the birth family is intact. The birth mother and father are together. Young children often fantasize that their birth families are wealthy or even royalty.

They often visualize the birth family searching the world for them. One little girl was sure she was the child of the lady doctor on the Star Trek series. She would stop people on the street to ask if they knew "Dr. Crusher."

One thing they all have in common is that when they

visualize the parents they've never seen, the faces are blocked from view. They can usually describe hair and eye color, whether they are tall or short, large or thin, as most children have learned the information from profiles the adoptive parents have shared with them.

The younger children exhibit no anger toward the birth family in group. They especially accept the placement if they were told that the parents were very young at the time of their birth.

The children are quite relieved to note that all of the other group members also have a fantasy and similar to their own. Many parents have told us prior to the series that their 7 or 8 or 9 year old does not talk about adoption or the birth parents and they are pretty sure that the child does not think about it. We have never seen one child in our series who did not have a well-developed fantasy about the birth family.

The parent group leaders ask the parents to talk about birth parent fantasies with their children and give them as many actual details as they can in an age-appropriate manner.

The birth mother visit

The young children are in awe as they come into the room and find a "real" live birth mother is present. They have known for weeks she was to come that night. Some children may have brought special treats on that night. Some children want to dress in their very best clothes. A few enter the room with great anxiety, expecting someone who resembles their "fantasy" birth mother. It does not matter to the children of color that she is Caucasian. The young children are more shy and ask less questions than the teens. They are never confrontational. They all leave with a sense that their birth mother loves them no matter what the reason for their placement.

Support and education benefits for young children

The result of the 10 weeks is that the young children have had an opportunity to meet and interact with other adopted children in an atmosphere that has encouraged them to reveal their feelings. They have also realized that other adopted children share the same feelings, thoughts, and concerns. This interaction helps to normalize their status as an adoptee. Their grief is recognized and addressed, and validated, often for the first time in their lives. They are allowed to reveal their anger and frustrations in a safe and non-judgmental atmosphere. They are able to talk about their questions and wishes to search as well as their fears of what they may find. Some of the fantasies are replaced with realities they can manage. Most importantly, it has opened communication within their adoptive family.

One parent said, "My children found the group experience gave them a sense of belonging, of being like everyone else, for the first time. As their parents, we found it beneficial and life changing for them, in a way that no traditional counseling had ever been. Of everything we tried, and we tried most of what was available, this group was the most valuable for our kids."

Children and teens come to the group series for many reasons and the results vary. The following examples are representative of the youth and the issues they bring to the group:

The latency group scenarios

Mark — Mark was 12 when he joined the group and determined to be a disruptive influence. He was loud, mean to the others and challenged the group leaders. Mark was adopted as an infant and had ADD, Tourette's syndrome, and was being treated for depression. When asked whether others treated him differently (friends, neighbors, family, etc. because he is adopted), he placed his head on the table and began to sob. He told us he was tired of everyone picking on him at school. He was called names. His homework was stolen and ripped up. He was rejected and humiliated at recess. He said this "group" is the only place where he has acceptance. No one treats him different here. After this episode he became the star of the group. His behavior was exemplary. His parents called a few days after the incident to say he was positive and happy for the first time in his life. He brought treats and actually corralled the others when they would try to act up. Several years later he remains positive. His parents told us they had been ready to give up and could not believe the change. He was truly our miracle!

Teri — Teri's single mom brought her to group because she was having attachment issues (unable to give affection), poor peer relationships, and talked about adoption a lot. She was adopted at age three after being abandoned at the age of 11 months. In group she said she felt her birth mother did not want her because she was not worth much. She only had one friend and thought no one liked her.

She was pleasant in group, although reserved. She said she felt more comfortable with boys, and did not want to be in a group with girls. She talked of feeling worthless like someone who had been given away. As the group progressed she began to talk about her gender issues and expressed the desire to be a boy. Further counseling was suggested as her depression and feelings of self worth were hindering her development.

Penny — Two very angry parents came to us with 10 year old Penny. She had been adopted at the age of six. Their 16 year old adopted son was a good student who excelled at every activity and he was a joy to parent. They had expected that Penny would behave much like their son after a short period of adjustment. However, Penny has had severe behavior behavioral problems (including temper tantrums, and fire setting) from the time of placement and now the parents and the older son were disillusioned and wanting to dissolve the adoption.

Penny was cooperative in group and openly fearful of her home situation. During one session she became upset and ran from the room. One of the group leaders found her crouched down in the hallway. She sobbed that she knew she was going to lose her home and family. She said, "They just don't know how hard I am trying. I go willingly to counselors and the hospital. I have tried with every thing they sent me to. Why can't they see how hard I'm trying?"

Sadly, the parents had already reached such a point of disconnectedness to the child that they failed to participate in the parent portion of the series. They dropped out after attending only 4 sessions. We were never able to re-engage them.

One parent who is raising two struggling teens stated:

Sometimes we parents get so caught up in the process of trying to help our kids that we don't realize what an overwhelming struggle it is for a child just to participate in all of the counseling programs we put them into. For a child to change long-term behaviors that may have become ingrained coping mechanisms many times requires abilities that our children do not possess. We need to do a better job of accepting the child we have and heralding the small successes.

The group series do not solve the youth's problems, or usually result in dramatic changes in behavior. The changes are usually subtle. The parent child communication improves, the teens and children understand their feelings and behaviors, and are more open to counseling. The participation in group offers a window to the professionals and parents to better meet the children's needs and offers a mirror to the child, to show that adopted children share many feelings and questions.

PART THREE

GROUP FAMILY PROFILES

Pseudonyms are used for all families who participated

Form Your Own Clan

Live like an Indian
With an arrow and bow
Follow the bison
Wherever they go

Live like a soldier
Fight in the fields
Disarm your enemy
Of the weapon he wields

Live like a ranger
Protect all the trees
Or live like a sailor
and ride the high seas

Live like a poet
Making words rhyme
Think very carefully
Take your own time

Live like a hermit
Stay all alone
Forget what has happened
And all you have known

Live like yourself
Follow no man
Follow your heart
Form your own clan

5

Parent Survey Responses

Six families from our long-term adoptive parent support group wrote detailed accounts of the histories of their families. They and the other group members provided information for this section to give the reader an opportunity to meet all of our members.

We have tried, by utilizing responses to a written survey, to present a composition of the family histories and outcomes. The resultant compilation of figures and information is by no means a research piece with controls and statistical analysis. It is meant to provoke discussion and encourage adoption education. It is meant to encourage preservation services for adoptive families.

Those who read the parent stories and who realize that some adoptive children and their families face great challenges and struggles may make certain assumptions about these families and whether they are representative of our members. We have surveyed all of the group members to determine their histories and children's' behaviors or difficulties.

Twenty six parents responded to the survey. There are 21 children in their families. The tables that follow provide a cross section of pertinent statistics.

Parents ages at time of adoption

Age	# of parents
23–29	12
30–39	9
40–49	4
50–56	1

Level of parent education

Education	#
High school	3
Tech or 2 yr. college	7
Bachelors	6
Masters	6
Post Grad/Ph.D.	4

Child's age at time of placement

Age	#
newborn	5
5 wks	1
3 mo	2
4 mo	1
11 mo	1
14 mo	1
18 mo	1
3 yrs	3
4 yrs	1
5 yrs	2
11 yrs	3

Placements prior to adoptive home

# of children	# of placements
8	1
6	0
2	2
1	3
1	4
1	6

Country of origin

Country	# of children
USA	17
Korea, Vietnam	2

Race of child

Race	# of children
Caucasian	15
Asian	2
Biracial	1
African Amer.	1

Method of adoption

Method	# of children
Public agency	12
Private nonprofit	4
Private/atty.	4
Private agency	1

Reason child was available for adoption

Reason	# of children
Voluntary adoption plan	13
Removal by human services	8

Developmental disorders or birth history problems

Diagnosis	# of children
No known genetic or congenital problems (at the time of placement)	14
attention deficit hyperactivity disorder †	9
fetal alcohol syndrome (FAS/FAE)	7 ‡
severe behavioral handicapped(SBH)	4

† (ADHD)   ‡ (suspected/or diagnosed)

Current age of adoptees ⋆

Age	# of adoptees
17	1
18	2
19	2
20	1
21	3
22	1
23	3
24	3
26	1
27	1
30	1

⋆ Two deceased, (at ages 15 and 19 in car accidents)

**Eleven Children required care
outside of the adoptive home** *

Age at placement	# of children
11	1
13	2
14	3
15	4
16	1

* Type of placement	# of children
Children services custody	10
Residential care	7
Foster care	7
Psychiatric hospitalization	6

Some children had several out of home placements

Approach to discussing adoption with child

Approach	# of children
Early informed	18
Open discussion	12
Read books to child	6
Didn't talk since told to raise as a birth child	1
Made major attempt to indicate adoption was positive	18

Pre-adoptive preparation and/or training

Preparation	# of parents
None	13
Classes through public agency	5
Was foster parent	1
Read *Adopting the Older Child* by Claudia Jewett	1

—

Types of interventions* sought for child and/or family

Assistance	# of children
Counseling	17
Temporary custody to county	11
Parallel education series	9 families
Medications	7
Psychiatrist	6
Psychological evaluations	6
Inpatient hospitalization	6

* Families may have listed more than one

Interventions# that were effective (open responses)

Assistance	# that worked
Parents united	All families
Parent support group	13
For child – nothing	11
Parallel Education series	7
Time to mature	3
Ritalin (in grade school)	3
Choose battles — concentrate on a few issues	1
Structure	1
Counseling for parents	1
Respite care	1
Sports involvement	1

Families may have listed more than one

What didn't work (no categories offered for this question)

Grounding, talking, rewards typical parenting techniques	All
Counseling	6
The county custody	5

—

How are things now? (open responses)

Good relationship between parents and young adult	9
Calmer	8
Is slowly maturing	8
Unable to maintain employment long	6
Severe emotional disability	5
Married	5
Working full time	4
Using alcohol and/or other drugs	3
Unknown /little contact	2
Deceased at age 15/19 (car accident)	2
Single parent	2
In college	2
Nearing college completion	1
In prison	1

How do you see the future for your child? (open responses)

Closer relationship between us	10
Child is continuing to mature	9
Unable or unwilling to work on issues	8
Still needs to mature and work on issues	8
Doubt will ever be completely dependable	7
Continuing dangerous associations and environment	6
Stable future	6

The following quotes were responses to the question: "What do you wish you had known prior to adoption, or done differently?"

"I wish I had known how big a role genetics play. We needed much more birth history information. I wish we had been more proactive in seeking information about his background before the adoption."

"I wish we'd known what we were getting into and that our impact would be minimal. We would still have adopted, but wouldn't have beaten ourselves up so much."

"We knew nothing of the potential problems."

"A united front for parents is crucial to success. We were so concerned about his problems that it nearly destroyed our relationship."

"Intensive education and resources by post-adoption specialists could have eased our way."

"We wish we had never contacted children's services, they made it worse."

"We trusted professionals whose knowledge was marginal, at best."

"We were rattled by demands of teachers who lacked the ability to cope with our son's problems. I wish we'd been more aggressive with the schools and courts and not taken so many attacks of, 'You're an awful parent!'"

"We wish we had focused more on building his self-esteem."

"I wish I had known it wasn't me. Second guessing myself didn't help. I should have trusted myself instead of blaming myself for their behaviors."

Words for others

Our parents offer advice and comments in the hope that they can help others who may be thinking of adoption or raising adopted children:

1. "Identify your expectations for the relationship. You cannot adopt the family you would have had biologically."
2. "Identify behaviors you can live with and endure (before adopting)."
3. "Keep your list of things you need to have control over to a maximum of 4-5 (e. g. child safety and your safety)."

—

4. "Keep telling them you love them."
5. "Present positive values."
6. "Learn as much information about the child and his history as possible before you adopt. If something sounds funny, question it."
7. "Be prepared for what you are undertaking. Find out everything about family background and have reasonable expectations. You'll need to understand and accept, that you won't have the same family with adopted children that you'd have had with birth children."
8. "It is important to seek knowledge and assistance when problems are first suspected, before they start school, perhaps even before the adoption."
9. "Get in touch with adoption specialists when the child is young, prior to the invasion of problematic behaviors. Don't take advice from 'rookies' or from people not trained specifically in adoption."
10. "We no longer look at adoption through the same rosy glow, but we realize there is still a need."
11. "Your children will need love, commitment, and the teaching of values; but that is not enough. You must learn all of the information about the child's history and raise the child you have, not the child you wish him/her to be. You must accept that your child may have dreams and a reality that does not fit your dreams, for example, education may mean little."
12. "We would caution other prospective adoptive parents that it is possible that loving your adopted child fully may not be enough. You need to know about adoption issues. You will need to understand that your child may be genetically programmed to think differently than you and you will need to respect those differences, even when they conflict with yours. You will need to understand that your child will have pain that you cannot fully appreciate or eliminate."

13. "We hope that we will someday be able to encourage parents with less fear for them, but right now we are still suffering heartbreak from our son's situation."
14. "Find a support group for adoptive parents."
15. "Believe in yourself! Be bold — you are in charge."
16. "Don't give up — it may take a long time — but we feel they are ours for life!"

Remember that this is not an easy journey: "Think of your family as a car, with you as the engine. You need to keep refueling. Too many of us don't look for help until we are running on fumes. It's important to take time to nurture yourself and for couples to nurture each other."

As another adoptive parent stated, "If you're going to last to the finish line, you have to learn to pace yourself so you can go the distance. This is not a sprint. This is a marathon."

Behaviors

Each family that completed the survey provided information about their child's developmental years. The short descriptions show both the range, and similarity of behaviors among our support group families. The families represented below are not among those who wrote extensive stories for the book.

The Albertson Family — The Albertson Family adopted two children as infants The early years presented no difficulties with either child. Their daughter had no learning disabilities, but was hard to motivate in grade school. Their son was diagnosed with attention deficit disorder and was very active. Sports helped him direct that energy until his mid-teens.

When their daughter was thirteen, school performance fell apart, she became sexually active, and began using drugs. An untimely pregnancy at 19 led her to make the decision to change her life. She is a now a good and loving mother who has sought further education and supports herself well. She has matured into a responsible person who now expresses appreciation for her family.

As a teen, their son committed thefts, vandalism, and abuse of alcohol. His parents became well known to all the police in their small suburb due to all the court appearances. He threw wild parties when they dared leave him overnight. Mrs. Albertson said, "He had multiple car accidents (possibly due to his attention deficit disorder) and calls from school about his behavior disturbed our work almost daily."

He has always refused to talk about adoption or his birth history. The Albertsons believe he harbors great bitterness toward his birth mother. He is now in college and is more responsible and affectionate toward his family. Both children, at deep risk as teens, are doing well now, despite how dark things looked a few years ago.

The Kramer family — They adopted their son as an infant. As time went on they suspected FAS. He had trouble with attention deficit and hyperactivity almost from the start. He destroyed almost every toy he had. After his third week in kindergarten, his teachers, his principal, even his bus driver, had called to complain about his behavior.

The chaos, anxiety, and disruption he caused brought embarrassment to their daughter, who was a well-behaved child. To about 8th grade she brought friends over, until one night when he lost his temper and her friends saw him twist his mother's arm in anger. The resultant bruises caused co-workers to ask if her husband was beating her. Their daughter didn't bring friends over again until he had left the home. Mrs. Kramer said, "I often regret that she was never able to express any normal teenage rebellion. I wonder if she sensed that if both of them acted out, her father and I would go over the edge."

He sabotaged any and all family activities. He would complain that the family never did anything together and then when they did, he would make it horrible. After he became involved with drugs and alcohol, they thought things had reached rock bottom, but their fears reached new levels when they found evidence of devil worship. He made suicide attempts at ages 15, 17, and 19.

There were few positives and if he started doing well, he would quit or sabotage himself. He burglarized a neighbor's home, causing an awkward relationship. He was so destructive that they had to lock things away. If he wanted them, he broke in.

When he was at his worst, social services told them to take him back home or lose permanent custody, and he would go to another adoptive family. (This is a tactic used by social services agencies with many of the families in our group. Some agency personnel try to frighten the parents into taking the child back into their home, where the child is often the most volatile and may harm himself or a family member). Mr. Kramer recognized this as a scare tactic, and told them to do whatever they had to do, but their son wasn't coming home until he was no longer a threat to anyone. Social services never brought the matter up again.

He is no longer at his last address and, and at age 23, they have no idea where he is.

The Bell Family — The bell family raised two adopted children and a birth child. Both children were adopted as infants, yet serious issues of identity, control, and attachment plagued the family. Their daughter was at times helpful and compliant, but in the teen years she ran away countless times, often living on the streets for months and doing drugs. Diagnosed with borderline personality disorder, she easily manipulated the system and social workers. At one point while living at home, she was so unable to function with people who loved her that she falsely accused her father of sexual abuse, knowing that would get her taken out of their home. Devastated, he found himself unable to even hug his other children without feeling paranoid. Social services believed her. They reported piling up legal bills and lethal levels of stress, before convincing the system that there was no basis for the allegations.

Their daughter sabotaged any chances of success and experienced four pregnancies; one miscarriage, two children were placed for adoption, and one she kept. This infant sadly died of sudden infant death syndrome (SIDS). The baby's death devastated the whole family as she and the baby were living at home at the time. She returned home a few months ago. She is now in her mid-twenties and still leads a nomadic life. She still can't hold a job for more than a few months, and still leaves any situation whenever there is a problem. Recently, she became engaged to a man in his late forties.

Their son (22) has attention deficit disorder and still struggles with poor impulse control. In his difficult teen years he excelled at sports, but was challenged by impulsively and short attention span. He related badly to authority figures. As an angry teen he once hit his mother in the head with a phone but she explained, "He didn't hit me very hard." The family handled the angry outbursts rather than involve the authorities and lose what ever control they had over their son. He always fell apart during birthdays and holidays, depressed and withdrawn. Expecting the upheavals made them easier to handle. The issues have now abated as he nears college graduation. He is of Asian heritage and chose a college in a city with a high Asian population. They believe he felt like an alien in our city of few oriental faces. He calls often, and now that they are physically distant, the emotional relationship is far closer. The support group members felt that no other home could have maintained him, but his adoptive parents were gifted at diffusing and working around his anger.

Their birth daughter struggled with the difficult behaviors around her while growing up. She resented the time and efforts devoted to her siblings. Like all our parents who also have birth children, they struggled with guilt about the chaos their adoptive children unwittingly brought into their lives. At present she is happily planning her wedding.

The Bells observed while sitting in support group that, "We all had different parenting styles, but many of the children have had the same behaviors and outcomes."

The Chambers Family — The Chambers Family adopted an eleven-year-old boy. Before coming to the adoptive home, he had endured his mother's suicide, abuse from his father, and three foster placements. The Chambers had never parented before and felt very positive about the first two calm and positive years. He had counseling throughout his teen years as control issues and manipulation became problematic. At 17 he fathered a child with a 13 year old, and before the year was over had attempted suicide twice. At 18 he received a fairly large inheritance, but as his parents feared, he spent it all in about 2 weeks. He attempted suicide again at 19, the same year his second child was born. He acquired a GED at age 20 having left school in the 10th grade.

For several years there were minor scrapes with the law and failure to keep a job more than a few weeks at a time. He called regularly for financial help. Crisis after crises became a pattern in his life. He is now at home temporarily while he saves money for an apartment and looks for a new job.

His parents stated, "We often baby-sit the grandchildren on weekends. We're unhappy about the children's' living conditions but are reconciled to the fact that we can't control the situation. He returned to our town to be near his children, and supports them as much as he can, emotionally and financially. We support him emotionally as much as we can, but let him face the consequences for negative behavior, hoping he'll learn from it."

The Miller Family — The Miller Family adopted a five-week old girl and a three-month old boy. They adopted after learning they could have no biological children. Their son was an irritable baby who required much holding. As a small child, he was likable, but couldn't follow directions and had poor listening skills. After years of struggle they had him tested. He was diagnosed with fetal alcohol syndrome (FAS) and attention deficit disorder. His teen years were troubled due to violent outbursts and drug use. He left home (after striking his mother and knocking her across the room) as the parents feared worse injury due to his outbursts. Drug use and the disabling effects of FAS are taking a terrible toll. He is unable to work and they do not currently know his whereabouts. Mrs. Miller reluctantly related, "We live one day at a time knowing tomorrow may bring news of his death. I avoid talking of him because when I do it brings tears."

Their daughter was a healthy, likable, easy-going child until the age of twelve. She then experienced a radical personality change that led to drugs, alcohol, and sexual promiscuity in her teen years. Her behaviors became so dangerous that her parents feel it was a miracle she survived. She snuck out at night, threw wild parties if they were away, and rebelled at any attempt to parent her. When she was sixteen, things got so bad that they literally threw her things out on front step, and told her to leave. They tried psychologists, grounding, and rewards; all to no avail. They feel that only time and maturity helped their daughter. She is now an adult in her middle twenties. She has a healthy marriage and parents her three children beautifully. *It is hard for the group to realize that she is the same person as that rebellious teen her parents were so heart sick about.*

Mrs. Miller says, "I look at my daughter now with her children and I see the closeness and the bond there and know it will always be there. That's how families are supposed to be, but it isn't how ours was." Mrs. Miller adds, "If I could go back in time I'd have blamed myself a lot less for the problems and I'd trust my instincts more. If anything, I'd be even firmer with them than I was. We found praying helped us to keep going in the tough times. We turned a corner as parents when we attended the education series and the support group. There was a radical improvement in our lives as we began to understand we weren't the cause of our children's problems." The Millers now find that time with their daughter and grandchildren nourishes them and brings great happiness.

Mrs. Miller advises parents to, "Seek help early on. Find an adoptive parent group. When you're not in crisis, keep attending to help others. Your children will find a guide (mentor) for themselves. When they are ready, a teacher (guide) will come along for them."

What are the positives about adoption?

The following statements are responses to the survey question, "What are the positives about adoption?"

Many of our children are doing well now: "Our son is in the army with a six-year-old step-son. Our daughter is on her own and working full time. We learned not to expect exceptional achievements and to take pride in their accomplishments. They both graduated from high school, neither fell into drug addiction or had children as teenagers."

They stay in touch and turn to us for emotional support:

"Our son calls every week. When our daughter skidded her car on ice, she raced to our home and into my arms for a hug. My daughter said, 'When it happened, the first thing

I thought was I wanted to go home to mom'."

<u>They will probably parent well</u>: "One thing we wanted to accomplish by adopting older children was to stop the cycle of abusive parents raising children who became abusive parents. Both of our children have shown signs that they are the kind of people who'll nurture and protect their children."

<u>A strong marital relationship</u>: "Most of us had time to build a strong foundation before becoming parents." Despite the stresses, most adoptive parents endure — only 11% will divorce.

Survey analysis

We do not present the survey or results as a scientific study. We present it as a window to the lives of those who have adopted and raised children who needed specialized care and attention. All of the families who belong to the group came to us in a period of crisis. The families represent a part of the adoptive population who have endured great struggles and pain to raise children who had very difficult childhood and or adolescent years.

The parents ranged in age from mid-twenties to mid-fifties at the time of the adoption. Their educational levels were from high school to Ph.D. level. They had all experienced success in their personal and professional lives. The children ranged in age from 2 days to nearly 12 years at the time of placement in the adoptive homes. Few parents had any practical preparation for raising adopted children. They all stayed committed through the most difficult of times. Their parenting styles varied greatly. They all dreamed of building a family through adoption and were dismayed to find that their dreams of an ideal family had to be replaced by the, sometimes painful, realities. Once they defined their problems, they each learned all they could about the them, the ways to address them, and then recommitted themselves to the child and the child's needs.

—

The parents all said that they wish they'd had extensive training, support, and knowledgeable professionals to guide them. The majority of them said they would still adopt, but would greatly alter their approaches, expectations, and methods of managing schools and other bureaucratic systems and institutions.

PART FOUR

ADOPTIVE FAMILY BIOGRAPHIES

This section contains the detailed adoptive experiences of six families from the support group. They were written by each family and are presented in their own words. Editing was only for clarity and the amount of space available.

Pseudonyms are used in all instances with the exception of professionals who interacted with the families.

Glaring Glass

Once I spotted them, I couldn't help
Staring at the check-out line
Next to mine.

They were a *Real* family:
Father smiled at Mother,
Mother beamed at daughter,
Merely a younger version of Mother.
They had the same brown curly hair,
Deep brown eyes,
Little upturned nose;
They even smiled alike.

I watched them with envy
Until they left the store.

As soon as I got home,
I ran straight upstairs, to the
Bathroom and locked the door.
Elbows resting on the cold,
Smooth porcelain,
Face resting on clenched fists,
Staring into the mirror.
The face reflected in the glass was
Glaring at me.
How I hated that face for being
Different.

Hours spent studying, scrutinizing,
Searching,
For even one similar feature;
My eyes, my nose, my lips,
my chin—
Not one feature resembles my mother's
or father's
This is what makes me so *ugly.*

A Foreword

to Our Adoptive Family Biographies

by Rosemary Haggerty

Six of the adoptive families in our support group wrote their stories for this book, with name changes to protect their privacy. While revisiting the past, at some point all of us hit an emotional wall and stopped writing. Some of us went back to it. Some found it too painful.

The Dugan, Brenn, Patterson, Kelly, Fremont, and, Brach family stories share many similarities. Most of the families were well into crisis situations before locating the support group. The common themes are the extreme behaviors of the children and the frantic search for help shared by all of the families.

We all discovered Parenthesis, an organization that supports adoptive families in crisis, after years of turbulence with our adoptive children. Most of us began our Parenthesis journey with ten-week parallel group sessions. Every week the adoptive parents talked about the chaos at home to adoption specialists leading our group. Was the problem our parenting; our inability to stay calm after hours of passive/aggressive behavior, or hour-long tantrums from our children?

"The problem isn't you," they told us. "It's adoption issues." Our children were acting out their grief and rage at the loss of their birth mothers and siblings.

Besides defining the problem, the group leaders gave us solutions that worked. They also affirmed what we adoptive parents had learned the hard way: regular parenting techniques only fueled the fires we were trying to extinguish.

We learned how out of control our children's lives felt since strangers had made life-altering plans for them. So they fought to control what they could, resisting any house rules or any parenting, turning school into a battleground with homework the weapon of choice. In group we realized that parents couldn't fix behaviors they weren't causing. But parents *could* alter their reaction to those behaviors, which changed everything. *If one of you gets off the seesaw, the game quickly loses its appeal.*

When adolescent hormones escalated our children's defiance into total war, my husband and I joined a monthly group for parents whose children lived away from home, for their safety and the safety of the other family members. In that group we met the families who contributed to this book.

One night a month we talked, laughed, and cried together, discussing the dilemmas we'd been dealt: children who raged over past abuse, children with diminished emotional control, who couldn't understand cause and effect because their birth mothers used alcohol during pregnancy.

We found anger and fear corrosive, so we laughed more than we cried, mining humor in every emotional landslide, helping each other to survive. One single mother came to group barely able to speak after years with a defiant, physically aggressive, hyperactive daughter. Her inability to solve her daughter's problems threw her into a major depression. While she struggled to accept what she couldn't change, we watched her evolve into a strong, resourceful woman who now helps other parents.

In group we pooled information while brainstorming problems. We learned that on birthdays, Christmas and Mother's Day, the behavior of all our kids took a dive. Those days resurrected thoughts of their birth families, which churned their grief and anger closer to the surface. Working together enabled us to recognize the patterns, anticipate the storms, and effectively head of some of the explosions.

We found other patterns. All our bank accounts had hemorrhaged money for legal representation, because the courts blamed us for our children's problems. Psychologists added to the financial drain and rarely helped, since most weren't trained in adoption issues. Did I mention adversarial social workers? We'd all dealt with at least one who assumed that all problematic child behavior stems from poor parenting. In group we told jokes, gained insight, strength and tenacity from each other, and became harder to manipulate, financially, legally, or psychologically.

We learned to accept that you can't mold a child's basic nature into something else in a different home. You can nurture his potential, but intellectual curiosity, or the desire to work hard to achieve a goal can't be grafted onto a child's DNA if he is missing that strand.

Most of our children are doing far better that we dared hope a few years ago, and we thank God for that every day. But we wonder how we'd have survived without the support group. We wonder how other families do, running into the same emotional walls with out feedback from other adoptive parents, and without the guidance of our group leaders.

We wrote this book for anyone considering adoption or on the adoptive journey, to share our experiences, our problems, and the solutions we found. We understand more than anyone how much you want children, and we know how much support your family will need. Support, we hope, will be more available to you than it was to us.

We also know how fiercely you will love your adopted children, and how lucky they will be to have found you.

With all our hearts, we wish you well.

6

Amanda

by Amanda, age 17

---

*This essay was written as a school assignment. The author (now
a young adult) hopes this will help adoptive parents and caseworkers understand the transfer from the child's perspective. Amanda
explains: "This piece, titled 'Moving On,' written in grade twelve,
expresses how I felt about leaving my birth mother and my foster
family."*

The thing that is most obvious about myself is how
hard it is for me to rely on others. I have to do
everything for myself even if it means cutting myself
short of an opportunity. I guess this is a personality that I
put up for myself as a guard from the outer world.

Sometimes to me the world is my worst enemy. This
is because of how the world treated me as a child. I was
two years old, too young to understand the intentions of my
elders. Everybody kept saying that they knew what was best
for me, but how could they? They only knew what was best
for themselves, not for me or any other person. But then the
court got involved, and about a month later I no longer had
a mommy, nor did my sister, Katie. I couldn't understand,

what had I done that was so bad. I thought that I was a good kid, so why did my mother have to abandon me? It was then that I decided never to put my trust and/or faith into another human being.

This, though, did not last long. Shortly after being placed with my aunt, my sister and I were moved into our first foster home. I grew very attached to the whole family. I had a mom, a dad, a brother, and two wonderful sisters.

I HAD A REAL FAMILY! I put my love, trust, and faith into them. But then again I was let down. My real sister, Katie became a problem to the family and was removed. I was very attached to her and her loss caused too much pain. I began to act out thinking that they would bring her back but instead they changed their mind and decided that they would no longer adopt me. In a little over a month, a family came to check me out. A few days later the people that I had become so good at loving were no longer a part of my life.

The children were moved from the birth mother to an aunt. She took them to children's services one day after learning she would no longer receive monies from the family for their care. The children were not told prior to any of the moves what was to happen to them or why. The move from foster care to the adoptive home occurred just before Amanda's 6th birthday and indicated the lack of preparation for a move to an adoptive home and loss of her foster family where she was attached. Amanda lost track of her sister and has not yet searched for her.

7

The Dugan Family
by Irene Dugan

People never said to me when I was young, "If you have children." They said, "When you have children," so I assumed I would. It's a given, right? From an early age I reacted to babies the way metal shavings react to magnets. When I was an X-ray technician I held any infant who needed films taken. Then I became a flight attendant. After serving dinner I'd take any baby on board, supposedly to give his mother a chance to eat in peace, but really so that I could hold him.

Somewhere in my twenties, I started worrying about world population growth and decided to have one child, then adopt a child of the opposite sex so each child would have a unique place in the family. But as someone said, life is what happens while you're making other plans.

I didn't meet my husband, Jonathan, until after I was 30. An accident and two surgeries postponed our wedding until I was 34. Barring accidents, I'd always been healthy so I thought having children would be a breeze.

My first pregnancy lasted three months. I was stunned when people dismissed my lost baby as though she'd never existed. If my body hadn't been fertile, my imagination had: I'd decided my baby was a girl, and in my mind I'd held her in my arms and rocked her; we'd read *Cat in the Hat* and watched *Winnie the Pooh* together; I'd even pictured her walking down the aisle, radiant in a white lace dress. Why did everyone expect me to forget her now, as though she'd been a flu virus instead of a baby?

A few months later we tried again, and again we lost the baby. Incredibly, someone at the hospital put our name on a list of new parents, and sold it to local businesses. I'd answer the phone and a salesperson would say, "Congratulations on your new baby!" and start a sales pitch for insurance or baby pictures. I'd go to the mail box and find diaper samples and tiny containers of baby food. After the second miscarriage, I started wearing waterproof mascara. Eating became difficult and most nights sleep eluded me. It seemed the world was filled with pregnant women and stories of abused children.

I finally made peace with the second miscarriage. When I was nearly 40 we decided to become parents by adopting a child rather than chance having a baby with birth defects I couldn't physically manage.

Now, much as I loved babies, I figured there were long lines of people waiting to adopt them. But what about older children who needed a family? Who'd give them a chance?

I'd read that neglectful and abusive parents often raise children who parent the same way and I wanted to be a part of breaking that horrible cycle. I thought that adopting an older child and showing by our example what a loving home is all about would do that. Our child would grow up with the skills to be a caring and loving parent. Sure, I thought, an older child will probably be distrustful and difficult at first because of the past. But our love and support will overcome that, and with time and patience we'll have a close-knit, loving family, just like everyone else.

—

So we contacted the children's services department of a nearby county.

Amanda — Several weeks before we met her, Amanda's social worker called to tell us about a five-year-old girl who would be available for adoption soon. When we asked why her foster parents weren't adopting her, he told us that foster parents weren't allowed to adopt their foster children. We were so naive we believed it, thinking the caseworker would always be totally honest with us. (We later discovered that the foster parents had considered adopting Amanda, but decided they couldn't commit to a lifetime of her difficult behaviors.)

I'd read *Adopting the Older Child*, by Claudia Jewett, so I assumed that during the six weeks we waited to meet Amanda, she was being given a chance to work through her anger and hurt at leaving the foster family she had lived with and loved for two and a half years. I thought that much time and effort were being expended, preparing her to become part of a new, permanent family, because that's the way it's done, right?

Apparently not at that agency. Her caseworker and foster parents knew that Amanda expressed grief and loss with anger. Most children do. Grief feels terrible and fury feels powerful, so which would you choose?

To avoid having to deal with Amanda's formidable anger, and the tantrums that would accompany it, neither her social worker nor her foster parents told Amanda she was leaving there until the night before she met us! She was so totally unprepared, she remembers having to ask them, "What does adoption mean?"

Happy in our alternate reality, we couldn't wait to meet Amanda. Minutes before that happened, her social showed us a picture of her, something it hadn't occurred to me to ask for, and she was beautiful. She had large, deep-set brown eyes, long brown hair with bangs cut to curve around her face, and one huge dimple in her left cheek, exactly like my sister's!

When she met us, I think she was in total denial about having to leave the only real family she'd ever had. Almost six, Amanda weighed only 36 pounds and wore a girl's size 4. We learned later that most older adopted kids are smaller than average because the turbulence in their early lives has taken up the energy normally put into growing.

That night she wore a pink and purple stripped mini dress, pale pink tights, and hot pink leg-warmers. (I saved that tiny dress and if our house ever caught fire, I think the first thing I'd grab is the box that holds it.) We spent a couple of hours with her, and when her foster brother seemed too rough with her, I felt like a mother bear with her cub. But Amanda, I noticed proudly, was fearless.

I brought pictures with me that I left with Amanda. Pictures of my husband and I, and of our dogs, a Toy Poodle and a Yorkie, and of all of the rooms in the house so that when she came to visit the next weekend, things would seem a little familiar.

The next Friday we picked her up for her first weekend in her new home. We'd bought a night light to make her new bedroom feel safe and cozy, and I put my Paddington Bear and Raggedy Ann on her bed. I remember Amanda unbuttoning their jackets and removing hats, and then dressing them again, making them her own.

It all seemed to be going so well. We said prayers together and tucked her in that first night, feeling as if we'd died and gone to heaven. I got up three or four times just to make sure she hadn't kicked off her covers. At least that's what I told myself, but I actually got up to drink in the sight of my beautiful little girl sleeping, her face as peaceful as an angel's. Her social worker had told us that Amanda couldn't wait to have a family of her own, and of course we believed him.

We shouldn't have, because Amanda thought she already had a family—her foster family.

She wanted to live with them forever, and they had given her the impression that she could, encouraging her to call them Mom and Dad, and to call their parents Grandma and Grandpa. Her social worker thought it important that she bond with her foster parents. Too bad he hadn't worried about her later ability to bond with her adoptive parents.

After Amanda had stayed with us again the next weekend, we were told that since things went so well, she could move in with us the following week. We agreed, sure that she wanted it as much as we did. On the day of the move her social worker, in his infinite ignorance, even had us go to the foster home to pick up Amanda, instead of having the foster family bring her to our house. If the foster parents had brought her to us, and the move been handled with more sensitivity by the caseworker, she wouldn't have felt we were kidnapping her away from them.

The drive home was a nightmare. Every mile of the way huge tears ran down Amanda's face and dripped off her chin. She saw us as terrible people who'd stolen her from the only real family she ever had. Desperately sorry for her, my husband and I wanted to turn the car around and take her back, despite how much we wanted her, but we knew they wouldn't keep her.

She moved into our home one month before her sixth birthday, and proceeded to do everything she could think of to be sent away, thinking that if she succeeded she'd be reunited forever with the foster family she loved. Her pursuit of this goal was relentless.

When people talked about using a "time out," I didn't know whether to laugh or cry. Amanda only went to her room when carried bodily, and left the second I did. She spent most of her waking hours trying to make me lose my temper, resorting to one provocative statement after another. If I said nothing, she repeated what she'd said several times, then screamed, "Stop ignoring me!" If I agreed with her statements she then took the opposite position. Any attempts to set limits brought on a temper tantrum. She'd rage around screaming, tearing things up, and throwing objects for twenty minutes or more

Three months with the "terminator-in-a-little-pink-dress" had me shredded, confused, and defeated. I wanted to give her a safe, loving home. How had I become the enemy?

When people ask now why we didn't give up and take her back to the agency, I remember how much Amanda craved affection. At night, exhausted from her daily combat, she'd relent and cuddle in my lap. I'd rock her and sing Daddy's Little Girl, and You Are My Sunshine, and she'd try to sing along. Each night I'd find the strength to believe that somehow we'd make things work out. Each morning, however, she'd declare war again.

"If I can't tell you what to do," I remember her yelling when she was barely six, "you can't tell me what to do!" All parent/child dynamics was lost on our Amanda. But with a retarded birth mother and an alcoholic grandmother for early parental figures, she'd done whatever she wanted for the first three years of her life, and Amanda saw no reason to change that now.

Desperate for help, I finally called her social worker, who'd had no contact with us since Amanda moved in with us two and a half months before. I found out later (a phrase you'll hear again) that he should have been visiting us once a week.

His response to our daily chaos was to send us to the psychologist used by the agency. Working with her did nothing to improve Amanda's behavior. Ultimately, we discovered that taking Amanda to that psychologist was one of the biggest mistakes we ever made, but that comes later.

—

My husband and I worked at staying calm. We set limits. Amanda overstepped them. We meted out discipline and consequences. They, changed nothing. We were fair; we were consistent. We were not accomplishing a thing.

During that first summer with Amanda, a friend, who could see that we were totally depleted emotionally, offered to take her for a weekend so we could get away together. I remember the long drive to our hotel, with the two of us so exhausted we could barely talk. If our friend hadn't given us that respite to recharge our batteries a little, I don't think we could have held things together. If there is one thing I've learned, it's that there has to be some kind of respite care for adoptive families. Especially those with highly problematical children and the unrelenting stress they bring with them. Otherwise the adoptive parents might not survive the experience, much less keep the family intact.

Soon after we returned from our weekend away, Amanda's psychologist, having run out of ideas on how to improve her behavior, arranged for a phone call between Amanda and her former foster mother. The foster mother told Amanda that she already had children of her own, and had never considered adopting her.

Knowing I was listening, Amanda painted a terrible picture of life at our house. "Please take me back," she pleaded at one point. "This lady hates me and she's mean! She's mean to me all the time."

My heart developed a major fault line when I heard how cheerfully Amanda would have left us, to return to people who'd given her up because she was difficult, when we loved her with all our hearts, despite behavior far worse than they'd ever encountered. But she'd given them that fierce little heart of hers, and couldn't let herself trust us enough to do it again.

Her foster mother repeated that she had no intention of adopting Amanda, and that she couldn't ever live with them again. Amanda continued to plead with her until the woman ended the conversation.

I drove Amanda home from that session with tears dripping off my chin. Amanda didn't know what to do, and I think she knew she'd burned some serious bridges talking with her foster mother, but she also seemed to know, on some level, that no matter how much she hurt me, I'd still be there when she needed me. Soon things were back to normal again, which means they were none too good.

With Amanda, control was the name of the game. Extremely bright, she worked far below her ability in school, never handing in homework. At one point I foolishly decided that Amanda simply needed help with her organizational skills. I had a conference with her teacher, and we decided that each day Amanda would write out her list of homework assignments and have the teacher sign it. I'd check at night to assure the work was completed, and each morning I'd see that it was in her backpack before she left the house. This way, I thought, she'll learn the skills she needs to do it herself, and soon her teacher and I won't even have to be involved.

Amanda threw her homework away for seven weeks, rather than hand it in. "I'm not letting you treat me like a baby!" was her explanation.

I told Amanda's social worker that she kept saying she did not want to be adopted. He insisted that we ignore her. Once she's officially adopted, he told, us, she'll finally be able to let herself trust you. And we believed him, because we wanted so much for it to be true.

Nine months after she moved in we went to court and became her legal parents. And no, she didn't finally trust us us then.

This next part is hard for me to believe, even now.

Michael — Nearly a year after starting to treat Amanda, her

—

psychiatrist asked if we'd be interested in an eleven-year-old boy who was eligible for adoption.

"All Michael's psychological testing is normal. He's a totally problem-free kid," she explained, and went on to say that his mother met a maniacal control freak through a dating service, married him, and the man hated Michael.

Amazed that she'd even asked, knowing our situation with Amanda, I told her that I could barely cope with my daughter, and couldn't even consider taking a second child, no matter how great he might be.

Two weeks later, I got a call from Michael's social worker, who could only have gotten our name and number from Amanda's psychologist. He said he'd heard we were interested in adopting Michael. Surprised, I once again found myself explaining that, frazzled as I was with Amanda's behavior, I certainly couldn't take on the responsibility for another child.

Yes, I should have confronted the psychologist about giving out our number, but naive to the death at that point, I thought it was over and couldn't see the point in making a scene.

A couple of weeks later, I took Amanda to spend some time with my family. I'd canceled her weekly appointment with the psychologist, telling her we'd be out of town visiting relatives. When I returned home, my husband told me the psychologist had called him while we were away. She'd told him that I really wanted to adopt Michael, but turned down the possibility only because I thought Jonathan didn't want a second child!

"Every man wants a son," she'd told Jonathan, pressing all the right buttons: imagine teaching your son to throw a ball, going to games together. Of course my husband believed her when she said that I wanted to adopt Michael. What sane person would assume the psychologist treating his daughter would lie about something like that? I learned that the psychologist and my husband had already set up a meeting with the boy.

I was flabbergasted.

For the first time in our married lives, what we had was a major lack of communication. Both of us knew we were barely staying afloat trying to deal with Amanda's behavior problems, but each of us thought the other wanted to adopt Michael, and we both felt great empathy for him.

How, I thought, can I cancel the meeting? I'd be putting this child through another rejection, and he's been through so much already. Besides, Jonathan wants a son, and how can I deny him that?

As hard as the psychologist's previous behavior had been to believe, it got worse.

She told us that she'd already approached Amanda about it, and Amanda really wanted an older brother. Amanda didn't contradict this, because, with her record on the truth, she thought we'd never believe her over a grown-up. We found out later (this phrase comes up a lot, doesn't it?) that Amanda had told the psychologist that she didn't want an older brother, she wanted a younger brother or sister.

Another thing we found out later was that moving an older child in with a younger child is almost always a mistake. It isn't a natural progression, since the newest child in a regular family is always younger. Plus an older child has more privileges due to his age, which a younger child may deeply resent.

Why didn't I confront the psychologist for going behind my back, and misrepresenting how I felt to my husband? Because I was stunned, and because I was drawn to this homeless child. A part of me did want to adopt Michael and give him a home and family, and that part muzzled all of the saner cerebral areas signaling: OVERLOAD!

Why did the psychologist lie and manipulate to have

Michael placed in our home? Well, she had told me how bright he was, and that she was concerned because his foster parents were simple people. She said they couldn't give him the educational nurturing and support he needed, or the social background. She tended to be elitist, telling me once what a pleasure it was to deal with someone who was intelligent, unlike all of her other referrals from the children service agency.

Flattery is one of the most effective manipulations, isn't it? And don't forget that Michael was a handsome, clever, well-mannered boy who really knew how to manipulate people himself. I think he charmed her completely. I've often wondered why, married and childless, she didn't adopt him herself.

She kept insisting that Michael was "problem-free and totally normal" and just needed a home and a family. Sounds too good to be true, doesn't it? But we had our psychologist's word on it and even with her track record, we believed her. She had to be telling the truth about something that important.

And I thought, who else will adopt an eleven-year-old? Most people want babies or toddlers. Michael might never have another chance for adoption.

Amanda's psychologist set up the meeting with Michael. Once again, I didn't have a clue what my future child looked like, and once again I didn't care.

He had curly black hair, beautiful, long-lashed brown eyes, and with his unusually white teeth, a wonderful smile. He was handsome, bright, and he had great manners just as she'd told us. Michael was part American Indian, and that really melted my heart. One of my favorite books as a child was *Jo's Boys*, and Dan, the character I loved most, was an Indian boy adopted by Jo.

Ambivalent describes how I felt about our psychologist. She certainly hadn't been honest with Jonathan about how I felt about adopting another child, and yet I couldn't believe she would lie about anything important. God, I was naive, but after a year with Amanda, I was running on fumes. My reasoning skills were, at best, dulled, and I wanted to believe that Michael was a totally normal kid who would be a good influence on Amanda. I wanted to believe we could give him the home and family he needed so badly. So I made myself believe.

Two weeks later he moved in with us. The next day he told us that his mother's sister and her sister's husband had wanted to adopt him too, but he'd chosen us. I couldn't believe my ears. We'd never been told there were family members willing to raise him.

It doesn't take a giant intellect to know that a child is often far better off with birth family members than with strangers. But no one had even mentioned to us that he had that option because if we'd known, we never would have agreed to the adoption. I found out later that, although they're delightful people, his aunt and uncle had less money than we did and we know how our psychologist felt about that! Michael said afterwards that he didn't want to live with relatives because his birth mother would know where he was. But she has never made any attempt to contact him.

If I'd had any sense, I'd have advised him to go to his aunt and uncle as he'd have been better served with biological family. However his aunt and uncle, being human, weren't thrilled that he'd chosen us, and I was paranoid about causing him any more rejection than he'd already endured.

We soon learned that our decision to take Michael was a mistake. As even a diehard optimist like me now knows, no child could be problem-free who's mother has chosen her new husband over him.

—

Amanda and Michael — From day one, Amanda and Michael were gasoline and a match. Michael's mother and step-father had favored his younger sister, apparently thinking that treating her with extra affection while punishing him would bring him into line. We didn't know of the sibling issues in the birth family. The psychologist had told us that he and his biological sister were very close. Of course, his anger about his sister's privileged position was played out with Amanda.

Now Amanda would rather be hated than ignored, so if Michael ignored her, she'd do whatever worked to make him angry, and get his attention. He retaliated by getting physical. When I found he'd used a choke hold on her, I told him sternly that it was never to happen again, because she could be badly hurt. He seemed sincerely upset and apologetic.

While the children warred with each other, they also warred with us, and at any given time one of them was acting out. The loving, peaceful home that Jonathan and I wanted to share with children felt like it had been time warped to 1994 downtown Beirut.

Books on parenting skills were like kindergarten reading when we needed Ph.D. level, their mild methods laughably inappropriate. Time-outs and gold stars were not what we needed. Our children were willing to endure any discipline, lose any privilege to avoid doing what we wanted and to accomplish what they wanted.

We've learned that being moved from family to family makes most adopted children feel like pawns, so they fight to control whatever they can. One way our children controlled was through school work. Michael and Amanda knew that parents want their children to get good grades, so they did everything they could to avoid that. We learned that parents can set aside time for homework and create an atmosphere for learning, but cannot make a child learn or get good grades.

Finally, I told Michael, "When you're in school you're not working for me, you're working for yourself. If you don't change what you're doing it isn't going to affect my standard of living, but ten years from now you'll be earning $6.00 an hour, living over a laundry, and driving an old used car." I figured Michael, who craved any obscenely expensive Italian sports car, might hear that.

Our children also had to learn every lesson the hard way, not once but many times before they got it. To illustrate: when most children touch a hot stove and get burned, they learn: Don't touch a stove! Ours learned: don't touch the stove on Tuesday. The next time: don't touch the stove when you're wearing a blue shirt. Then: don't touch the stove when it's raining. Their learning methods followed this pattern in most of life's lessons.

And their anger was boundless, especially towards me. I know now that most adopted children are angry with their biological mothers for the loss of their family, and they focus that rage on the adoptive mother, partly because she represents a mother figure and partly because it doesn't seem right to focus that hate on your birth mother.

I didn't realize how depleted I was until I went to the family doctor with a sore throat, and when she asked how things were at home, I burst into tears. I was appalled when I couldn't stop crying. She suggested that Jonathan and I attend a 10 week education and support series she'd heard of for parents of adoptive children with behavior problems.

Finding that adoptive parents' group saved our sanity.

The education series

There was one room for the parents and another for the children. One of the mothers said later, "The parents sitting around that table looked like they'd just come out of a concentration camp." All of us had been fighting losing battles to establish "normal" families with our children, and dealing with levels of defiance that were incredible, and unheard of when we were growing up. Since none of our friends with biological children were experiencing anything even remotely similar, we were all blaming ourselves to some extent, thinking that if we could just figure out how to fix things, we could become a normal family too.

During the series we found that all of us were having the same experience. As one parent said, "you'd swear the same child was going from house to house."

Each of us had been told by the children's services people from our various counties, "All of your problems are due to your lack of parenting skills and your unreasonable expectations."

The most important thing I got from the series, and the one thing adoptive parents need desperately to understand, is that many adoptive children cannot be parented in the same way as biological children, because it just doesn't work.

At some point all of us had attended basic parenting classes, but they were designed for parents whose children hadn't experienced the losses and/or abuse our children had, and whose children were behaving within normal limits. None of the regular parenting techniques worked with our children, and our expectations certainly weren't unreasonable.

Like all those attending the adoptive parenting series, we had long before lowered any expectations we'd ever had for good grades to the point where we were happy with anything above an F. We'd all lowered any expectations for good behavior to the point where we were happy if the children weren't screaming profanity at us, throwing things, or shoplifting. Some parents had lowered their expectations so far they were happy if the child wasn't physically attacking them or practicing devil worship.

—

I can't tell you what a relief it was to hear that we weren't alone in the ordeal we were facing. We learned from the group leaders about our children's adoption issues: an inability to attach with adoptive parents due to past rejections, feeling disloyal to their birth families if they allowed themselves to become close to their adoptive families, their inability to deal with the rage they felt towards their birth mothers, and their transference of that rage to us.

The monthly support groups

All of the women in the group adopted a child imagining that now Mother's Day wouldn't be a sad experience. And it wasn't. It was much worse. On Mother's Day our adoptive children weren't thinking about their adoptive mothers, they were thinking about their biological mothers. All the sadness, loss, and rage surfaced, and it became one of the hardest days of the year for everyone concerned, especially the children. Then come birthdays and Christmas. We'd all learned to dread the days other families loved, because when our adoptive children were sad, they said it with anger.

Although Jonathan and I had assumed that most of our problems were due to our children's ages when we adopted them, other group members who had adopted infants reported many similar problems, because their children had experienced rejections and losses too. We learned that newborns turned toward their mother's voice moments after birth. They knew that voice. But for our children, that only-important-person-in-the-universe had disappeared.

Many were then placed in foster care, to give their mothers time to change their minds about adoption. The infants gradually became accustomed to their foster mothers' love and care, and attached to the families. Then they disappeared when the children were moved to adoptive families.

—

Unable to understand their previous losses, why would these babies trust that their adoptive parents wouldn't disappear like everyone else? Many emotionally fragile children can't bring themselves to risk one more connection to someone else they expect to abandon them, and whether it's convenient for society or not, what a child perceives when his mother leaves, and then his foster mother(s), is that he's been abandoned.

Did you know that if a child doesn't bond emotionally with his parents, he may be unable to internalize their values or develop a conscience? That was why so many of our group's children were constantly lying, stealing, and seemingly had no moral compass.

Another thing we discovered in group was that all of us had been misled or told only partial truths by the placing agencies. We were told that Amanda was neglected. We weren't told that she was physically and sexually abused. Many parents weren't told that their babies had been born to alcoholic or drug addicted mothers. If they'd been told, they could have expected, understood, and planned for the developmental and behavioral problems that resulted. Sadly, the code still seems to be, "Don't tell adoptive parents anything that might influence them not to adopt a child."

What's even sadder is that agencies seem to place the most behaviorally or emotionally impaired children with single parents who have little or no support system for when the going gets tough. The other mistake is placing such children with couples who've never parented before. Then they compound the problem by not providing them with the special parenting techniques they need. and give them no ongoing support.

One single parent in our support group recently called me to say she had finally pressed unrulyness charges against her 14-year-old daughter after experiencing years of being hit, punched and almost stabbed by scissors once. There

were also classroom disruptions, truancies and countless runaways. The child's attachment disorder specialist, also an
adoptive parent, said he couldn't live with the child. When
I went to court with her the next day, a caseworker from
children's services told the mother, in front of her daughter,
that the girl was just exhibiting normal teenage behavior!

Her experiences, along with others from our support
group, have taught us that a single person considering adoption will be more vulnerable and have less resources than a
couple. There may not be someone there to say, "You aren't
imagining it; this child is out of control." Becoming part
of an ongoing parent group can give feedback, emotional
support, and help with problem solving skills from people
who've been in the adoptive trenches themselves. And on
days when you're looking for a building to jump from, you
can pick up a phone instead and call someone who, unlike
your family and friends, understands what's going on in your
home.

The support group Jonathan and I joined has helped
us in a thousand ways. We've learned so much over the years
from those who had older children, and who could advise us
how to deal with behaviors they had already learned how
to manage. Behaviors our friends had never encountered as
parents. We learned from group that you have to let the
children own their own problems and to let school be your
child's responsibility. Trying to make them get good grades
is like trying to teach a pig to sing. It won't work and it
annoys the pig.

Besides the support, and the understanding we could
never find anywhere else, listening to other adoptive parents'
stories has kept us from making some of the same mistakes.
When Michael ran away the first time, I remembered one of
the mothers in group whose child had run away more times
than she could count.

"There's only one thing I wish I'd done differently,"

—

she told us. "I wish I had pressed unrulyness charges on the second runaway, instead of waiting so long to do it and putting everyone else in the family through hell."

I had a lot of respect for her opinions, so when Michael returned the next day I told him that I wouldn't play the run-away game with my children." You get one free runaway in this family," I said, "but don't do it a second time, because I promise you, and you know I never break my word, if you run away a second time I'll call the police and press charges."

When he did run the second time I pressed unrulyness charges with the court. When he refused a drug test, saying that it was his constitutional right not to, my antennae went up.

I asked him a direct question, and found he'd been smoking marijuana at a friend's house. He'd never tried it at our house, he said, "Because you'd have known right away."

While he was in detention over the weekend, our friends who had taken the children occasionally on weekends, told us Michael had used choke holds on Amanda more than once. They hadn't wanted to tell us because they knew how difficult things were at our house and, they said, "we hated to add to that."

When we questioned Amanda about it, we found that he'd nearly broken her finger the week before. He'd told her that if she ever reported to us that he was hurting her, and he was removed from the house because of it, he'd return and kill her.

We then found ourselves in court trying to have him kept out of the home because he might seriously hurt Amanda, even if it wasn't intentional. With some detective work, I managed to obtain some of Michael's old psychological testing.

The results far from mirrored the information given us by the psychologist who'd encouraged us to adopt Michael.

—

We followed up with new testing. The specialist who tested him informed us that Michael saw any connection to us as a weakness, and that because of his poor impulse control and his anger toward Amanda, there was a real probability that if he returned home he could hurt her. In court, after I brought that up, the judge asked Michael repeatedly to tell him that if he sent him home, he would not harm Amanda. Three times Michael told the judge that he could not make that promise. I'll always be grateful to Michael and proud of him for his honesty that day, despite what it would cost him, and despite a judge who seemed determined to make him lie.

Both the juvenile court system and children's services are programmed to deal with neglectful and abusive parents, and both had immediately taken an adversarial position with us. In order to keep the court from sending Michael back home, we had to spend thousands of dollars on attorneys. Frustration and anxiety filled our days; the feeling that we'd failed our son robbed any rest from our nights.

Finally, working with the court, we found a unique foster home for Michael with people who were adoptive parents themselves, and specialized in fostering adoptive children. She worked and her husband stayed home. This role reversal was a plus with adoptive kids, because their "mom" was a dad, so their rage toward the mother figures got dissipated there. I don't think Michael would have done as well anywhere else.

Then we discovered that Jonathan had cancer.

One morning I noticed that an over-developed muscle on the back of his thigh looked larger, and ominously different. I insisted he see a doctor, and that "over-developed muscle" turned out to be a cancerous fatty tumor. The oncology surgeon said, "According to what we know, a 30 year old fatty tumor can't suddenly become malignant, and if it had been malignant from the start, you'd be dead by now.

This is really one for the medical journals."

When a group of cancer patients took part in a survey, the results disclosed that over 95% of them had been under abnormal stress the year before being diagnosed. No kidding! We'd been doing daily battle with the county children's service agency and the court, both of whom saw Michael's behavior as "normal teenage rebellion." Sound familiar?

We found out that the cancer hadn't spread yet, and that Jonathan didn't need chemotherapy or radiation. When he came home after the surgery, Amanda's anger filled the house, because his illness scared her. I talked with her, trying to help her understand that yelling and chaos would keep her father from healing. Her behavior grew worse by the day. I called every possible respite source, but nobody who'd ever taken Amanda for a weekend would take her back, even for a few days, despite knowing about my husband's surgery. His pain increased, and we found he'd developed phlebitis in the affected leg. We felt there was no other option than temporary foster care for Amanda, and then we worked with a new counselor to prepare her to return to our home, which she did.

Around age nine Amanda's behaviors got worse. Limit setting of any kind brought on anger marathons. If I suggested she try the relaxation techniques her psychologist recommended, she'd yell, "I don't want to!" Fury would ratchet up to rage, with Amanda slamming around the house screaming insults, swearing, tearing things and throwing things. When she was yelling at me if I tried walking away, she'd follow me from room to room. I'd finally stop moving and find Amanda back in my face. I tried going to my bedroom and locking the door. She stood outside yelling, pounding on the door until I came out, genuinely afraid she'd break either her hand or the door.

I was advised, "If she won't leave you and give herself

a chance to calm down, you should leave." It was a hard concept to swallow, but I figured I had to try everything. The first time I left the house she made no effort to stop me, and had calmed down by the time I returned. I was so grateful I'd given the technique a chance. The second time she followed me to the garage door. The third time she followed me to the car. The fourth time Amanda grabbed for the door handle, and when I pushed the door lock, she hung onto a door handle until I'd backed out of the garage.

What, I wondered, will happen the next time? Will I have to fight her off to even get in the car? Or will she just keep holding onto the car door so that I'm forced to stop the car?

I fought with everything I had to keep it from happening, but by the time she was thirteen she was totally out of control, and we had to press charges for unruly behavior.

Once again we were in juvenile court. Once again our child was taken out of the home and placed in foster care. I kept remembering my parents telling me that I could do anything if I was willing to work hard enough. And because I was willing to work hard, I'd been successful at every important thing I tried to accomplish, until I watched my son and then my daughter leave our home to live somewhere else. Nobody had explained that in a relationship with another human being, you can only do your part of the work.

One of the post-adoption specialists told me that adopted children who can't let themselves attach will feel safer and will behave better in mediocre foster homes than they will in good adoptive homes. Their foster parents are being paid to take care of them, and the children don't feel required to develop emotional ties to them.

I wish hearing that had helped, but all I felt was an overwhelming sense of having failed my children.

What did help was the support group. Other adoptive parents telling us about their children, who five years before when we first joined the group, had to leave their adoptive homes because of their out of control behaviors. These same teens were now starting to become part of their family again.

When Amanda left after six and a half years with us, I sent her a card every week to remind her that we missed her, and we still loved her. She never acknowledged the cards, or sent one to us, but I found out years later that she'd saved every one. Deep down I always knew that no matter how hard Amanda fought it, or how hard she tried to deny it sometimes, she really does love us.

Amanda's return from foster care at age 12

She began acting out within ten minutes of her arrival back home. There have been daily tantrums of: stamping feet, tearing and throwing things, and hurting herself. Her behavior was so argumentative and unruly on the second day that I left the house to avoid escalation. The third day brought more tantrums. She began slapping herself repeatedly in the face as hard as she could, four or five times on each cheek. It frightened me that she'd deliberately hurt herself.

While she was in foster care, I'd arranged to attend a conference in New England, not knowing she'd be back home. She had several tantrums about my plans to go away. I tried to calm her and assure her of my love. She insisted I'd come back from the conference loving writing more than I loved her. I tried reassurance, reminding her that I'd done no writing for days, but had taken her to movies, shopping, and swimming. She just kept saying, "I just don't want you to write!" The raging went on for days.

One day she came to me crying, "I don't know why I'm so mad all the time" she said. It broke my heart to see she was as confused and upset about her behavior as we were. The psychologist advised my husband and I to tell her that she had a choice: stop the behaviors and stay, or continue and we'd have to press unrulyness charges.

The next day a woman revealed to me that our daughter wanted to live at her house. The mother of Amanda's friend, she was also a foster mother. Amanda had figured that by acting out, she'd be placed in foster care, in their house. All of the rages and tantrums had been a plan to live at another house because a friend lived there.

When I returned from the conference, the outbursts only intensified as her behavior escalated. One day I took her shopping for clothes She didn't like the store I'd selected, stomped out and swore at me on the ride home. That day she scratched, "I HATE YOU!" in big letters on her wall.

It had to stop. We called the police. As the officer led a defiant Amanda out I looked at her fierce little face as she passed me in the hall. "Why am I the only one crying? I asked her. She said, "I've cried all the tears I'm going to cry!"

★ ★ ★

We tried two more times to have Amanda live at home, but each time her behavior started to fall apart in the first few days. The arguing and temper tantrums would resume, and at one point she lost it and knocked me right off my feet. We finally learned that no matter how much we love each other, we can't live together. At least not yet.

But against all odds, both of our children graduated from high school, neither developed a drug habit, and neither became a teenage parent.

Those things alone should make us feel that we've accomplished a lot, but it's hard to feel like a successful parent when your child has had to be raised, part of the time, in someone else's home.

I can't imagine loving any biological child more than I love my adopted children, and I once asked a parent in our support group, who has both biological and adopted daughters, if she feels differently toward them. She said that if anything, she loves her adopted child a little more, because they've been through so much together.

It's hard to believe, but thirteen years have passed since we began our adoptive journey. Michael is in the Army now, and just married a lovely African American woman who was part of his unit in Germany. She has a five year old son who is handsome, incredibly bright, and well-behaved. Except for being geographically distant, he's everything you could hope for in a grandson.

We're thrilled that our daughter graduated from high school, and is in her first year in college. Amanda shares an apartment with several friends and works almost full time. Whenever anything happens that upsets or hurts her, Amanda comes over, and when she walks through the door she walks into my arms. We listen to her problems without being judgmental, give lots of hugs, and she leaves feeling better, which makes us feel better. I love knowing that our home is where she comes when the world hurts her.

Part of being a successful adoptive parent is accepting that your child has other parents and other allegiances, whether your child feels secure enough to share them with you or not. When they don't feel comfortable about sharing their feelings about the birth family with adoptive parents, most children search for their birth families in secret, not wanting to hurt their adoptive parents.

Michael knows where his birth family is, and helped put his stepfather in prison when he discovered that he'd sexually abused his biological sister. Unfortunately, despite his being found guilty of the sexual abuse of her 13 year old daughter, his birth mother again chose her husband over her child. He's out of jail and they're together again.

Amanda knows where her birth mother is, but hasn't chosen to see her yet. I've offered to help her find her older sister, who was adopted by another family, but both her

mother and sister are retarded, and so far Amanda has delayed contact. I can understand her ambivalence, and how
torn she must feel about what to do.

I wish we could have had specialized parenting courses
before we adopted the children, parenting courses that could
have given us the special skills one needs to be an adoptive
parent, but they weren't available then. They are beginning
to be, and if you're considering adoption the best thing you
can do for yourselves and your adopted child, is to find a
good adoptive parenting course.

There are now courses for school-age adopted children,
where they can discuss being adopted before it becomes an
issue, and before problems start. I wish our children could
have had that kind of help.

Jonathan and I have let go of the dream of being a
"normal family, just like every one else." We realize that
what we have is different, but we went into adoption wanting
to stop the cycle of abuse, and I hope we've accomplished
that. We wanted to make a difference in the lives of our
children, give them a chance to have a successful, happy life,
and I hope we've achieved that.

It isn't the family I thought we'd have, the kind you
hope for and dream about, and the hardest thing was letting
go of that dream. But you leave a burden behind when you
do.

Recently Michael was in town, and all of us were able
to spend a day together. We met his new wife and son, and
watched the boy who said, "Nobody's ever going to control
me," trying to control his five year old stepson.

We watched him take Amanda to a tire store and make
sure her new tires had good, deep tread for winter driving.
The boy who once wanted to strangle her had evolved into
a man who wanted to keep her safe.

We watched our impatient Amanda sit on the floor
and do the same puzzle over and over again with her new

nephew because he loved it, and because she wanted to make Michael's son happy.

We may not be your average family, but against all odds we are a family. We may not have always been their parents, and we may share them with parents from the past, but they will always be our children.

An open letter to Amanda

I can see you now, the way you looked when we first met: a tiny child with beautiful brown eyes and a dimple in your left cheek, wearing a pink and purple striped dress and light pink leggings. I've always felt lucky to have you for my daughter. On the worst day we had together, I've never once wished I'd adopted some other little girl, because I've loved you since the night we met. I'm so glad I saved that little striped dress. I'll always have a piece of the first hours we spent together.

My favorite memories of you, when you were little, are the thousands of times I rocked you in my lap, singing "You Are My Sunshine," and "Toora, Loora, Loora." It wasn't long before you were able to sing along with me.

I remember that first summer, when we played waitress. You'd take my order, and pretend to write it down, even though you couldn't write yet. Or you'd be Dr. Amanda, wrapping my ankle with a roll of elastic bandage.

My mind and heart are filled with memories of you: holding my breath as you'd roller skate at breakneck speed, then fixing your scraped knees after you fell. You were so tiny when you first moved in, you could "swim" in the bathtub. That summer, in your Mickey Mouse bathing suit, you'd play in the sprinkler, and eat frozen green grapes or the ice pops we made.

One day I let you splash in the pouring rain in every puddle in our court until you were filthy and muddy.

—

Then in the winter, I'd bundle you into your snowsuit, and you played outside till your cheeks were bright red.

I can see you so clearly, coloring at the table, playing with your Cabbage Patch Kids, or swimming like a mermaid, your teeth chattering when you left the pool.

I remember how you loved Quiche Lorraine with bacon on top and Grasshopper pie. And who could forget the day you learned to ride a bike? You smiled all the time it fell over sideways, because I was snapping your picture.

I remember millions of hugs, and the time you came back to your hospital room on a stretcher after the surgery you had when you were nine. I was so relieved that you were okay, I nearly cried. When I asked how you felt you said in the tiniest voice, "I'm fine, thank you. I'm just feeling a little droopy."

I have a million happy memories of you tucked away in safely in my heart. I know we've had difficult times, but I wrote this because I want you to remember we had thousands of wonderful times too. If and when you have children, you'll understand that since dad and I first saw you, you've had a home in both our hearts, and that won't ever change.

All my love, Mom

8

The Kelly Family
by Linda Kelly

I remember first hearing about adoption when I was about seven years old. My mom and I were watching a TV newsreel showing the Holts bringing their newly adopted children home to the United States. I remember my mother commenting on how cute the children were and what a wonderful thing it would be to adopt. The idea of adoption must have been planted in my mind at that time and continued to grow more and more appealing to me as the years passed. The time came that I married and began a family of my own. After giving birth to two children, a boy and a girl, the idea of adopting a third child began to take shape. I convinced my husband that instead of bringing another child into the world, we should adopt a child who would want us as much as we wanted him or her. Because we had two birth children already, an international adoption was the fastest way to get a child at that time. The war in Vietnam was raging so that was where we felt our child was waiting.

The adoption process began. Everyone was excited. Piles of paperwork and the long wait for a child occupied our plans and thoughts for the better part of the next year. Then we received a picture of our "son." We had requested a toddler and this was a six month old baby! Everyone quickly agreed—a baby would be a great addition. We made all sorts of plans, even named our new son Jason. But at the last minute, because of health complications, our baby was not allowed to leave Vietnam. We could wait, maybe for years, or we could go on with another adoption. After mourning our loss and talking among ourselves, we decided to continue our adoption in another country. We were impatient. We were told Korea had thousands of toddlers available.

My husband and I were called to the adoption agency a few weeks later and were shown a picture of a beautiful little girl with a tear on her cheek. We loved her immediately— and we were sure she needed us. Our children would have a little sister!

Before too many months had passed, we were on our way to Chicago to pick up our new toddler. After hours at the airport, our daughter finally arrived. She was the first child off the plane, and she was beautiful. I grabbed her and did not let go for hours. She, on the other hand, was not so wild about me or any of us. She was about eighteen months old and tiny for that age (malnourished). She could not walk and did not understand any English. Of course, she was terrified by these strange looking and sounding people. We weren't too concerned. This was to be expected. We would love her and everything would soon be great. Everyone knows love conquers all.

We traveled home and started getting to know each other. My son and I were the only ones Leisa would go to. My older daughter and husband felt hurt but didn't give up trying to earn her affection. After months of sleepless nights (and days) and fits of frustration, Leisa calmed down and we became a normal family. She continued to be my "little shadow," always at my side or on my lap. I was convinced she really loved me! We found one baby-sitter brave enough to stay with the children on the rare occasion we could tear ourselves away.

From age three on our daughter didn't talk about adoption or "her people." We (mistakenly) thought that was great. She wasn't concerned anymore. We'd done our job well integrating her onto our family. It worked—love had conquered all. She had found the family she needed. During this period from toddler to 13 everything went just as we had dreamed. This adoption business was easy. Then the bomb dropped.

Out of the blue, our daughter told us she'd been fooling us all along. She actually hated all of us, and wanted to leave our home immediately. She would live anywhere except with us. She insisted that if we wouldn't find a place for her, she would run away. Needless to say, after recovering from the shock, our hearts were broken!

The hunt for a therapist started. After having two teens, we knew that this behavior was not typical. It must be the adoption. The first therapist did not agree, saying our daughter was a typical teenager trying to spread her wings a bit. "Give her some space," he said.

Leisa got her space a few nights later when we found her packed bags outside the back door. Since she was determined to leave, a shelter for runaways was our only alternative. We dropped her off that night with the agreement that we would all get together for counseling in the days to come. After two nights of having her possessions stolen, Leisa decided to come home. She let us know, though, that she was only there passing time. She still hated us.

Fortunately, our next therapist was an adoptee who'd been through similar teen age adoption problems. Leisa refused to cooperate, saying "Adoption is your problem, not mine!" Some of her problems were: she was not like us; we treated her differently; she did not choose us to be her

—

family; if we had not wanted her, she could still be with her *real* mother; she wanted independence; she wanted to smoke—and the list went on. She became more intolerable and aggressive every day. Suddenly she could no longer keep friends and didn't want to go to school. She complained of illness much of the time. She ran away several times, but usually went to a friend's home where she felt safe and could have time away from us.

Our house had become a battleground. No one wanted to be there with her. We loved our daughter, but (and the feeling was mutual) we couldn't stand each other! If we could have found her birth mother, Leisa would have been on the first plane back to Korea with our blessings.

For our own sake, my husband and I continued counseling without her—for years. We then joined a support group where we discovered we were not alone. There were lots of families enduring the same struggles with their adopted children. Most of the kids had been adopted at birth. Most of the other parents' problems were worse than ours.

What a relief! We weren't failures as parents—we just didn't understand a thing about adoptees. Finally, we saw a light at the end of the tunnel. Our adoption therapist said "Give her three years and she'll be all right." She loved you once and she'll love you again."

At last there was some hope. We could hold on.

We were referred to an adoption education group for a ten-week series. Both parents and teens would attend in separate classes. Leisa went to one or two groups and quit because she felt the other kids were "crazy." I suspected it was because they all had worse problems. Besides, as she said, we were the ones with the problem—not her! We continued attending the classes without her and began to learn about the feelings many adopted kids had. We found there was a reason for the lack of trust; she was grieving and full of anger for a reason. She hoarded food and money

—

for another reason; to provide for herself. She might be afraid we were going to dump her so she was trying to dump us first. There was an explanation for every behavior we had struggled with. We heard stories from adult adoptees who had some of the same experiences and went on to have normal lives. They told us our daughter did love us. What great news! We were still committed. We would hang on.

We had been told that when most adopted teens act out it can last for three years, then the situation resolves. Our "three years" of turmoil turned into six, but we stuck it out. Times were getting better as we went along, with longer periods of calm between the crises. Of course, friends and family were pretty sick of her behavior and didn't understand why we kept putting up with it.

We were determined to help her get on her own. I went to the support group longer than anyone else and soon became a leader. Leading the groups seemed to help me as much as it helped the other members. I also became a co-leader of the parent education series along with a talented therapist. Each session also provided therapy for me too.

I worry about families who don't have these services available. I often wonder how families survive on their own. I fear many don't "hang in there" and the adoptions fail. We were lucky to get the adoption education when we desperately needed it. Without this help, I believe our adoption would have failed.

Our story ends well. Leisa went off to college and got the freedom she wanted. Apparently she decided we weren't so bad. She was back home after two quarters. We were friends again. Not family—but, what an improvement. She was pleasant to be around.

She's married now and expecting her first child and is so happy. She has a family of her own now, and she is looking forward to seeing a little someone who will, in her words, "look like me." A baby of her own!

—

She still keeps a physical distance. For both my husband and I, some hurt still lingers and the fear of rejection is still great. Although she still doesn't say so, she does love us. She calls us Mom and Dad now.

9

The Brenn Family
by Mark Brenn

P aula and I were married in 1978. She was 34 and I was 40. We wanted a family and thought about adoption from the beginning. After a miscarriage in 1980, we thought about it more seriously. In 1981, we began a series of classes with the county children services agency in preparation for adopting a child.

A friend told us of an opportunity for the private adoption of an infant yet to be born. We waited hopefully through almost the entire pregnancy. The baby was due in May of 1981. On the 24th of May, Paula said she had a feeling the baby had been born that day. By the 28th, we couldn't stand the suspense any longer. We asked our lawyer to get in touch with the expectant mother's lawyer. We learned that the baby was indeed born on the 24th, but had Down's Syndrome and a heart defect. We were told at that time that a child with such health problems could not be adopted through a private adoption. What a tremendous disappointment!

During the classes we learned through another friend of three boys who were in need of an adoptive home. In the

Spring of 1982, we adopted the three young brothers, Eddie, Mike, and Andy. They were fast approaching their 5th, 4th, and 3rd birthdays, respectively. At this writing (1997), Eddie is deceased (in 1992 at age 15), Mike's whereabouts are unknown, and Andy is living in a foster home. So much has happened in 15 years. There were both happy times and tremendous amounts of pain for all of us. We now know that love was not enough.

My older brother and sister and I were raised by a non-social father and a controlling mother. She rarely saw anything positive in anyone or anything. My father's philosophy of life was, "I don't bother you, so don't you bother me." But we were kids, so we did bother him, especially me. I talked and talked. I was probably hoping that someone would pay attention to me. He was never what I considered an appropriate father to any of us. Mostly, he ignored us. They both appeared to regard us as miniature adults and thought we should act as adults at all times. At the time of the adoption, they lived 800 miles away. My mother died in 1982 without ever meeting the boys. My father died in 1990.

As I eagerly approached parenthood, I felt I was an expert on how not to raise children. I was determined not to make the same mistakes.

We were told that the birth mother of our boys was dull normal with a flat personality, and that if you spoke to her, she might not answer you. She completed 10th grade, then did not return as she was pregnant with Eddie. She bore two more sons after Andy who were also removed from her care. We were told that the birth father was tall and slim with red hair. The agency assumed he was of normal intelligence based on the fact that he had a job.

Again we waited months, this time for the wheels of the system to turn. We were able to learn some things about the boys and even saw a picture of them. They had been severely

—

neglected, physically abused, and possibly sexually abused in at least one case. They were left alone on Christmas Eve in 1979, and just after midnight Eddie (2) set the Christmas tree on fire with a cigarette lighter. The resultant fire left all three boys with scared faces and bodies.

They never returned to their biological parents. For the next two years, Eddie and Andy were in one foster home and Mike in another. A hearing was held in February of 1982 to select an adoptive home. I had asked our caseworker to call me at work so I could use the three-way phone hook-up and Paula and I could hear the news together. I emphasized to the secretary the importance of interrupting my meeting when the call came. I was so excited that my boss had to caution me to calm down. The call came to say we had been chosen. We were overjoyed!

We then had to wait another month. During that time I prepared an announcement to send to out-of-town friends and relatives. It said, in part, "Just to share our joy," because we were indeed joyful. We were encouraged to prepare "lifebooks" which would give the boys some idea of who Paula and I were. Instead, I prepared a bulletin board for each of the two bedrooms. They contained pictures of Paula and me at different stages of our lives, and other pictures that told something about us and our interests. Between the pictures I placed colored cutouts of numbers and shapes.

Finally we met Eddie and Andy at their foster home. They served us pretend "pannycakes" and fish on their toy dishes. The two boys visited us in our home for two days with an overnight stay on the second day. I held Andy's hand while he cried himself to sleep. On March 19, 1982, Eddie and Andy (4 and 2) entered our home and our lives permanently. That night, Andy went to sleep with no problem, but I had to comfort Eddie while he cried himself to sleep, telling him this was the "forever home" God had chosen for him and his brothers. Later that night, I wanted to sneak into their rooms and just look at them—and I did.

A few weeks later, we went to Mike's foster home. He served us a cake he had baked, and this time it was real food. Mike visited several days and the noise level in our house rose dramatically. He was very resistant to being there. Mike (3) joined his brothers and us on April 5, 1982.

During the next few years we did all the fun things families do. We went on picnics and fed the ducks. We went to the zoo and to theme parks. We went to the circus. But Mike was frightened by the noise and wanted to go home. I waited 43 years to have children to take to the circus, and he wanted to go home!

I loved reading to the boys. Eddie in particular would sit transfixed during a story, and would be able to repeat it back to me in great detail. I took time from work to go on a school field trip to an ice skating rink with Eddie's class. I love ice skating, and now was getting to do it with my son. What a treat for both of us.

Our first encounter with the mental health system occurred after Mike (4) set a fire in the wastebasket in our family room. Paula took him to a counselor who worked with children involved with fire. The counselor said he did not take pleasure in seeing things burn, but was fascinated with fire. It seemed strange that a burn victim would have such an interest, but we later heard of other similar situations.

In the spring of 1983, the psychologist at Mike's (4) preschool expressed concern over drawings of himself because the parts were not connected. We took Mike to an educational/optometric center. He commented on every sound in the building and talked his way through all the tests, even though he couldn't do much of what was asked of him. Mike had to walk down a beam wearing glasses designed to distort his vision. He did this with obvious difficulty. He came to hug Paula and then me. My heart ached for this beautiful little human being. He had to repeat the process three more times with other glasses.

The report described Mike as very outgoing, extremely polite, bright (no surprise to Paula and me), inquisitive, and in constant motion. His perceptual age was slightly below his chronological age, and he was diagnosed with a visual motor dysfunction for which glasses were prescribed.

In July 1983, we took Eddie (5) to the same center because of his difficulty in translating directions into action and in expressing his thoughts. He was described as very shy (not at school, and not really at home), pleasant, co-operative, and a hard worker, but with a short attention span. His perceptual age was significantly lower than his chronological age and he did not trust what he saw. He was diagnosed with binocular vision dysfunction and glasses were prescribed. Eventually Andy underwent the same tests and was prescribed glasses for his visual motor dysfunction. All three boys were fairly good at wearing their glasses—at first.

We then began the long journey through a maze of mental health centers and counseling. Andy visited a psychologist who placed him in a program to improve his social skills. His behavior did not improve.

In June 1984 Paula and I separated. The boys (now 7, 6 and 5) remained with me for four months until the Court awarded temporary custody to Paula. Of course, I didn't want to be separated from them. In 1985, Paula and I were divorced. I fought hard for permanent custody of the boys, because I wanted them with me, and I felt that Paula could not work to support herself and take care of the boys too. I lost.

I found being a part-time father (every Wednesday evening and every other weekend) quite painful. It bore no resemblance to "real" fatherhood.

Paula had Andy (7) evaluated by a psychiatrist in the

—

spring of 1986. He was diagnosed as having oppositional defiant disorder (ODD). He was found to have an average IQ. He tolerated testing very poorly.

In 1986, I took the boys for a two week vacation to Boston and to Cape Cod where we had a wonderful time on the beach and in our little cabin. During this time Paula realized she was no longer able to parent the boys alone. Eddie, Mike, and Andy had raised sibling rivalry to a high art. At least two of them were with me at all times. Several weeks later, at ages 9, 8 and 7, the boys moved in with me to share a tiny two bedroom house. In the months that followed the change of custody Paula could not tolerate the bickering. She decided to take one of the boys for an overnight visit every other weekend.

During the boys' elementary school years, I was fortunate to have access to a latchkey program. There were frequent complaints about their behavior and occasional long letters describing their actions. With two weeks left in the 1986-87 school year, I picked the boys up one night and was told not to bring Mike back. After the first year, there was a wonderful latchkey teacher who seemed able to handle anything. Things were successful because of our cooperative efforts.

All three boys were having difficulties in school, both academically and behaviorally. Mike and Andy were placed on medication for hyperactivity. Over the years, both boys took a variety of medications (stimulants, anti-depressants, mood stabilizers) to help them cope with life. When matters didn't improve greatly, Mike started seeing a psychiatrist and continued the visits until early 1993 when he was nearly 15. A few months later, Andy began sessions which with a psychologist that lasted until 1991. Neither of the boys ever engaged in meaningful therapy. They were never able to deal with their feelings.

All three boys underwent a series of neuropsychological tests in 1987. Eight-year old Andy was found to have receptive and expressive speech difficulties as his greatest problem. His IQ was low average.

Mike's IQ was in the high average-to-superior range, but he had difficulty focusing and sustaining attention. His personality testing showed him as unusually dependent, self-effacing, non-competitive, with sometimes obsessional thinking, with overwhelming anxieties and fears of separation and rebuff, leading him to suppress his anger. He saw himself as a weak, ineffectual victim in a threatening and hostile world.

Eddie had an average IQ, but a significant delay in his mental processing. He had difficulty putting his thoughts into words. He was assigned to a specific learning disability (SLD) class in middle school.

The school system would not accept the test results, so the boys had to undergo another battery of tests. Andy's psychologist and I were astounded when it was concluded that Andy had an average IQ, was performing at an average level, and needed no help!

Many adoptive parents are stretched to the limit when they are overwhelmed with the behaviors of the children and are barely holding it together. When a traumatic event occurs, parents may react in a manner that surprises and dismays them. At this time in Mark's life, his marriage is over and he is struggling alone. There is no real support system for him. He is faced with the fact that his dream of "a family" is shattered.

It took great courage for Mark to tell his story, but he did it because he wanted to try, by his experiences, to help others prepare and ensure support for the tough times.

The period following my father's death in March, 1990 was difficult for me despite that fact that we never had a significant relationship. The boys got into new kinds of trouble beyond anything they had tried before, at a time when I was least able to cope. That is not an excuse for what happened.

—

Eddie (then 13) stayed home from school one day because he was not feeling well. I talked to him from my office several times during the day. The last time we talked he asked me what time I was coming home. A repairman was scheduled to fix the attic fan, but he called me and said there was no one at my home. I came home and confronted Eddie about leaving the house. I completely lost control and struck him on the back repeatedly with my fist. I was furious. Only later did I realize why I was so angry. The stresses and losses had overwhelmed me.

Eddie was rightfully upset and had Paula pick him up at school the next day. She took him to a hospital. He was fine physically, except for the bruises on his back. I received a call telling me not to go to latchkey to pick up Mike and Andy because they would not be there. All three boys were placed in the foster home where Mike had lived before his adoption. When I saw them several days later, I feared what Eddie's reaction would be. He met me at the door with a big smile and, when asked, said that hugging him wouldn't hurt him. He and Andy wanted to come home. Mike (12) wanted to stay and be adopted by his former foster parents. He even signed his Father's Day card with their surname. They were prepared to adopt him, at least until the boys burned their barn down. All three admitted adding straw to the fire.

The boys and I were separated for four months, despite letters from Mike's psychiatrist and Andy's psychologist stating that the separation would be harmful to them. We made six trips to court and I spent six hours in jail.

The boys were much more hyperactive when they came home. Eddie made the honor role one grading period, but other school problems resumed. Mike took a knife to school and they wanted to expel him. I fought hard to keep him there because I felt any further disruptions in his life could only be harmful. Mike and Andy did little or no work and received both in-school and out-of-school suspensions for various infractions.

A post-adoption support group was recommended to me, and has been invaluable to me ever since. What sanity I have left, I owe to those people. The boys each went through a series of ten sessions designed to help children deal with adoption issues. I went through the parallel parents' series three times. Once more, the boys weren't able to get in touch with any of their feelings.

I finally agreed that a severe behaviorally handicapped (SBH) placement was appropriate for Andy. The first few months were spent in a school where he was repeatedly robbed of money and clothing, and intimidated to the extent that he asked Eddie to come to school with him for protection. At my insistence, Andy was transferred to Eddie's school. I frequently got calls at work about Andy's behavior, which did nothing for the remainder of my workday. I finally had to tell the school not to call me during the day unless there was some action I needed to take immediately, such as pick him up if he had been fighting. Andy was transferred to an SBH school and finished middle school in this placement.

Mike (13) and Andy (12) went to summer school in 1991, where Andy got two F's and tried to get thrown out. Mike accumulated one more F to add to his collection.

Andy began to have anger attacks, brief outbursts of door slamming and foul language, sometimes directed at me. Afterwards he would be remorseful. He spent two weeks in a psychiatric unit after summer school with the hope that we could determine how best to help him, but the outbursts continued. He was diagnosed as dysthymic (depressed) but not in a major depression. He was again found to have an oppositional defiant disorder, an unspecified learning disability, and attention deficit hyperactivity disorder (ADHD). While in the hospital he was competitive and antagonized his peers in a way that seemed to say, "I feel bad, so you have to feel bad too." His self-esteem was very low. He began to get in touch with his feelings about being burned and being adopted, which turned out to be a mixed blessing. He was trying to put a family back together again. He wanted me to find his biological parents and his two younger brothers and have them move in with us. If I couldn't remarry Paula, he wanted me to marry someone else. Just what I needed! Andy returned to school and had six suspensions in a three week period.

Unfortunately, the hospital had separate departments for inpatient and outpatient therapy. Although an inpatient and therapist might establish some level of rapport, it was a given that the relationship could not continue. We began family therapy with a child psychiatrist, but after a few months he was rotated to inpatient therapy and no longer available.

Soon Eddie began having the same kind of outbursts. One morning he threw a cup of yogurt on me. He found it hard to say he was sorry, yet he was the only one of the three who ever seemed to understand how difficult the children were to parent. The other two said they didn't think being their father was so difficult a job.

At the end of 1991, Mike spent two weeks in a different psychiatric unit at the same hospital Andy had been in, with the same hope that we could determine what could be done to help him function better at home and at school. He was diagnosed as having ADHD and a conduct disorder (solitary aggressive type). During the exit interview, I was effectively told that Mike's only problem was having me for a father, and that neither of us was going to change so we might as well just go home. It was a far less positive experience for everyone than Andy's stay.

Eddie's personality was just now beginning to blossom. Girlfriends had entered the picture and changed often. Once

—

when Eddie announced he had a new girlfriend, I pointed out that he'd just had a new girlfriend the week before. His response was, "Nothing lasts forever, Dad."

On November 3, 1992, Eddie was a passenger in a car that was hit by a train. He died instantly. He was only 15. Two of the other three boys in the car were also killed.

The night Eddie died, the other two boys took up woodcarving. Andy (13) carved Eddie's name into the headboard of his bed, and Mike carved it into his desktop. I guess that was one way of dealing with their feelings. Andy also sobbed that he loved Eddie and would miss him. He has never expressed any feeling as well, before or since. At Eddie's wake he completely shut down and built an impenetrable wall. I felt pretty helpless. The boys and I went for grief counseling in separate groups. Mike and Andy disrupted their groups and had to discontinue their sessions.

In early 1993, Andy (13) and I drove 150 miles for a screening interview for rage reduction therapy, also called holding therapy because the psychologist and an assistant hold the child throughout the sessions.

Andy was resistant at first, then as I observed the session on closed-circuit TV, he began to loosen up. I left elated, thinking we had finally found something that would work. He began the eight-day treatment two months later. He was required to write letters to his birth mother and Paula, then read them aloud. He wrote a very angry letter to his birth mother saying, "If I ever see you, I will kill you." His letter to Paula was also angry, but he only read it with reluctance. He never did share his feelings with Paula. Over all, the process did not go as well as the therapist and I had expected. The assistant said she had never seen such a scared child. This time I was discouraged. The occasional outbursts of extreme anger did cease, however.

Several months later, Mike (15) was confronted at school with the fact that he had brought two knives and a pellet gun into the building. He took off and walked to the railroad tracks looking for a train to kill him. His psychiatrist recommended hospitalization and he spent $2\frac{1}{2}$ weeks in a psychiatric hospital. He resisted all attempts to help him. He was again diagnosed with ADHD, but not with a conduct disorder. The psychiatrist thought he also had a personality disorder, but didn't have enough time to determine which type. I feel sure the doctor was right. Mike just doesn't see the world the way most of us do. After being convicted some years later of robbing Paula, he still planned to become a law enforcement officer. When asked if he thought that was a realistic goal, he said somewhat indignantly, "I only have one felony."

A few days after Mike entered the hospital, Andy said to me upon returning from work with, "If you go out tonight, I'm going to kill myself." We played twenty questions as I tried to determine whether he was suicidal, or just wanted to be with Mike, or what. I took him to the hospital for evaluation and he was admitted. A year later he told me he only went to the hospital because he didn't want to go to school. His little respite cost us $15,000.

Mike did not want to come home. He went to stay with a friend of Paula's who brought him back two months later because he wouldn't follow her rules either.

After their discharge, we tried family therapy with a social worker at the hospital. Once again little was accomplished.

In the summer of 1993, Andy (14) entered the house next door and stole some alcohol and two rifles. He was placed on probation for two counts of aggravated burglary.

In the fall, Mike (15) enrolled in an Air Force ROTC program as a freshman in high school. Mike refused to go the learning disability tutor assigned to him, and got into various sorts of trouble—including being robbed at gunpoint after leaving the school grounds.

—

I began to socialize with Parents Helping Parents, and Paula and I had put a team together to ensure that the boys' needs were being met. It consisted of a representative of an umbrella agency designed for that purpose, the children services caseworker, the facilitator of my adoption support group, Andy's probation officer, a mentor for the boys, Paula, and me. Unfortunately, once again little was accomplished for the boys and I was exhausted.

I had been in therapy off and on again since the divorce, and was now seeing a psychiatrist and taking medication for depression, anxiety, hypertension, and difficulty sleeping. The cumulative effect of years of struggling to deal with and help the boys had worn me out. I felt as though the boys had fallen into a whirlpool, and that I could be pulled down with them. It was at this point that I gave temporary custody to the county children services agency.

Sometimes it seemed like I had a second, part-time job filing and canceling missing persons reports. There were always academic and behavioral problems in school. Mike failed one subject in sixth grade, three subjects in seventh, and three more in the eighth grade. Then came damaged fine cutlery and the twenty-odd knife slits in the month-old furniture, followed by slashes in the furniture, walls, and deck railings from a sword fight. I bought a cabinet and locked the cutlery and alcohol in it. The boys broke into it, so I moved it to my bedroom and put a lock on the door. They broke into the bedroom on several occasions.

There were the three large holes in the walls, one made by Mike's fist in a rare display of anger, one made when Andy put another boy's head through it, and the third one made by Andy has never been explained. There were the numerous holes in the linen closet door and sundry other walls in several rooms made by a Chinese throwing star. There were dishes, glasses, and silverware under the ivy in the back yard. There were the battered flashlights from roaming the neighborhood while I slept.

Andy was placed in a residential treatment center to provide the highly structured environment he needed. Andy and I, and sometimes Paula, engaged in family therapy once again. He did make some progress this time.

Mike was placed in the home of Paula's friend again. Things did not go well. He ran away several times, once for a month. He brought a knife into the house, made phone calls, some to a pornography line in Hong Kong totaling nearly $1000. He was sent to a special school program for behavioral problems. It was eventually necessary to place him in the same treatment center as Andy.

Mike and I attempted family therapy with a social worker who soon decided that it wasn't working mostly because Mike was only interested in blaming me for everything that was wrong with his life. There is no question that I was hardest on Mike, and I sat and cried and told him how sorry I was that I had not been a better father to him. However, his behavior was not only problematic, but sometimes bizarre. He had replaced a fascination with fire with an obsession with knives. He was sexually active with a fourteen year old girl and had stuffed girls' underwear with the crotches cut out, under his mattress. He had put spoons laden with peanut butter in bureau drawers with clothes and books.

At the end of 1994, Mike (16) was ready to be dismissed from the treatment center. This time he wanted to come home, but I was not prepared to have him come home. We tried joint therapy one more time, but again Mike refused to take responsibility for his behavior. In early 1995, Andy (15) came home from the treatment center.

Another team was established and it looked like we would have help at every turn. In fact, we only had one social worker, and then only until she left for another job. Andy was enrolled in a unique day treatment program, another highly structured environment where he could succeed.

—

He did quite well there. However, when summer came he decided to stop taking his medications and ran away to join Mike. Mike stole cars and motorcycles with members of his birth family. Mike said he felt bad about stealing the cars, then followed with, "It's funny, I didn't feel that way about the motorcycles." No charges were ever filed.

Andy was always immature and playful, and seemingly without guile. I'm sure I blamed Mike, at times, for things Andy did. I should have known better. Andy blamed Mike for taking part in things he may have done by himself, including the last time my bedroom was broken into, through a deadbolt lock. He was apparently in search of a check belonging to him. He eventually found it in the family room, endorsed it, and left it sitting there! Then he called me and said he saw Mike coming out of the house. That was the proverbial last straw. When our annual routine visit to court came around, I asked the children services agency to take temporary custody of Andy again. At this writing, he has been living in foster homes and I talk to or visit with him, but it is difficult to maintain a connection in his very detached state of mind.

In February, 1995, Paula was reading obituaries in the newspaper and saw one for the boys' biological father. The boys' names were listed as survivors in the hope that we would appear. He had died of cancer, as had his parents and eight of his twelve siblings. I took the boys to the funeral where they met their down-to-earth Appalachian relatives. The father was laid out in jeans, red suspenders, and a white sweater. The family was extremely grateful that we came, and all of them were gracious to us. When Andy met his birth mother, her eyes were filled with tears and she hugged him, but never said a word.

Paula, the boys, and I sat down with her several weeks later. She was exactly as she was described to us in 1982. I showed her a stack of pictures of the boys and invited her to take as many as she wished. She didn't do so until her mother selected some and handed them to her. She is in denial as to why the boys were not returned to her. She says that caring for them after the fire would have been too difficult, and nobody would help her. I didn't ask why her other two sons were later taken from her. The boys have maintained some contact with her. She has harbored them on some of their runaways.

In late 1995, Mike (17) ran away from his group home. Sometime later, he was picked up by the police for entering an abandoned building with a birth cousin and setting fires. The police did not hold him, even though there was a current warrant for his arrest, because he used the name he was born with.

Andy saw Mike a few times after he first ran away. Paula and I did not see or hear from him for eleven months. He called each of us and said he was OK, and that he was in town for a week. He wouldn't say where he would be going. He didn't sound good and admitted to being a little depressed. I asked him to call me again in a couple of days, after I had a chance to look into the status of any warrants. I was hoping he could come out of hiding, get a job, and get on with his life—with a 10th grade education. He didn't call.

On two visits in late 1996, Andy (17) made calls to pornographic phone lines totaling several hundred dollars. I confronted him but he denied making them. He didn't call or visit after that, and I didn't call him. I waited for an apology but it never came.

I received word through a caseworker in the spring of 1997 that Andy did not want Paula or me at his high school graduation. I wrote him to give him my perspective on our relationship and told him I was coming to his graduation anyway. He was very pleasant on graduation day.

Unfortunately, Andy decided not to take his Ritalin

anymore, and he began acting impulsively. He returned to our city from his foster home, but never moved into the apartment that the emancipation staff had set up for him.

I had no way of getting in touch with either Mike or Andy. From what I could gather, they were living with their birth mother or members of her family. Communication from them was rare. There was a tearful, panicky call from Mike because he had been accused of assault, then there were collect calls from jail to borrow bail money while I was away on vacation. When he finally reached me, he had decided to stay in jail until his day in court. He was arrested for involvement in an armed robbery. He denies any wrong-doing in either the assault or the robbery. He was released from jail in the middle of 1997, pending trial, after serving two months.

Andy eventually called me because he wanted something: a birth certificate so he could get a job. For six weeks he "ran around and had fun" rather that look for work. When I asked why he hadn't moved into the apartment, he answered with the ever popular, "I dunno!"

And the Summer of 1997 came around and my sons, now 18 and 19, decided to show some filial devotion—at least I wanted to think that's what it was. On a very hot Saturday, Andy walked to visit Paula, and then me, a total distance of more than ten miles. He stayed ten minutes with me. A week later I answered my doorbell to find both my sons there. We had a pleasant visit for forty-five minutes. A week later I called Mike's beeper number and talked to him and Andy. Neither one had a job yet. The next night I got a collect call from Andy asking me to bail him out of jail. He says he didn't do anything except be with a guy who robbed an apartment. He called again the next day, and I told him that I didn't think he would learn the lesson he needs to learn—to stop making poor choices—if I bailed him out. I think that was the right thing to do, but it didn't feel very good. Who knows what comes next?

I had read a poem by an unknown author at Eddie's funeral:

For All Parents

"I'll lend you for a little time, a child of mine," He said.

"For you to love while he lives, and mourn when he is dead.

"It may be six or seven years, or twenty-two or three

"But will you, till I call him back, take care of him for me?

"He'll bring his charms to gladden you, and shall his stay be brief,

"You'll have his lovely memories as solace for your grief.

"I cannot promise he will stay, since all from Earth return,

"But there are lessons taught down there, I want this child to learn.

"I've looked the wide world over in my search for teachers true,

"And from the throngs that crowd life's lanes, I have selected you.

"Now will you give him all your love, nor think the labor vain,

"Nor hate me when I come to call, to take him back again?"

I fancied that I heard them say, "Dear Lord, Thy will be done.

"For all the joy Thy child shall bring, the risk of grief we'll run.

"We'll shelter him with tenderness, we'll love him while we may;

"And for the happiness we've known, will ever grateful stay.

"But shall the angels call for him much sooner than we'ed planned,

"We'll brave the bitter grief that comes, and try to understand."

★ ★ ★

—

"And from the throngs that crowd life's lanes, I have selected you." That's the line that choked me up the first several times I read it. Why me? Was there ever anyone less suited to nurturing three very needy children?

One of the most important things I learned as a parent is that despite your determination to be a very different kind of parent, you will behave much more like your own parents than you ever imagined possible.

I read that one of the things about children that drives parents crazy is that children want to be nurtured in ways that their parents never were. How very true. When I'm feeling remorseful about my inadequacies as a father, I try to console myself with the fact that Eddie, Mike, and Andy were hugged, kissed, and told they were loved at least once a day.

Neglect, abuse, being burned, separation from birth parents, foster care, adoption, divorce, a change of custody, more abuse, loss of a brother, the death of their birth father, not being able to live at home. That's enough trauma for several lifetimes, and theirs have barely begun.

The rage reduction therapist had asked me whether I found myself emotionally distancing from the boys. He suggested that I would have to in order to survive. I had never thought of that before, but I realized that he was right. What a sad thing.

I can imagine what prospective adoptive parents might be thinking as they read this: "But we're going to adopt one child, not three." I know families who adopted one child and still had severe difficulties.

"Our child will not have known so much tragedy." You cannot depend on adoption agencies to tell you the whole story, even if they know it. The breaking of the nine-month bond between a mother and her newborn through adoption is in itself a severe trauma.

Do all adoptions involve so much pain? No, but many

—

do. If I had it all to do over, would I adopt children? I never would have become a parent had I known how unprepared I was.

Am I discouraging you from adoption? Absolutely not. However, I would urge you to examine very carefully your motives for wanting to parent an adopted child, and your expectations of the parenting experience.

Do I feel guilty for my deficiencies as a father? Most definitely. Do I think the outcome would have been significantly better if the boys had had ideal adoptive parents? Strange as it may seem, I don't. Paula and I, and so many others, were very naive and thought that love would be enough to overcome any problems that arose. I've learned that the boys' genetic heritage and early deprivations had a much greater effect than anything Paula and I did or didn't do. Love was not enough. The most important thing I have learned is that love can never be enough.

10

The Patterson Family
by Grace Patterson

When writing one's story, the hardest part is where to begin. For me, it began as a very young child. Adoption as a life choice was made at the age of four as I "assisted" my mother in caring for newborn foster children. "We" cared for them for a few weeks until they could enter their new adoptive home. I thought they were so sweet and smelled heavenly. From my much older perspective, smelling sweet hardly sounds a profound cause for such a decision. However, over the years I never wavered from the wish to adopt. My school-age fantasies were to be a mother of birth children and have a United Nations of adopted children. The husband was merely a shadowy figure, necessary only to provide the money to support us.

As fate would have it, the only way I could have a family with my first husband, Mitch, was to adopt. We had a baby girl by birth one year after our marriage. She seemed to develop normally till about one and a half years of age. Then we discovered she had a terminal disease called Hurler's Syndrome. All we were told was that she would stop growing and developing, and that she would not live beyond the age of seven (although she did live to age twelve). My husband and I carried a matching recessive gene that causes Hurlers. The devastation, pain, and helplessness of watching our child slowly die was terrible. The story of our Leigh-Ann deserves it's own book and I only refer to her to let the reader understand our later pain.

Zachary—After long discussion, my husband and I decided we wanted more children and would like to adopt. We first approached the childrens services office in the county where we lived when our daughter was two years old. We were well aware of the challenges of raising a child with catastrophic illness and our only request to the agency was that the baby be normal and healthy. (We much learned later that our request was ignored).

When Leigh-Ann was four, we adopted a three month old boy named Zachary. He only weighed 10 pounds, and was, to me, a dream come true. The caseworker told us that his mother was a freshman in college and her father was a minister. The birth father had returned to college to get a master's degree in civil engineering. They decided not to marry and the girl and her family believed that she could not adequately raise the child on her own. (When our son was 16 years-old I went to the county offices and read a very different account of his birth parents).

He was healthy and ate well, although he was always just below the bottom end of the "appropriate" size for his age. We only had our daughter to compare him to, and he seemed normal in infancy. The only thing we noticed was that he would not let us cuddle him.

He would tolerate being held to take his bottle but as soon as he could hold it himself, refused even that closeness. He would sleep well at night, but during the day would scream if we left him alone even for a minute as I went to another room. We bought a portable crib on wheels that I

—

moved from room to room as I worked. Even as he matured and would go out to play, he would come in every few minutes to check to see if I was there He was a very pleasant child and did show great affection toward his sister. He did not seem to care if his toys were broken. He was not destructive, but had no feeling at all about the loss of even a favored toy.

Zach was three when our son Andrew was born. He was a great surprise as my husband had been injured in an industrial accident and I was told he was sterile. We had been informed that any child we had would have a 1 in 4 chance of having Hurler's. Andrew was diagnosed with the disorder at six weeks. Andy was a cheerful little guy and Zach showed him much affection. Andrew died at the age of ten. Both he and his sister never weighed more than 36 pounds and were only about three feet tall. Though Leigh-Ann's development slowed after the age of one, she did not show signs of retardation or begin to lose physical abilities until age three. Andy never walked or learned so talk. Andy remained at the developmental age of about nine months, but Leigh-Ann achieved the abilities of a three year old. As a result of Zach's experiences with his brother and sister, he is still quite comfortable around people with serious illness or disabilities, and as a young teen volunteered at an MDA camp.

When Zach was four, Mitch and I separated. Leigh-Ann and Matt's illnesses and other stresses had taken a terrible toll on him. My husband lost his grip on reality and became dangerous to me and the children. Zach experienced the loss for many years in denial. He always believed his daddy would return one day. He never saw Mitch again after the age of five.

As a toddler, he would not sit still long enough to be read even a short child's book, but we were not knowledgeable about ADHD and did not realize what these behaviors predicted.

Zach seemed well adjusted during the divorce and loved the two years that we lived with my parents, while I worked and attended college. I remarried in 1972, when Zach was five. He had been such a cheerful little boy and seemingly well adjusted until my remarriage and his entry into kindergarten. He soon became violent and destructive in the classroom. He resented sharing me and my time with my new husband, Jeff, and his teenage son, Mike.

We now know that his behaviors were partly due to the losses he was experiencing. He lost his first father but loved living in a large household that consisted of a great grandmother, grandparents, teenage aunt, and mother. When I remarried we moved away from his extended family and his neighborhood friends. He had attended a play school for over a year that was also lost in the move. By the time he was five, both his brother and sister were living in nursing homes as their fragile conditions made home care impossible. There was no home care assistance in those days.

When he was attending the daycare center, as I worked, he was well liked by the children and the teachers. Their only concern was that he seldom finished projects, preferring to play instead of doing activities seated at the table. When we moved to a different neighborhood, it was time to start kindergarten. He was soon in trouble for disrupting the class, fighting with other children, and was asked to leave.

He also began bringing other children's toys home from play visits. He would go to play and forget to come home. His behavior at home was always pleasant and obedient and other parents found him well behaved when in their homes. We could tell he was very unhappy but he was unable to express the reasons.

When Zach was seven, we got a new puppy. He was outside alone with the dog for a few minutes and when I looked out the window, he was lifting and dropping the pup

—

to the ground repeatedly. I hurried to the dog and rushed it to the vet, but it died. I found Zach's treatment of the animal frightening. He did not seem to understand that his actions would harm the dog and seemed confused but not remorseful.

Any one of the behaviors he was exhibiting might not have alarmed us, but the combination of violence in school, attempts at fire setting, thefts of toys from friend's homes, inability to learn cause and effect, and inability to remember a task long enough to complete it caused us to seek assistance. We had him admitted to Cleveland Babies' and Children's Hospital for tests as we were puzzled and dismayed by his behaviors. They told us he had an antisocial and sociopathic personality and would most likely end up a criminal who would spend time in prison. His IQ was about 79. He was dyslexic, had ADHD, and other learning disabilities. There was speculation that he had suffered brain damage in-utero.

I did not take the diagnosis well. It was impossible to believe that such a prediction could be made about a small child. I was already losing my other babies to a terrible disease. The doctors were telling me that there was nothing I could do to stop a horrible future for the child that was my greatest joy.

Zachary was also diagnosed with a conduct disorder, weak ego, with no self controls. What they did not diagnose, as little was known at the time, was fetal alcohol effect. A few years after Zachary reached adulthood, I read the book *Broken Cord*, by Michael Dorris. When I reached the description and photos of children with FAS, I was devastated to recognize my son in the traits and one of the photos in Dorris' book. It finally all made sense then about the behaviors, and the lack of cause and effect thinking.

Zach's childhood years during the 1970s saw us at many counselors, psychologists, and psychiatrists. None of

—

them ever mentioned adoption issues, genetics, or pre-natal effects. Instead Zach was given Ritalin. We were not informed about parenting techniques for his problems. The psychologist du-jour would usher him in, spend an hour, and receive my check. We were given no insights at all.

After the age of seven fewer moms in the neighborhood would let him come to play and he once tried to set a neighbor's house on fire as retribution. Fire fascinated him. We hid all the matches, but he always seemed to have an endless supply of lighters. Each time we took one away, he'd produce another. When we moved out of the house, there were burn marks all over the carpet in his room.

We were ostracized as "bad" parents by neighbors, friends, and relatives who chose to believe we were causing his behaviors or failing to control him. In later years, we became acquainted with many other parents who lived through rejection by friends, family, neighbors and their church due to the behaviors of their adopted children. The self-blame and guilt we felt was exacerbated by the opinions of others who did not understand our great challenges. There was no one we could talk to. We felt very alone.

Zach was assigned to special education classes for his first four grade school years. I felt he was learning little and that whatever talents he had were going untapped. I took a leave of absence from work and tutored him. I found he could do average work. However, when I attempted to get the school to give him more mainstream work, they refused, accusing me of being an interfering parent. After much research, we transferred him to a residential parochial school, where he attended with regular students. He received average and some above average grades. The church-sponsored school offered a military drill team as an extra-curricular activity and he excelled in learning the complicated routines. He did not advance in rank as steadily as others due to his lack of self-discipline, but in his fourth year, he was promoted to second in command. He remembers those years in a highly structured atmosphere as the happiest of his childhood. At the end of his eighth grade year the school closed and we tried to find an acceptable high school.

We did have enjoyable times during his childhood years. We traveled with Zach each summer. He especially loved boating and fishing. We spent many summers from the time he was seven till he was 15 with extended family at a resort on Lake Erie. During the summer, his behaviors were not problematic until after he graduated from the eighth grade at age 15. In his early grade school years he also attended a camp for children with learning disabilities and scout camp. His stepfather and I were active in scouting for several years. Holiday preparation and the family gatherings for Easter, Christmas, and birthdays were delightful times. He unselfishly bought gifts for family and friends.

Zach had not seen my first husband since he was five years old. My husband and I believed that if he adopted the boy, he would feel more secure. My first husband readily agreed to relinquish custody as he would no longer be responsible for child support. He had not paid any since Zach was four. My husband then adopted Zach when he was 12 years old. Unfortunately it did not help.

The teen years were difficult for Zach as he was unable to adjust to high school. He attended three high schools in six months of his freshman year, was labeled a trouble maker and terminated from all three. He seemed very angry, but his anger was undirected. When we tried to talk to him, he was unresponsive. We had devised an elaborate lighting system over our bed at night to tell us when Zach was sneaking out of the house. We felt we had to be his jailer and watch his every move. There was great identity confusion. He shoplifted, committed acts of voyeurism, and finally took a knife to school to "hurt" a girl who had turned him in for bringing pornographic magazines in to the building.

—

The psychiatrist felt he was dangerously violent and should be arrested. He spent the next three years in a residential teen facility. He ran away many times. He ran on foot, on horseback, and by train. They always let him come back but they admitted that no counselor had ever reached him. One counselor said Zach had a "wall of steel" around him that they had never broken through.

Those years were very difficult for us to understand because we never observed any violence or aberrant behaviors. He was always polite and well-behaved at home. We found a stash of knives in his room after his arrest at age 15. He had begun talking to other youth about devil worship and we found a small shrine in his room. At age eighteen, after leaving the residential facility, he attended a gathering, where the image of a medallion was burned into his upper arm. He would listen quietly while we tried to reach him through discussion, as we told him of our fears for his life. He never lashed out, just sat with his wall fully intact.

As Zach's troubles accelerated, I became more desperate to find "the key" that would unlock his heart and free all of us from our problems. When he was 16, after trying all we knew to help him, I decided to examine his adoption records to see if they would provide any clues to his baffling behaviors. It took several months to achieve this as the county agency refused to show me even the non-identifying information. After we hired an attorney, they did supply records that had large blacked out areas.

My heart stopped as I read of his history. It was nothing like we'd been told. Zach's mother was 22 at the time of his birth. She was mildly retarded and had the equivalent of a sixth grade education. She and her siblings were all removed from their parents' home because of alcohol and physical abuse and neglect. The birth mother had sought no pre-natal care till her seventh month, when she entered a home for unwed mothers. The caseworker noted that when she signed the relinquishment papers, she showed no emotion at all. The worker had never seen this lack of feeling before.

As I read the account of the mother's personality, I began to see my son's personality traits mirrored in the reports about her. His behaviors and difficulties began to make sense. I wondered why we had not been informed about his birth family, but then I remembered what we had been told by caseworkers at the time of his placement. This information certainly did not agree with the story of an unwed college freshman and a master's level student.

This new information staggered us. We talked to an attorney and were told we had a good case but decided a suit would only bring money. It couldn't give us the child we thought we adopted, or help Zach. We feared we could further damage this boy who was already greatly troubled. The copies of his birth history and his mothers personality are still in a file drawer. We told Zach it was there when he was 18. He has never looked in the drawer. He says he may want to search some day, but at age 29 (at this writing) that day has not yet come.

When we were attempting to adopt there were no education classes, nor were there any practical books. At the time of placement we were told to "take him home and love him as your own." That is what we did. We had no idea that genetics or events in-utero could have such permanent and damaging effects. After all, in those years the theory of the "blank slate," and that the environment was everything, was in vogue.

I haven't spoken much of our feelings or the effects on the family because that is much more difficult than reciting facts. After my divorce in 1971, Zach seemed to be doing well as we all lived in my parents' home while I attended college and worked. I remarried in 1972 to a man who had three sons, one of whom is severely mentally retarded. Only

—

the fifteen-year-old son, Mike, lived with us. Zach, who was five at the time, refused to accept the marriage, and insisted in talking to my husband through me. He seemed more accepting by age 12, when my husband adopted him, hoping to better cement the bond. In truth he has only recently begun to accept him, but their relationship remains strained and distant.

They tell us that adoptees, birth parents, and adoptive parents all grieve the losses that bring us to adoption. I had to grieve the loss of my daughter, Leigh-Ann, my son, Andrew, who was born in 1969 with Hurlers, and also the "loss" of the son I thought I had adopted. Zach was my great hope and the person that gave me the will to get up in the morning. His diagnoses and years of troublesome behaviors took away that dream. In his teen years we feared for his very life and sometimes our own. Leigh-Ann died at 12 and Andrew at age 10. They each lived the last few years of life in residential facilities. There were no home-care possibilities in those days, so I worked to provide top insurance.

Zach cared deeply for his younger brother and older sister. He would show them affection openly. I still do not know how their losses affected him. We talk little of them with him.

After his 18th birthday, we tried several interventions, but he was on his own only a few weeks before he and a newly released ex-con stole a TV and other items from a handicapped man. He was given probation, but decided to have several free meals at the same restaurant and was sent to prison for eight months. After prison he lived on the streets, both in Hollywood, California and in our home town. For several years he would work a short time and then live off others for a while.

At 24, Zach seemed to be maturing and was holding jobs longer, keeping himself cleaner and trying harder. Then, he started a new job at a fast food restaurant where a co-worker introduced him to crack cocaine. The next two years he spiraled downward into an addiction that had him near death. He stole money from his grandmother's wallet and from us. He looked dirty and smelled terrible. When he came over, he paced the floor. We tried to provide understanding, love, and yet intolerance for his addiction. He denied any problem most of the time. We did get him to a couple of NA meetings but he refused to continue seeing a professional after one visit. He continued to live on the streets and stay in shelters. The teeth we had put braces on at age 13 began to rot till he now has less than half of them. His weight went from 135 to 113.

In the depth of his addiction, he married a street person who had lost her children due to neglect and substance abuse. They lived together on the streets and occasionally with her relatives. They separated several years ago but have just recently divorced.

At age 26 he met an unsophisticated 20-year-old girl who became pregnant a few months later. Three months into her pregnancy, he was coming down off a cocaine high and robbed a small specialty store, with a very large knife. He was caught attempting to make his get-away on a city bus. He was sentenced to 10-to-25 years. At this writing, he has never seen his son, who just celebrated his third birthday. However, he has made the best of his time while incarcerated as he got sober, joined AA, attended college and received an Associates degree in business. He plays acoustic guitar, composes music, and is the head of the prison music association. He also has discovered a wonderful artistic talent. He specializes in drawing flowers. He will be 30 years old this year (1997) and comes up for parole again in a few months.

We talk often by phone. Zach sounds mature now and our conversations are adult-to-adult. We are comfortable with one another. I still worry that when he is released, he will use cocaine again and that when the structure that prison provides is no longer there, he will have difficulty taking charge and managing his life.

This seems a very sad story as I write and it is very painful to review the history of this beautiful baby that I first held at three months of age. He was supposed to be my hopes and dreams. He was to grow up as my birth babies never would. In my dreams, he would go for career education, marry the girl down the street, have children and a dog and a house with a yard. He was to bring his family for Thanksgiving dinner and be the continuation of myself and the "environment" of values and love and all that we taught him was important in life. It has been a long time since I cried in the night to ask God, "What happened?"

Would it have made a difference if there had been pre-adoptive education classes, or support groups, or honesty on the part of the caseworkers? Of course it would. We could have understood about ADHD, FAS, and adoption issues and known that when a baby pushes you away it is an attachment issue not a failure to love him enough. We would have known that there are methods to work with the baby to achieve attachment. Would we adopt again? Yes, we would and we did.

Christina—In 1988, we investigated the possibility of adopting an older child. We took classes this time. This time we had extensive profiles to review. This time caseworkers were fully honest and assisted all along the way.

We met a chubby ten year old who was very bright but had a rough history. She and her older and younger brothers had been removed from the birth home for the last time when she was six. She has little memory of the early years. She does remember being hungry and days of being left alone together while mom and dad went off to bars. Most of her clothes were ill-fitting hand-me-downs donated by her birth mother's sister. Christina had been taught to steal at garage sales for other needed goods. The caseworker told us that when they went in to remove the children, the rooms of the house were knee-high in trash and dirty clothes.

Christina was two years old the first time she was removed from the birth home. Over the next six years she was moved ten times and lived in six different settings. She had experienced sexual abuse by family members and friends of the birth parents. Her father physically abused all of the children and the mother. She was placed in a residential facility at age nine, where she encouraged boys to be sexual with her. These seductive behaviors continued through all of her growing years, although she did learn not to exhibit these behaviors within our adoptive family.

Christina and her two brothers were placed as a group with an older couple who had never parented before. The baby, three years younger that Christina, adjusted well and attached to the parents. Christina told many lies even when it would have been easier to tell the truth. She had nightmares and fearsome temper tantrums, wet the bed, hoarded food, and took hours of the mom's time to assist with homework, which she then threw away on the way to school.

The mom's things began to disappear only to be found broken among Christina's things. When they blamed Christina, the tantrums escalated. The three-years-older brother seemed to be doing well, but Christina was removed from the home and placed in a residential treatment facility where they repeatedly scolded for not admitting her guilt and refusing to take responsibility. The family declined to take her back and finalized with the other two boys. Later they discovered it was the older boy who was taking and depositing the mom's broken items in Christina's toys. She had been innocent of the thefts. The older boy had planned to get her out of the home so he could have the attention of the parents. Although innocent of the thefts, her other behaviors were so extreme that the parents felt she could not return.

—

She was then placed with a birth aunt who promised to adopt her. Within a few months the aunt decided to allow the county to find a permanent home as she and her husband were too old to deal with the problems that might come with the teen years. We read her profile and decided we could work with her and attach to her.

She moved in one month before her 11th birthday. We had heard of honeymoon periods, where the child demonstrates angelic behavior for a time. Our "honeymoon" lasted about an hour. I made a dinner designed to appeal to a child, sloppy Joe's and french fries. She immediately informed me that she only ate those made by her birth aunt's recipe (a well-known canned product), and that I could make her a peanut butter and jelly sandwich. My husband and I recognized this as a control issue and informed her that we all eat together or not at all. She could chose to eat with us or go without. She grumbled that we were unfair, but sat and ate the meal. We never had the issue arise again until I served liver and onions. We did allow her to eat something else on that occasion.

She had been diagnosed with somatic disorder, but we were surprised to find that her suitcase contained four well-used ace bandages. She would complain of an ache or pain somewhere on her body almost daily and wrap the leg or arm with a bandage. One day she complained of a headache and we (feigning seriousness) suggested she use one of her ace bandages. She turned to follow the suggestion, then realized we were teasing her. We rarely saw the ace bandages after that.

The first month no one got any sleep. She had nightmares and feared being alone. We had to have lights on all over the house. I would have to return her to her room many nights after she came crying into our room. I noticed a difficulty in breathing and looked in her throat. She had monstrous tonsils that were affecting her breathing in sleep.

—

After a tonsillectomy, the nightmares stopped.

However her imagined injuries continued to be a daily routine. One day she came home from a friend's house complaining of an injured wrist after attempting a hand stand. Due to her regular complaints, no one believed her claims of injury. We checked it, as we checked all of her "injuries" and discovered she really had broken the wrist. Her complaints often included stomach pain, so when she doubled over in 1990, we assumed it was another one of her attempts for attention. We shortly realized our mistake and she had an emergency appendectomy that same night. She was in real pain and realized how self-destructive it was to make false complaints. After the appendectomy, she rarely complained unless the pain was real.

Christina had several assessments prior to the placement. All suggested delayed social development, extreme lack of organization, a speech defect, extreme attention seeking behaviors and perhaps, depression. The ability to attach had been severely strained. Strengths included spelling, rote memorization, and a willingness to get involved in new experiences.

Christina met the adjustment to an upper class community and school, where achievement was stressed, slowly and with great reluctance. Christina carried her book bag every school day all day for six years, until the day she graduated. She did not take her coat off the first year and used her locker for hoarded food. Her counselor said she could have used one for each of her food groups, sugary and salty. We would work with her for hours every evening to complete homework. She would cry, stomp, throw things, including books and papers, and made the experience hell for all of us. Each morning she would toss the homework sheets or project in the trash on the way to school.

A tutor was assigned, but the homework horror continued for two years. We had to obtain direct information from teachers as she would always say there was no homework or that she had completed it in class. We finally stopped the attempts after two years. Her grades neither went up or down as a result. But our home became much more peaceful.

The strain was incredible as we attempted to teach her appropriate behaviors and deal with her resistance. She would cling at the most inappropriate times, gave us painful "bear" hugs. We had to give lessons about how much pressure was appropriate for hugging. She wanted to sit on her father's lap like a small child, though she weighed 140 pounds. She also would try to caress and kiss him the way she had seen on romantic TV scenes. We conducted extensive lessons on appropriate affection for each category and age group of friend and relative. Her bathroom habits were unbelievable. A roll of toilet paper would last for weeks in her bathroom. We had to throw out her underwear every three months. She would fill the tub with only hot water and get in. No amount of talking could get her to turn on the cold tap. We had to turn the temperature down on the water heater so she would not be injured.

Many of her problem behaviors stemmed from the fact that Christina believed that if she behaved badly enough we would give her back and she would be returned to her birth mother. After a year, at age 12, we took her to the caseworker, who explained that she would never return to her family of origin. If she left us she would be placed in foster care until age 18. After hearing that she began to accept the placement. We met the adoptive parents of her brothers and developed a visitation plan. The couple were still struggling with letting her go and Christina would sometimes manipulate them to believe that she wanted to be with them. Our two families had to struggle mightily to keep her manipulations from causing rifts. She would tell each family that the other had made derogatory statements about them. This continued until she married at age 19.

—

School continued to be a great problem. She did not like studying, but went faithfully every day because she loved the social contacts. She was in the band, school plays, and other activities in middle school. She loved band in high school, but hated playing the clarinet. She had played the clarinet before we met her. We bought one and discovered that she had been playing for several years with the hands in reversed positions.

Every day was like living in a war zone. She opposed every request by being passive-aggressive or having a temper tantrum. We assigned a few daily and weekly chores such as emptying the dishwasher, vacuuming carpets, and setting the table. She would forget to do the chore and needed reminding daily for three years. We tried rewards; no response. We tried removing privileges; no response. The idea of taking responsibility for herself or her actions was abhorrent to her. No possessions had meaning. No rewards had meaning. No discipline was effective.

In order to get her to do anything, I had to shout, to get right in front of her as though she had a hearing problem. She would then argue, whine, stomp, and then go into a full temper tantrum. After about a half hour, she would come for a hug, announce pitifully that she was sorry, and complete the requested task. These behaviors lasted for several years. I thought my husband and I could outlast her—after all we were older, educated, and experienced at parenting. We consulted the agency case workers often, took her to counselors, called a post-adoption specialist but did not attend any classes or a support group. At the time she was growing up, there was no support group for us.

The behaviors reached a crescendo in her sophomore year when she had some dental work and the dentist told her she could take Tylenol for pain. She took 28 in a few hours and had to be taken to the emergency room for assistance. She told us and the medical staff that she did not think

Tylenol was a drug. She said she did not believe they could be harmful. She insisted it was an accident. A few weeks later her friends called me to say she was talking about suicide. She was going to throw herself in front of a truck. A discussion with counselors and a psychiatrist resulted in a hospitalization for an assessment for depression. She was placed on an antidepressant.

She did function better on the medication and the hysterics reduced in number and intensity. Her school work did not improve, but her ability to make and keep friends did. We really began to attach after she calmed down, and she later told me that she had finally accepted us as her family (after three years).

There were fun times. When she first came to live with our family, she had never been outside central/eastern Ohio. We soon took her on trips as far away as Florida and California. She had never been on a plane or boat. Some of the joys were introducing her to new places and activities. Her first palm tree, first concert, and other experiences that widened her world also changed the way she looked at the world. Unfortunately, she continued to see herself as an ugly duckling who could not find a place in our world.

The summers, after school was out, were pleasant. She was quite calm and cooperative because there were no pressures to perform or conform in a school setting. But within six weeks of each new school year, the extreme behaviors would begin again. We had many meetings with school personnel as we worked cooperatively to ease her anxieties and help her to adjust to the requirements. She liked the tutor she had for several years, but she spent much of their time together manipulating ways to avoid school work. She still needed the tutor in high school, but was embarrassed when other children teased her about being retarded. She refused to work with a tutor after her freshman year.

My husband took an active role in her parenting and

—

could remain calm regardless of her efforts to enflame situations. I began graduate school one year after she came to live with us and (for a year and a half) my husband was the one who had to help with homework and manage the tantrums. His calm demeanor could quickly deflate her anger most of the time but other times she saw it as a challenge to try harder to make him angry. I am extremely grateful that he was an equal partner in the efforts to raise her. Even today, she turns to me when she is agitated and seeking confrontation. However, over the years, I have also learned that the way to still her hysteria is to listen quietly and speak very slowly in nearly a whisper.

Christina could talk intelligently about appropriate actions in various situations, but always descended to attention seeking behaviors of a much younger developmental stage. She would have an adult conversation, followed by baby talk and clinging behaviors. She kept repeating the same negative behaviors, even though they had not worked for her the twenty times before.

When she became interested in boys, we noticed that the boys who caught her eye were ones who were familiar with the juvenile justice system. They dressed punk and smoked. They were often in trouble in school and she would brag about their actions. She continued to have a weight problem. We had been able to assist her in maintaining her weight until her freshman year. We could not put her on a weight loss diet as she was still in her growth years, but managed to keep her from gaining. However, the freshman year brought more opportunities to eat away from home. She went to 198 pounds at a height of 5'1". She was ridiculed by boys. They would see her in private, but deny it in public while ridiculing her to their friends. She became convinced that the best way to have boyfriends was to be sexually active.

Christina wanted to have a baby. She announced at

age 13 that she would get pregnant as soon as possible and that there was nothing we could do to stop her. We discussed the reasons to abstain, reasons why she could not yet parent. It all fell on deaf ears. She continued these behaviors, but was unable to become pregnant. From the age of 17 she would announce, with great regularity, that she was having symptoms and would go to a doctor for a test or buy home test kits. In the summer of her 18th year one of the kits read positive, but it was a false alarm.

Several positives occurred in our years together. After her first two years with us she diminished the angry behaviors that she thought would make us relinquish her. We traveled extensively and did all of the fun mother/daughter activities that I had dreamed about. She played clarinet in the school band for five years. She participated in school plays. The most positive experience was her membership in a girls organization that she joined at age eleven. The organization requires public speaking, holding offices with increasing responsibility, and a time commitment for outside activities. By the age of 17 she had achieved the highest local office and presided for a six month term. This activity gave her poise, self-confidence, and pride. It took a great deal of effort on our part to keep her on track, but it helped her sense of belonging and feelings of self-worth.

She began working at a fast food restaurant at age 15. They complained that she talked a lot and that supervisors had to maintain a tight rein, but she felt successful as they scheduled her often. She even saved enough money to buy a car by her 18th birthday. She planned entry to a beauty school in the fall after graduation, but faltered when some of her college-bound classmates made fun of her choice.

After high school graduation, at age 17, she felt she no longer had to adhere to the structure we provided. She left her regular circle of friends to associate with very troubled youth. She began dating a 30-year-old man. She started

—

beauty school in the fall and seemed to like it. However, she was staying out till very late at night and was kicked out of the program after missing three days in the first two weeks. When we stated that she must either work full-time or go to school full-time, and made other rules in order for her to remain at home, she moved in with the older man. They broke up in two weeks, and she moved in with a 20-year-old man the same day.

She soon quit her job and began writing NSF checks for cash. At first they were accidental, but when she realized that stores would take the checks even after the bank closed her account, she continued the behavior. She did this for four months, until warrants were issued for her arrest. She did not work again for one and a half years. The relationship with the twenty-year-old broke up as soon as she stopped writing checks. Against my better judgment, we let her use the funds we had saved for school to pay off about $2000 of the checks. She felt no remorse and responded that she wrote the checks because "I needed the money." She did not see it as theft at all. (When she was arrested a year later on the bad check charges, she whined loud and long about the unfairness of two nights in jail and probation requirements.)

When she was eighteen, she tried to return to the Appalachian community of her birth family, but discovered that she no longer fit there. She moved in with the same aunt who had promised to adopt her many years earlier. They soon argued over her unwillingness to get a job.

She then made the rounds of her birth family, living a few weeks in each of about six different homes. Each would take her in with the understanding that she would work to pay her way. Each evicted her after a few weeks. She seemed to be able to find someone to take her in each time. We were hoping it would stop and that she would be forced to take responsibility for her life, but she seemed to feel that others should take care of her as though she were still a child.

—

One month before her 19th birthday, she met a 29 year old man from Pakistan who wanted a wife. When they married five days later, he told her he didn't want his wife to work, she was in heaven. After their marriage he was, at times, verbally abusive, deepening her depression. She talked about suicide. They had many clashes in culture and religion. He told her she is not worthy to be the mother of his children. Friends and relatives tried to help her see how destructive this arrangement is but, she felt a kind of security in the relationship. We finally convinced her to seek the assistance of a psychiatrist and a counselor. She began taking anti-depressants and was more calm. She takes the medications sporadically and has mood swings from euphoria to despondency.

The relationship between her and her husband is changeable from day to day. They are now separated. She is desperate to stay married, feeling the fear of further abandonment. She wants him to love her and takes every small gesture as proof of his commitment. He too, is uncertain and gives her mixed messages. She will occasionally obtain a job and work for a week or two. She drifts from one enabling friend to another and then to family. We have tried to get her to have a psychological assessment as she may qualify as disabled. She vacillates between cooperation and defiance, never following through with any plan.

Where are my husband and I after all these years and all the struggle, which is far from over?

Our efforts often felt futile and there were times my husband and I had very little energy to continue the struggle to work with her. We asked ourselves if we were really making a difference. There were times in the first few years when we believed we should dissolve the adoption, especially when she would remind us that she really belonged with her birth family no matter how problematic because that was the only place she felt comfort and a sense of belonging.

—

The best way to convince ourselves to keep trying was to imagine her growing up in foster care. Her behaviors would have surely caused many moves. She would not have had us or our friends and family for role models, with only her birth family to look to after age 18. We know that we have had some influence. We cannot say that there was a better way to raise her. We know all of the adoption issues and all of the parenting methods and have tried many of them over the years. What we have learned is to accept the child we adopted. The dream is long gone, replaced with the hope that she can accept herself and find her place in this world given the very different environments, values, and all of the input from those who have touched her life.

We struggled to instill values, ethics, and an identity that would allow her to function well. What we did not know in 1988 is that genetics and early history is forever a part of the child, and that a child cannot be remolded in the adoptive parents' image. She was a month from her 11th birthday when we became her parents. It would have helped if we had known then that it would be easier to accept her as she was. However, we would still have struggled to educate her and instill some values and ethics. It is too soon to tell just how much we were able to contribute. We love her and support her in the positive things she does and no longer rescue her or enable the destructive or negative behaviors. She will be twenty soon and has now been married for a year. She is our daughter for better or worse. The commitment is for our lifetime.

11

The Brach Family
by Anne & Jon Brach

We are of German heritage and were raised in devout Roman Catholic homes. We were married in September, 1967, one week after the end of Jon's last undergraduate class. Jon obtained his doctorate in chemical engineering in late 1971.

We wanted a family, and infertility led us to adoption. In September, 1973 we were delighted to welcome three-month-old Elizabeth Anne, just before our sixth wedding anniversary.

We were given medical information about the mother's birth family, but there was very little information about the birth father except that he was part Native American. The day we met, she was wearing a little yellow smocked dress, had slightly curly dark brown hair and the most startlingly huge brown eyes we'd ever seen. She knew something big was going on in her little life. She did not cry, but very solemnly observed us. She became then, as she remains today, "Daddy's little Princess." Elizabeth immediately initiated me as a mother by spitting up all over my dress.

The social worker read to us part of a letter written

by the 19-year-old birth mother. We could picture the birth mother's anguish as she explained to her daughter that she was dearly loved, that she (the mother) simply could not give her beloved baby the life which could only be provided by two loving parents. We were profoundly moved by her words, and have always thought of Elizabeth's birth mother in the most compassionate and positive way.

We soon grew adept at the mechanics of diapering, feeding, and transporting a baby. She was a delightful and much-photographed infant.

In 1976, we were hoping to adopt another child. To be brief, it was one of the most heartbreaking experiences we have ever had. We were asked repeatedly if we would care to adopt a child of mixed racial background, or one of Puerto Rican heritage. Each time our answer was yes: Our extended families had a successful history of such adoptions. The final and most stupid statement by the social worker was that they couldn't possibly place with us, who were so highly educated, a child whose parents had not graduated from high school.

After this major disappointment, Jon accepted a position in central Ohio because it seemed a good place to raise our family. We moved here in 1979, after Elizabeth's sixth birthday.

In the spring of 1980, we met a colleague of Jon's at church. He had with him his children and an adorable baby boy who was a foster child. He was a special needs baby, having had a highly traumatic premature birth to a teenage alcoholic which landed him in intensive care for the first three weeks of his life.

We fell in love with this beautiful baby, but were also forced to consider the more practical aspects of daily life with a brain-damaged child. Tom had APGAR readings of 1 and 5, respectively. He had a long list of birth problems, including breech presentation, and cord being wrapped around his

—

neck for an indeterminate time. Custody had been turned over to the county by the young birth mother's father when the extent of the baby's problems became known. Upon his release from the hospital, he was in two foster homes before being placed with us at the age of $10\frac{1}{2}$ months. We consulted experts and decided we were willing to confront whatever came along. Thomas Jonathon was in our home in September, 1980. Another wedding anniversary gift.

Elizabeth was entranced with her new brother, and elected herself his protector, teacher, and second mother. She was in second grade, and loved to read to him. He was healthy, and sunny, loving interaction with people. At 16 months, Tom's adoption was finalized. He made splendid progress that year. Elizabeth spent the summer encouraging her little brother to crawl, walk and talk. She regarded each little bit of his progress as her own personal victory.

He was not quite two in September of 1981 when we again attended a picnic and quite casually met Tom's biological sister.

While waiting with Tom in a long line for the pony ride, Jon struck up a conversation with the man ahead of him who had with him a little girl. Jon was told that the little girl was their foster daughter. When Jon heard the little girl's unusual birth name there was no doubt as to her relationship to our son. Jon scurried to find me. Once the foster mother heard us refer to Tom and found out that he was 11 months younger than Emily, she too, knew of the relationship. Emily had been with them for two years. Could you ignore the proximity of your adopted child's biological sibling, and take no action? We certainly couldn't. We immediately called the caseworker requesting Emily's placement within our home. Welcome Emily Mary and happy 14th wedding anniversary to us.

Unlike Tom, Emily had been a full-term baby with no birth complications. She had come to the attention of human services only when the birth mother approached them for help in the last half of her pregnancy with Tom. Until then, she and Emily had lived a nomadic existence. The mother would leave the child with someone, state that she would be "back this afternoon · · · ," then not show up again for a few days. Emily was removed in late 1979.

We worked with Elizabeth quite a bit because she would have to share her bedroom with Emily. She was reservedly agreeable.

We found Emily to be a bright child who already knew her colors, letters, and numbers, and was quite verbal. She was a chubby, little blue-eyed blonde. We firmly believed that this adoption, as with the other two, was the right thing to do, and that the love of our family as well as the environment and education we could provide would far outweigh any negative forces in place at the beginning of these young lives. The feeling of the day was that "nurture would rule over nature." We were not counseled otherwise; indeed, we were not counseled at all.

Placement Day was in November 1981. The foster mother was upset because Emily was so attached to a certain red dress that she would wear nothing else for our big day. Problem was that Emily(3) had outgrown the dress. With little time left, I made a soft red corduroy dress and delivered it via the "Daddy Express." The day passed happily, and we felt we were truly "walking into the sunset" with our new little family.

Emily's treasured possessions included a scrapbook lovingly put together by the foster mother and the "family book" we made for her. Looking at these books was one of her favorite activities.

We were given no advice about how to impress on this little one the fact that we were now her family. Our desire to have Emily blend with our family only seemed to make her more insistent on holding on to her previous ways. Looking

—

back on this time, it is obvious that Emily was afraid of "losing herself."

Soon after placement a very strange and alarming incident occurred. The children were in bed and suddenly Elizabeth called out to us in alarm. We went running into their room. Both girls were terribly upset. Elizabeth told us that Emily had tried to walk through the bedroom wall. Elizabeth got her back into bed, and almost got back to sleep when Emily got up again and tried to wrap the lamp cord around Elizabeth's neck! It took a lot of effort to settle the girls down, and it was difficult for Elizabeth to understand why we were comforting rather than punishing Emily, then age 3. We knew we needed help ASAP. We called the caseworker, who made an emergency appointment for us on the following morning at a mental health facility.

We began family guidance sessions with Emily that lasted through the next year and half. The sessions were somewhat helpful to us as they focused on Emily's manipulative behaviors. For instance, we were told that one form of manipulation is Emily's "soft" voice, which is barely above a whisper, so that one must drop what they are doing and pay close attention to her. We had never thought of that as "manipulation." The solutions were to give her a catchphrase prompt to speak up; to state that her request would not be considered until she spoke properly; or to ignore her completely. Hmm · · · this is whole new territory for us! And we were learning a new vocabulary, terms like "oppositional behavior."

Another manipulation was to balk when time was of the essence. Often this occurred on mornings when Elizabeth, nine, had to be driven to school. Emily was asked to do dressing chores she was capable of doing herself while I prepared myself and squiggly Tom, then age two. Emily, three, would stubbornly refuse. The suggested solution was to bring Emily along just as she was, even if she was still in her nightie, and let her get dressed in the car. The experts call it "consequences."

Our marriage had been established as a true partner-ship, and compromise was an essential component. Jon tai-lored his travels to minimize conflicts with family activi-ties as best he could. He was an active parenting partner. We discussed what had to be done, and divided up the du-ties. We maintained a united front on disciplinary and other parental matters, to avoid the ploy of "playing" one parent against another.

1982. Elizabeth, now ten, enters fourth grade and Emily starts preschool. I need the break, as Tom is becoming more active and "into everything" now that he can walk.

1983. Sessions at the guidance center with Emily have helped us cope with her prickly personality. Looking back on those early years, we can see the beginnings of a ten-dency in her life which we find hard to understand: That of sabotaging any chance at success, be it in relationships, academics, or athletics. It still amazes us that such a young child can be so adept at emotional distancing. We did not recognize this at that time, nor was it ever brought out in counseling. After years of counseling, we can't say there was much progress; perhaps we merely got used to Emily's be-havior. It certainly did not seem to improve, and combined with Tom's growing impulsivity, Emily's behavior was not easy to take. Because of this, we had still not finalized her adoption.

We consulted another professional about Emily's be-havior. After three appointments with the psychiatrist, we were given the unadorned pronouncement that Emily was a very strong-willed child. Period.

1984. Elizabeth, eleven, is quite a young lady. She feels like she's in the "big time" because she's in junior high school.

Tom, now five, likes school. The past summer has seen

—

an increase in his impulsivity and activity level. Nothing we do seems to alleviate it.

Emily, six, does well in kindergarten. While life has not exactly been tranquil, it seems a bit more settled. So, late in the summer we started final adoption proceedings. Emily's finalization was a very happy occasion, celebrated with a picnic. It's been a long three years · · · maybe there are better times ahead.

In December, Tom's teacher calls a conference with us. He has become increasingly wild and undisciplined, even hitting the teacher. She suggests a complete evaluation. During the testing process, the team leader shows us pictures of children with classic symptoms of fetal alcohol syndrome. Of the fifteen or so physical manifestations of the syndrome, Tom has six or seven, including his long body and facial conformation. Final diagnosis: Tom has fetal alcohol syndrome and is hyperactive. A Ritalin regimen is recommended.

The teacher is astounded at the change in five-year-old Tom. He was a bit groggy, but alert enough to follow through on directions. When it came time to do written work, he actually stayed in his seat.

Wow! It was quite obvious to us that Tom was truly hyperactive, who really needed the benefits of Ritalin in order to function well. We felt that anything that would help him settle down long enough to learn and be successful in school was worth any amount of criticism we would encounter · · · and we did hear quite a bit over the years, usually along the lines of "I would *never* let my child take Ritalin." Tom does well, and breezes through the remainder of the school year. We have great hopes for his future.

Behavior, sibling interactions, etc.

There had been no doubt in our minds that Tom was a very bright child. But the behavior we saw at home and at pre-school between the ages of three and four gave us a glimpse of more difficult future challenges: that of dealing with a child with distinctly disparate ages all wrapped up in one little body—that of high intellect, with emotional and social development lagging behind on a far younger scale. An annoying factor about Ritalin was that I had to brief each new teacher on its effect.

To this day, we remain happy with our decision to begin a Ritalin regimen. The problem was that the Ritalin basically controlled his behavior at school—at home, when the day's dosage came to its abrupt end, we were left to deal with a hyperactive child. This took a toll on family life. The girls still hold the perception that our lives revolved around him. We tried mightily to provide special times for each girl.

Emily, at $7\frac{1}{2}$, remained emotionally distant from us. It seemed as if she permanently replaced the word "want" with "need." She would lobby for her perceived needs with vigor even when it was obvious that the answer would be negative. It seemed to us that Emily was a tightly walled little entity who carefully calculated her reactions and alliances according to what she perceived as being good for her. Declarations of affection were usually followed by a request or demand. We now realize this to be a serious emotional problem, maybe a result of her first chaotic months of life when it was a survival skill.

Emily's social interactions mirrored her emotional distance from us. Her peer relationships were always rather bumpy. We believe that an emotional barrier stopped her short of forming firm friendships.

Elizabeth, on the other hand, was reliable, somewhat on the quiet and thoughtful side. She was well liked by all her teachers, and peers regarded her as a valued friend who was trustworthy, and sweet, with a wonderful sense of humor. She had little patience with Emily's manipulations and often expressed frustration with Tom's behavior.

—

1986. Tom starts first grade. He has been chosen for the Reading Recovery program. He thrived on the one-to-one regimen, and completed the six-month program in three months.

1987. Elizabeth started high school. Tom's teacher has her hands full. Tom's not an instigator, but would gleefully respond to the slightest disturbance. He was becoming the class clown. Tom perceived this as social acceptance. Despite the distractions, he was completing the academic material. His clowning became out of control, and changing his medication could not solve the problem. He is at maximum dosage. Consensus is that the situation is untenable and unlikely to improve unless we move him to another school. He was transferred in December.

1988. Tom has done his schoolwork well. However, at the end of school, an at-home behavior shows up in the classroom. One of his most annoying habits was taking things from other family members. He had been engaging in this behavior for about four years. He would usually be caught. His explanation was "I took it because I wanted it." No amount of scolding imparted any change. Now, he had taken a workbook and was punished by losing the privilege of attending the Fun Olympics.

1989. For the annual science fair Emily and Jon do a project involving momentum. Emily won a "Superior" rating. Way to go, Emily!

Life has finally settled down somewhat, and Elizabeth successfully obtains her driver's license. She is a reliable, careful driver. But she is not easy to get along with at this stage of the game. Sixteen year old female hormones? In any case, we've only got one nerve, and at the moment, she's on it. Even Jon is pushed to his limit, and angrily suggests that she take herself out into the community and not return until she either has a job or at least several applications. I

—

am relieved when she returns two hours later to announce that she has a job at the local steak house. The job is great. She is good at waitressing because she enjoys being around people.

In September, Tom, now nine, takes the "California" or "Metropolitan" tests. Once again, as in kindergarten and second grade, he scores right smack at that time in his life: 4th grade, 2nd month. As the year goes on, he is more attentive and interactive in class, and his grades - never totally bad—seem to be going up.

These past few years have been exhausting for me. Trying to stay one step ahead of Tom's hyperactivity, Elizabeth's adolescence, and Emily's stubborn mindset has taken its toll. Outside of being a mother, what have I done lately on a purely adult level?" I am not pleased with this mini-retrospective. So I take an adult "return to school" seminar and register for one class.

1990. Elizabeth is both amused and embarrassed to have a mother in school. In March I aced my English course, and sign up for Spanish and World Geography. At this point a hot topic of discussion around our house revolves around Elizabeth's college plans. Her grades are lackluster. We tell her that if they don't improve, she can plan on attending the branch for a year or two while she lives at home. To put it mildly, that proposition didn't sit well with her. "I wouldn't be caught dead going there! It's OK for you, but not for me!"

But Elizabeth's prom preparations had to be seen to. She and I go shopping, and she spots a dress she would love to wear to the prom. It looks great on her—a strapless dress of electric blue metallic stuff with a tiered skirt. All we need are the accessories. One Saturday I assigned Jon to take her to buy shoes, purse, and other accessories. They came home quite pleased with themselves, crowing about the fantastic

—

sale they'd encountered. And what was this fantastic purchase? Something I would not have even considered for Elizabeth, much less for myself: a gold chain, which cost "just under \$200"! Hmph. Now I still had to take her out for shoes, hosiery, purse, and the whale-boned undergarment, and still have fights about all of the above. That's the last time I sent those two out shopping together!

In May, I take my head out of the Geography book long enough to observe the end prom product. What happened to our little girl? She is suddenly so beautiful and grown-up. We took pictures at home and at the beginning of the dance, and our chaperone stint at the post-prom party. Then it was back to business as usual. The Cinderella glamour faded into geography textbook and Spanish.

Late in May, Tom got embroiled in a clash with his reading teacher. He refused to do his reading homework. Unfortunately, this will cost him dearly. At the awards ceremony on the last day of school he receives merely an achievement certificate instead of making the 4th grade honor roll. Of course he was furious, blaming the whole world, and most especially the teacher. What would have been a glorious end to the school year turned into a portent for the way things would go at home all summer.

In October, Elizabeth enters a program in which seniors take over posts in local government. She is placed with the city engineer's office, and came home with an aerial view of our section of town including our house and a new found respect for the complexities of keeping city streets operational. Because she threw herself wholeheartedly into her assignment she was rated one of the top students in the program. Mom and Dad were very proud.

November: Elizabeth's (17) grades are amazing. She makes the honor roll for the first time. Mom's threat of being her locker partner at the branch seems to be working! Tom's medication is again in question, it doesn't seem to

—

control his outbursts as well as it used to.

1991. Tom's behavior deteriorated over the holidays. He is now eleven years old. It seems that his whole personality and outlook on life has taken on a hard edge quite unlike his usual happy-go-lucky attitude. We had hoped that the holidays would smooth him out, but he continues to irritate his teachers and peers—and living with him at home is no picnic either. He is angry with his teachers, and his revenge is that he won't do his homework.

It seems that his medication is totally ineffective, just as if he's taking none at all. We've thought over the years that he occasionally seemed to metabolize his Ritalin too quickly, but never has that resulted in this type of behavior. We make an appointment with a new pediatrician who declares that another thorough evaluation is needed to update neurological, psychological, and physical baselines; to determine whether there is a true need for medication. He suggests the children's psychiatric unit of a local hospital.

After giving the matter serious thought, we make arrangements to have Tom admitted. We are devastated because we feel there is very little if anything we can do to help Tom normalize his life. We tried to explain to Tom that this was the best way we could help him.

We were interviewed before seeing Tom's room. I remember being shocked by the fact that there were two locked doors to go through. The hardest thing we ever had to do was leave him there. Our feelings were complex and corrosive: guilt, and then great anger that this was even necessary, anger toward the birth parents whose selfish, addictive lifestyle had caused such unnecessary difficulty in our son's life, such pain for all of us.

Life at home bumps along. We try to get to as many of the girls' events as possible. I make time to work on a quilt for Elizabeth's graduation. I am so distracted by the other issues that it takes about 30-45 minutes to relax enough to concentrate on the work in front of me. I cry a lot these days.

We visit Tom two or three times a week. When it dawned on him that there was no escaping the scrutiny and the annoying routine and rules, he became very angry with us for taking him there. But life got better for him as he progressed up the incentive system. We even allowed ourselves to hope that this would be a positive experience for him.

In the end, they released Tom with a diagnosis of fetal alcohol syndrome and attention deficit hyperactive disorder—just as we told them at the time of his entrance—and placed him on Tofranil (a drug that we found totally useless and were later told, by more experts, was not recommended for Tom's condition). The staff promised they would be available for follow-up counseling and drug therapy, and then proceeded to either leave out the unit or the hospital entirely.

So, we were left alone with a time bomb and with no help or guidance! We felt betrayed by the hospital; we felt ourselves to be victims of our pediatrician's incompetence, and felt that he was the unsuspecting cause of a major setback for our child. (In looking back we could see that we were too trusting of the professionals we dealt with because of our unfamiliarity with FAS and ADHD and because of our upbringing, which held that these professionals were always working in our best interests and with the most up-to-date information.) As bad as we felt, we had no idea of the hell that lay ahead.

I felt/feel that the doctors were reluctant and even downright unwilling to treat ADHD issues. Granted, a psychiatrist and/or psychologist must be part of the picture—but it is preferable for a physician to admit that he cannot adequately treat a certain problem than it is for him to just go ahead and attempt to do so. Perhaps I was overly sensitive, but I felt like they only wanted to treat nice average pediatric cases, and that Tom was somewhat of an anomaly—they treated his more normal physical symptoms, but refused to even speak of the ADHD issues.

We soon determined after that the Tofranil did nothing to suppress Tom's impulsivity and negative attitude. Again, it was as if he were taking no medication at all. We speculated that maybe this continuation of previously undesirable behavior was due to his hospital stay, and hoped that a return to school would help. The first few days were OK. Then I began hearing troubling things from classmates and teachers. The principal called to tell me that his behavior had garnered him an in-school suspension. I was shocked; this was something I had never, ever encountered. The principal also called in the school psychologist to evaluate Tom.

There was soon an out-of-school suspension. Why couldn't we figure this out and stop it? Why was there no halting this spiral? We finally got the school psychologist's official word: Tom's problems were definitely not academic, he scored at or above his level in school, with reading, writing, and verbal skills his highest scores. The problems were behavioral and social, with his social skills lagging behind his grade level. So what do we do?

We call the hospital to have them shed some light on the dilemma and are told that they don't do follow-up because they are purely a research and diagnostic unit.

Toward the end of April, the principal called. Tom had become angry on the playground and continued yelling in the hallway. He ranted and raved in the principal's office, and tried to throw a chair through a glass wall. They had to physically restrain him. They told us his behavior was escalating, and a ten-day out-of-school suspension followed by expulsion were the only alternatives. We were absolutely stunned? We admitted him to the neighborhood elementary school at the end of the suspension. We had hopes that the sudden change in schools would work for him as it had in second grade. The cold water of the expulsion seemed to rattle Tom. He was quieter and reasonably good during the ten days.

It is with a high level of apprehension that I deliver Tom to the new school that May. He soon becomes a regular at the principal's office. This administrator has little or no experience with ADHD children nor cares to know about how these children function or respond to discipline. Tom lasts for barely $2\frac{1}{2}$ weeks, and is then suspended for the rest of the year and "placed" rather than "promoted" into the sixth grade.

The one bright spot in our lives is Elizabeth, who is starting to do everything for the last time at school. She made the honor roll for the last quarter of her senior year. and had been accepted by her university of choice, to pursue a major in psychology.

I finally get her gift quilt together the day before graduation. I am quite proud of it, and feel as if this gift is the only right, sane, and useful thing I have done for a very, very long time. Elizabeth, now 18, cried when we brought out the quilt. And later on, when her friends came to pick her up for the graduation parties, she dragged the quilt out to show them, saying, "Look what my Mom made for me!" I cried too · · · I had actually done something that made at least one of my children proud of me, and temporarily glad to have me around.

The pleasurable activities are soon over. Tom is basically unmedicated. We bugged the psychiatric hospital once again, and they insist that they simply cannot offer us any follow-up help; they do not even offer suggestions. Dandy! Our pediatrician won't do anything, so here we are, swinging in the wind. We don't know where can we go for help. We are desperate. We have this off-the-wall, out-of-control

—

11 year old, and must get him on track before fall.

Tom is to attend the middle school. We are deathly afraid of what his behavior will be like. I certainly can't take the strain of any more suspensions or expulsions! A major brain storm leads me to call the pediatrician who headed Tom's diagnostic team at in 1984. He is sympathetic with our plight and gives a prescription of Ritalin. He is definitely a refreshing well of compassion in the midst of the impersonal, often uncaring medical community.

Elizabeth is all excited about going to college. It finally sinks into us that our time with her is short. In September, we move Elizabeth into her dorm room. It is hard to believe that the time has now come to say good-by and launch our first child into the world. Tears and pride abound.

Elizabeth winds up her exams and comes out of her first quarter of college with a 4.0 GPA. I believe that Emily, 13, might also have hit the honor roll. She, like Elizabeth, is very into basketball, and must keep up her grades. We can't recall for sure, but we believe that Tom, twelve, actually got to Christmas without any sort of suspension.

1992. Jon and I recall 1992 as being the year Tom once more exploded into more problematic behavior at school— life became a never-ending series of in and out-of-school suspensions. After serving a detention or suspension he often repeated the same infractions thus incurring the next most severe consequence on the punishment ladder. This business of Tom's not understanding cause and effect is making us absolutely wild with frustration.

Once again, we were stonewalled with Tom's Ritalin dosage by his weight. and we still had to live with the Ritalin drop-off at home.

One positive interest of his is long overdue for mention. For as long as he could read, he was absolutely fascinated by maps. Obviously, we encouraged this. His love of reading maps soon had him making his own, starting early in second grade. His maps became more and more complicated as he grew older. In fifth or sixth grade, he "went dimensional" and created in our basement an entire city out of large toys, boxes, and anything else he could get his hands on (including items he took without permission from all over the house). His city had a municipal building, hospital, parks, and an airport, just to name a few features. For a long time, there was not a box in our house unembellished by him.

Tom was instrumental in driving his sixth grade teacher bananas. She told us that Tom was not necessarily the instigator of a disturbance but was good at carrying through on someone else's lead. There were a good number of detentions and suspensions that year.

We were rapidly becoming anesthetized about the constant complaints from school. Ironically, Tom still maintained a grade range of B to D. We needed—and felt we had actively sought—help in dealing with his and our frustrations, yet none was forthcoming from the school or the medical or counseling communities. We felt as if our son was regarded as just a piece of annoying garbage which the school was compelled by law to tolerate until he could be legally discarded. Who the hell cared about him or about us? As the years pass, that feeling has intensified to an unbearably painful level. Outside of the help given by Barb VanSlyck, Dr. Dupre-Clark, and one other psychologist who came into our lives in early 1993, we have yet to get any real and useful assistance or consolation.

The stupid psychiatric resident we were assigned, is really annoying us This young man does not seem to be knowledgeable about ADD/ADHD issues. Indeed, we feel that we and our insurance company are paying him $120.00 an hour for the privilege of educating him—help certainly isn't flowing OUR way.

—

Do psychiatrists, psychologists, social workers and teachers even hear about ADD/ADHD, much less get direction on dealing with it? I wonder. Perhaps a crusade ought to be launched to require 10-20 credit hours of study AND proven proficiency in this area before a professional license or certificate is issued, with continuing education mandated to keep up with new developments in related areas such as medication. Our experience is that professional education in this area is sorely lacking, or at best, of dubious patchwork quality. ADD and ADHD-related disorders are at an epidemic level in our schools and society. The disorders are insidious because there are so many varying degrees and varieties of manifestation. Requiring competence in diagnosing and adequately treating these disorders will go a long way toward getting a handle on helping these people become fully functional. — Jon.

At the end of this month, just when I need it most, Jon comes home from work with incredible news: In April he must go to Europe. At the very outset of his arrival, he must spend six days at a conference in Paris. Since this is the year of our silver wedding anniversary, he rather figured that I should accompany him. April in Paris? Yes! We immediately call his mother to baby-sit.

Beth and I have finished our winter quarters. She is once again on the honor roll. Now I can concentrate on our trip. Isn't it weird that after I go through four quarters of Spanish I travel to Paris, France? Wish we had known we were going to this conference earlier, so I could have studied French instead. Oh, well. Suffice it to say that April in Paris was absolutely wonderful, except that I spent the entire trip saying "por favor" and "gracias" instead of "s'ilvous plait" and "merci." Jon used his last bonus miles to upgrade my return flight to first-class. I was wined (champagne), dined, and pampered all the way home. Then it was back to my real world.

1993. Elizabeth returns to college for the second quarter

—

of her sophomore year. Emily is into basketball. Tom is becoming noticeably more organized in his writing. Math comes easily to him. Tom is actually helping Emily with some of her math.

In February Tom's behavior once more weighs heavily on us, but we get two little rays of hope. First, we finally hear from the private psychiatric facility: They have assigned Tom's care to another psychiatrist. She is a lady of whom we have heard good things. This leads us to believe that she will move us out of our medical dead end. Our new psychiatrist, Dr. Kim, offers us new hope for Tom. She continues Ritalin but in a slightly different dosage.

In a casual conversation, the school's guidance counselor mentions a seminar he attended dealing with ADD/ADHD given by a very dynamic lady who is herself ADD. She is a Ph.D. psychologist in practice. I am on the phone that afternoon, setting up an appointment. The psychologist is a lady with much to say. The underlying theme of her suggestions and treatment is that we must work in mini-steps, over a long period of time. Tom likes her, and Jon and I are jubilant. We feel we have actually found the knowledgeable help we have sought for so long. Dr. Rose is definitely a "keeper."

In May Elizabeth decided to take a year off from school and live at home, working to save up money for an apartment when she returns to school full-time. We are happy with this decision. It will be good to have her back.

Emily graduates from 8th grade, and accompanies the family of a friend to Myrtle Beach for two weeks. She returns in mid-June and asks to stay over at her friend's house another night because other friends are coming over to welcome them back.

It seems we have unwittingly let Emily slip into a group which negatively impact her values. She is entranced with the new friends. The next few months are fraught with

—

pleas to go to her friend's to "help baby-sit," and that is a clue that the girls are seldom if ever supervised by responsible adults. We get inklings which indicate that her new friends often congregate there.

As the weeks go on, Emily is getting calls from a young man—who, when he manages to annoy us, has his friends call for him. He was the first in a long line of "boyfriends." We wondered what was going on, and later became numb at the thought that Emily had become sexually active. We tried to limit her contacts and phone calls, but her friends had access to vehicles which they used to help her sneak out at night.

August: Tom had seen Dr. Kim, and was given a new prescription for impulsivity control: A time-release Clonidine transdermal patch which can be worn all day, plus another medication. We are thrilled with this change—we no longer see the obnoxious "edges" and limits of Ritalin. Our son is calmer. He is also doing well with Dr. Rose. He relates well to her, and is fond of her form of "office" visits: sometimes at a fast food restaurant, as he seems to talk more freely in that venue. NOW can we start hoping again?

Elizabeth, 20, has been working as a waitress now for quite awhile. Emily, 14, seems to be enjoying high school. She has gotten a part in a play. We hope this is a distraction from her unbelievable summer activities (at this point, we still are not aware of their scope). But her friend of the Myrtle Beach trip is a classmate, and it is impossible to eliminate contact between the two. She and her friends devise new ways to circumvent our efforts to re-direct her energies.

In October Tom comes home with a flyer about being a delivery person for our newspaper. We decide to give him a crack at this. Collections are a riot—they take FOREVER, because with his blue eyes, cute smile, and the "please" and "thank you" we've drummed into him from a very young age, he is invited in by every little old lady on the route for cookies and milk. This newspaper routine lasts for almost a year.

At Halloween, it seemed the kid's take was unusually large and we were sorting in the living room when a young boy knocked on the door asking for Tom or his sister. A few minutes later, another stronger, angrier knock came at the door. I did not recognize the man, and was reluctant to open, but he yelled that he wanted to talk to my children. I told the children to please stay inside. The man told me they had something that belonged to him.

Emily ran behind me and out the side door. She had grabbed an aluminum baseball bat on her way out, and was now approaching the man as she brandished the bat, yelling at him and calling him names. I thought, "What in the world is going on?" The man yelled back, claiming that Tom, Emily and their friends had taken his sons' candy. He wanted the candy back.

Everything happened so fast it was a blur. I took the bat from Emily, told her she was not permitted to talk to any adult in that manner, and firmly ordered her into the house. She reluctantly complied. I asked the man to repeat his allegations. He did so, asking me to return the pillowcases that had held the candy. I told him that I did not have them. He left.

Emily told me that his sons had bugged Tom on his paper route. Our children had decided to get even. What happened here? Looking back on things with the perspective of the next four years' events, I wonder whether Emily, and Tom had used marijuana. They acted differently, and this whole ugly scene was a total shock to me. I had never seen Emily act (or react) in this manner, ever; and this was the first time I had heard about kids bugging Tom on his paper route. This is the last Halloween we observed—a sad ending to a festive family tradition.

Emily's aggressiveness, blatant use of force, and verbal

abuse were like a bolt out of the blue, but we soon recognized it as an inherent feature of her (later) drug-related behaviors. Three years later Tom boasted of that night in such a way that we finally had a factual account of the evening's events, and it did indeed prove that our suspicions were correct.

As we look back to the beginning of Tom's (age 14) school year, we see that things are a bit calmer for him in 8th grade.

1994. Tom receives his tentative schedule for next fall's freshman year, and is angry to find that he is in low level math and language arts classes. He is REALLY upset · · · says he's going to kill his new advisor and a whole long list of other people who "did" this to him. We and his teachers bluntly inform Tom that he did this to himself. We challenge him to obtain higher grades for the rest of the school year to achieve a better schedule. He seems to like the idea of proving an authority figure wrong, and accepts the challenge.

Tom's grades perked up. We are quite pleased. We actually observe the child studying before tests. And he finished the last quarter with a 3.2 GPA. Isn't this reason enough to hope that he will shape up in high school? We smiled for quite awhile that summer.

In late summer we get phone bills for over $1000.00. There is a long list of 900 numbers, mostly to the Caribbean and Central America. We confront Tom. At first he denies the calls, but finally admits to making them—then brags, "Wait till you see what I do next." Needless to say we are stunned and confused. A feeling of apprehension settles in.

We tell Tom he must pay for the calls, and ask him why he has committed such a deed. He replies with a smirk, "to hurt you!" What is behind all of Tom's anger? Could it be the issue about the friends he was hanging out with in 7th and 8th grade? They thought he was funny. Tom, in turn, perceived all of the "strokes" from this group as positives. These girls, and one other boy, were all "social outsiders." He had not mentioned our opposition to his friends, so was this really the major issue triggering his explosion of anger?

Tom's continuing friendship with these kids was an ongoing subject with Dr. Rose. She, of course, was telling us to "pick our battles," and to put up minimal opposition to the connection, lest major opposition give the relationships far more cachet than they deserved. Common parental wisdom, but oh, so hard to follow!

But why those hurtful words? Perhaps this was an extension of the anger about being in the children's psychiatric unit, the "extension" being that he had apparently made and successfully carried out a phase of a deliberate plan to hurt us. Heretofore, we often got an apology from him for thoughtless, hurtful behavior. There was no apology even implied here. We were at a loss to understand.

We removed all the phones except the one in our bedroom. Of course, the girls complained mightily—though frankly, limiting or eliminating Emily's time on the phone was also a positive in our eyes.

In August we help Elizabeth, 21, move into her apartment near school. Another apron string has come untied. This marks the end of Elizabeth's living with us though we are not yet aware of that fact. There is a hole in our hearts and house.

In August, Tom and Emily go to the public high school. Tom began his freshman year backed by the hopes his last quarter of good grades had spawned in us. His schedule had been modified to his satisfaction.

Alas, our hopes were once again dashed. Tom irritated his English teacher in a major way the first day of school. Tom considered the man's way of doing things stupid and let him know it. Tom had a one-day in-school suspension by the fourth day of school. So much for turning a new leaf.

—

He bonded even more closely with his group of friends, who turned out to have, as with Emily and her chosen friends of the past two years, a perverse influence.

The Major Crisis Period

September 1994—Pandora's Box Opens. On one Friday, Tom did not show up at the usual meeting place after school. Emily met me at the car, and claimed she did not know where he was. We did minimal searching, then went home. At almost 8 p.m., five hours after he was to have met me, Tom called. Unfortunately for my blood pressure, I answered the phone.

"Hi!"

"Where are you? Why didn't you meet me? We were worried sick!"

"Calm down. I'm all right."

"Where are you?"

"I'm at my birth mother's house."

I went cold · · ·, I swear blood simply stopped flowing through my body. He'd certainly found THE most shocking thing possible to follow up the incident of the phone calls.

By now Jon was eager to hear the other half of the conversation. I numbly repeated Tom's remark, then handed him phone and sat down. Jon elicited an address and we were soon driving to our destination a scant two miles away.

There, sitting on the cement stoop of a tiny house, was our son and an older woman. Just before we got out of the van, a moment of panic set in. For years we had had strong feelings amounting to hate for this woman who had so selfishly lived a lifestyle harmful to her children, with no thought for their well-being. Her bad choices had certainly impacted our lives in a major and negative manner. Now we were forced into meeting her "cold," with absolutely no preparation.

We each took a deep breath and stepped out. Tom

—

introduced us, "This is Marilee, my mother. This is her father. I'm named after him, Daniel Eugene Johnson the Second. This is Hilda, Marilee's stepmother. And this is a cousin of mine, Clyde. And that dog you hear barking in the back is Buck."

We never thought we would be the position of having to make small talk with the object of our bitterness, let alone meet her family. Tom is pleased as he can be at finding her, and greatly aware that we can do nothing to undo this latest wonderful "accomplishment."

Marilee told us how happy she was to have finally found her babies after so many years of mourning their loss. To hear her tell the story, one is led to believe that they were stolen - taken illegally from her. She thanked us—not once, but several times—for raising "Danny and Starr" together in our home.

Tom has opened a Pandora's Box, and there is no undoing that. Perhaps Marilee should know about their lives with us. Maybe she will see the advantages of not interfering with what we are offering these children. Perhaps this will actually enrich their lives.

We asked Tom, "How in the world did you find Marilee?" "Well, one of my friends showed me a picture of a girl in her mother's yearbook who she thought looked like Emily. I got to thinking that maybe we have family real close to us. So today I went to check it out at the library. I looked at the 1977 yearbook. Then I looked up the microfilm newspaper birth announcement for Emily. The day Emily was born, four ladies had babies. Three of them had husbands. The one who didn't matched the name in the yearbook, and she had a baby girl. So I took down the address and went to find her. She wasn't at the address in the (1978) newspaper. I saw a cop on the corner and asked if he knew Marilee Johnson. He said 'Sure, I know the whole family. Marilee lives in that house right there'." "I went to the house and knocked on the door. I asked her if she'd once had two babies and gave her our birthdates."

Marilee interjected in at this point, "I told him it was none of his damned business and who the hell was he, anyway? When he told me he was my son I almost decked him. My baby boy died. He couldn't possibly be my son. Then I looked at him again. He did look just like the birth father. He's got the eyes, the hair, the face · · · and he's skinny like Jake. It was like my baby come to life. And when he told me his story, and all about Emily, I just knew it was him. I couldn't believe it. We talked. I cried and cried. Imagine— after all these years · · · · . He's a pretty damn smart kid to find me like that, ain't he?" (This, said with a wide smile at Tom, who sat there, looking as proud as Punch, and with a triumphant look at us.)

The comment about her baby boy dying immediately caught our attention. For years we had harbored intense resentment with the county adoption agency for placing these children so close to their birth family. We had been told only that the birth family resided in our county, then, with Emily's placement, had received the curious admonition to "watch where you shop. This family tends to shop at (naming some area stores)." For years we had feared that their resemblance was so similar to that of biological family that someone would literally accost us in public. Also, we had visions of vengeful family members stalking us; we knew Emily was taken from the birth family's custody with the help of the sheriff's department because the family had put up fierce resistance to her removal. NOBODY should have to live with the fear we had felt.

Had children's services REALLY lied to Marilee? Much as I hated having this conversation at all, I had to piece together what had really taken place fourteen years ago. So I asked, "Why do you say that your baby boy had died? He had a very traumatic birth, but after three weeks in

—

the intensive care nursery, he was sent to foster care, where he actually began to thrive. Who told you he died?"

Marilee responded: "Well, I started having contractions early, so I went to the emergency room. (Tom was born a month premature.) My obstetrician came to see me. My water broke all of a sudden, and he was so angry about the mess on his nice suit that he just shoved the baby back up my birth canal and then tried to turn the baby around inside me. God! That was the worst pain I've had my entire life! I needed so many stitches from that. Anyway, Danny was real sick when he finally came out. My aunt told me the baby died. That's what I thought all these years. So you can imagine how shocked I was when Danny actually came to my door today." (She smiles, and our son bristles with pride.)

One of Tom's major birth complications had been a breech presentation. An RN told me that the doctor's quick action had been "standard operating procedure" for that particular problem. So an aunt had told her the baby was dead? Interesting. In speaking with the social worker who had worked with Marilee at that time, she recalled that Marilee had angrily confronted her with the "information" that the baby was dead. The social worker told her that the baby was NOT dead, but alive, well, and in foster care. Marilee just chose to believe her relative.

At a later date when I confronted Marilee with responsibility for Tom's fetal alcohol syndrome, she brought up the doctor's response to her water breaking, claiming that the doctor was responsible for Tom's fetal alcohol syndrome and hyperactivity.

I proceeded to tell Marilee about Tom's young life, mentioning our struggles with his hyperactivity and hoping that she would make the connection with her drug activities. She said that Tom sounded just like her younger brother, who also had trouble sitting still in school and behaving. "Oh, what does he do now?" I naively inquired, hoping for a flash of insight into a possible view of my son's future. She replied after a slight hesitation. "He's in jail."

Marilee chose that particular point in our conversation to show me the old needle scars on her arm, and to declare that she is clean, and, no longer drinks or partakes of drugs, "and I just got a part-time job. At a bar downtown."

It's getting dark outside now. We tell them that we must go home to meet Emily. We ask if Marilee would like to meet Emily · · · of course, the answer is a resounding Yes! We state that this might well be a shock to Emily, and we are not sure how she will react, or what she will choose to do. Marilee must understand that Emily will make the decision as to whether, how, when, or even if she will meet with Marilee and the birth family, and that they must not force the issue. We promise to tell Emily this evening.

Tom has asked if he may stay awhile longer, and we consent to his staying till about 10 p.m. We need a little time alone to better absorb the emotional shocks we have just sustained, and also because at the moment we still harbor angry feelings for Tom for the cruel surprise he has sprung upon us. We drive away feeling numb, and wonder if whatever it is we feel isn't akin to being mugged in a dark alley and left for dead?

We tell Emily. "Tom has located the woman who is birth mother to both of you." Her face crumpled and turned white. She had been leaning against the door. She just slid down to the floor and started crying, sobbing her heart out wordlessly. We all liberally draw from the box of tissues.

When Emily regains her composure, we give her a sketchy account of our evening's events, leaving out any mention of our feelings (which we couldn't identify, even if we wanted to). We tell her that she alone decides whether or even if she wants to meet her. For a moment, she is again our little girl, and we intend to protect her if that is what is needed. Emily decides to come with us to pick up Tom. She

—

fusses about her puffy red face; I tell her that anybody with a grain of compassion will know the emotional impact of the news she has just gotten, and will certainly understand her tear-stained face.

As we approach the little house, Emily tenses up. We can see the group gathered on and around the stoop. There are more people present than had been there earlier. We pull the blind on the van window, telling Emily that nobody will force her to get out, that this meeting can be postponed until she is absolutely ready, that all we really must do now is to pick up Tom. Once again, she sobs uncontrollably. She gulps and asks if this means she must leave us and our house. "Of course not! Life can and will go on as usual. We are still your parents, and we love you, orneriness and all (a tiny smile from her at that). We will always love you (more tears)."

After a few minutes of eternity, she dabs at her eyes and slowly gets out of the van. Marilee's 5'10" baby girl, whom she has not seen since the age of 11 months, tearfully hugs her, and they walk a little distance away, with Tom. We keep an eye on the three of them, while we meet Marilee's husband, Rory. He, too, thanks us profusely for raising the two children in our household, and talks of Marilee's anguish over the years. She has never had any more children.

A fleeting thought: Do they all consider us to be delivery people?—"Get your ready-made teenagers here."

We tell Rory, "Of course, we will extend the courtesy of making prior arrangements before visits, and if our children show up without such notice, please call us at once. They should not inconvenience you."

Emily, Tom, and Marilee all look like excited little kids as they re-join us. They ask if Tom and Emily can stay overnight, so some friends and other relatives can meet them.

This is unexpected. Jon and I are divided: He thinks

this a major bad idea; I am thinking that maybe this whole reunion could be a good thing, that maybe they need to get to know their biological family. We step aside to discuss the matter. We wonder what could possibly happen in an evening. Tom has his paper route; perhaps that will be a good reason to come get them at 7:30 in the morning. From 10:30 p.m. till 7:30 a.m. the next morning is nine hours. Not an unreasonable length of time for long-separated relatives to get together, especially when about $\frac{2}{3}$ of that time will be spent sleeping, right? Jon is still wary, but I doubt bringing them home will solve anything. So we go away with heavy and confused hearts. We had no clue then what we were dealing with.

Emily and I talk for a few minutes after they come home the next morning, while Jon and Tom do the paper route. Apparently they were up most of the night, talking. Emily is amazed that she and Marilee both like country music, and says Marilee thought it was cool that Tom enjoys '70s music because she listened to a lot of it while she was pregnant with him. I try to tell Emily how hard it was to walk away without them last night; it was very hard to keep all the years of resentment out of my words. Emily solemnly tells me that it was "very trustworthy" of me, thanks me, and gives me a kiss.

It is only much, much later that we find out more about that night. (Marilee freely shared beer and marijuana with our children, and they gladly partook of it.) September 1994 was certainly a bittersweet month for us. We celebrated our 27th wedding anniversary, but lost our two beautiful, children for whom we'd had such high hopes.

Post mortem of "Opening Night"

How we loathed that day! How we loathed the county human services for placing those children so close that a simple library search could find them! If ever there was a lesson

—

that needs to be given an agency about placement of children, this is the one. As much as we wanted these children, we would have passed if we had known how close and extensive the birth family was, and how hard and dirty they fought to prevent human services intervention, then later waged expert guerrilla warfare against us. The placement was either gross negligence at its worst or plain stupidity at its best.

In putting together fragments of conversations from that night and subsequent conversations during the early days when we were still being polite to one another, we found out a bit more about the birth mother. Drugs, alcohol, and prostitution to support Marilee's addictions already comprised her lifestyle when she was barely sixteen.

Our mistake when we met Marilee was to let our middle-class upbringing get in the way of our survival instincts. We decided that Marilee should be treated as any other adult who had a place in our children's lives. We thought she could be an influence for good. We now know that Marilee was not an adult emotionally or intellectually, nor an influence for good. All she wanted was to justify her position that human services had wronged her. The children were tools to whom she finally had access after all these years of attempting to "prove" this position. She wanted them for appearances only.

She was definitely a street-smart addict, and accordingly used bribery, deceit, and innuendo to create in the children's minds that her way was the way to their future. And because it was easy, free, and totally different from the ethic we were presenting, and because they felt they were born to it, it became their lifestyle.

Tom's friends had encouraged him to find the birth family. And what inspired them? In 1994 the rage among daytime talk shows was to reunite families who had been broken up by adverse circumstances and subsequent adoption.

They romanticized reunions. So, in a way, the misguided adolescents who encouraged Tom's actions were actually victims of the media, who usually failed to show any adverse aftermath of such "wonderful" reunions.

September through December 1994

Within two weeks of meeting the birth family life has deteriorated quite a lot. The week afterward, Emily and Tom come home later and later. I find myself running to the birth mother's house in search of them, usually with little or no success. (The extended family regularly hide them.) We feel marooned in a sea of insanity. Any attempts to connect with the birth family are met with indifference or stonewalling.

We soon receive another jolt: official notice that our children have been truant and must serve a Saturday detention. (What in the world is that?) How could they be truant? They are always on time for school; Jon drops them off. Answer: They get out of the car and then simply walk off to spend the day partying with the birth family or with friends in homes unsupervised by responsible adults. Of course, the truancy picks up speed, and soon Emily and Tom are suspended.

In the course of these three months both Tom and Emily start openly and defiantly smoking cigarettes. We discover that Emily has graduated to smoking pot. Later, alcohol and other drugs come into play, and we are positively sickened to find out that she has become sexually active on an indiscriminate basis. Tom does not use pot or other drugs, nor is he involved in sexual activity. It is from Tom that we get tidbits of information on their activities and whereabouts. They are staying away from home overnight, then for more than one night. We fill out many missing person reports. We entertain a procession of police in home in the process of filing such reports. One happened to be the officer who initially directed Tom to Marilee's house. He indeed knew the whole family. He tells us that he came to the force around the time Marilee's activities came to the attention of the authorities, and has arrested most of the family at one time or another.

We still can't figure out what hit us, but as time goes on, we see that Emily's response to finding the birth family is different from Tom's. She emulates Marilee in looks, attitude, and values yet does not run to them as Tom does, to obtain "stuff," generally cigarettes. She uses them to leverage favors from us; indeed, she historically uses everybody and anybody to get what she wants. She won't let anyone close to her. We feel that she is the classic detached child who has reached adolescence with little or no ability to give, or accept love.

October: We tell Dr. Rose about the reunion. We tell her we can't believe that our kids are not seeing the error of their ways and getting their acts together. She rummages in her files of professional literature, and pulls out a flyer about a local group called Parenthesis, which deals with adoption problems. She's heard some good things about this group, and recommends that we call the post-adoption services director for further information.

We are both amazed and relieved that there might be a knowledgeable, sympathetic group near us, and call. Barb (the post-adoption specialist) sends us literature, and tells us about the education series conducted by her and Dr. Dupre-Clark. The classes sound like they were made for us. It is from her we hear for the first time about things like respite care and subsidy funding. We feel that some control has crept back into our hands for the first time in ages. It feels good to have some positive direction in our lives once again.

November, 1994 Jon has once again gone through the charade of dropping off our children at the high school. He just barely arrived at work when I get a call from a counselor at the school Emily, 16, attended last year. She tells me that a friend of Emily's is terrifically upset about a conversation with our daughter. Emily and she were talking on the phone last night, and Emily was despondent about problems with the boy with whom she was still sneaking out. Emily had suspected that she was pregnant, and had told him. A few days after that she told him she had a miscarriage, and got nasty with him—probably because he wasn't terribly sympathetic. (This pregnancy ploy will crop up again several times). She told her friend that she had gotten a gun from her street sources, "and I'm gonna use it—promise you won't tell anybody." Once again, my blood runs cold, but now I am more conditioned to responding quickly to unpleasant surprises.

I speak with her friend to elicit details. I then call the high school to have security detain Emily. Then I call Jon to dispatch him to the school. Before we hang up, we discuss our options. We decide that the best thing is to get some psychological or psychiatric care for her, possibly residential. But where?

I call Dr. Rose. We value her advice. Until Barbara, Dr. Dupre-Clark, and Parenthesis came along, Dr. Rose was our sole source of navigation. She recommends the programs at two medical facilities nearby. The second call is to our employee assistance program. She tells me the private psych hospital will offer us the best residential assistance. I explain our mixed feelings about the placement, but she still thinks it will work best for someone Emily's age. I am skeptical— nothing has gone smoothly for a very, very long time, but I get busy on the phone. The hospital personnel tell me to bring Emily in. Upon arriving home, Jon and I are utterly exhausted, but we do take time to look for the gun, but if there is one hidden in this house, we cannot find it. We

—

never do find it.

Emily is scheduled to spend seven days at the psychiatric hospital for observation and analysis. During that time we are to be part of the therapy—working with a resident social worker. Our first session sets the tone for the whole stay—the social worker doesn't show up for the appointment. On the second visit, it gets even worse. Emily, during her solo visits with the social worker, had convinced the woman that we were ogres who had mentally abused her all her life. The social worker verbally attacks Anne to the point where Jon must call time out. Jon reprimands the social worker for unprofessional behavior and demands that she either apologize or leave. She gives a less than adequate apology and without notice takes herself off the case. Emily again sees that she can manipulate naive ill-trained professionals with her acting ability.

On her sixth day at the hospital, a large, male patient attempts to attack her. The staff was barely able to prevent any damage, thanks to quick action by other male patients. Emily was physically scared to the point she could not move without support and was trembling and sobbing uncontrollably. Jon rushed to the facility as fast as he could (actually hitting a deer in the fog) and stayed with Emily, walking her around the campus over and over until she regained her composure. Next morning, they released her before she could be seen by the post-care psychologist. The whole situation was a fiasco—poorly run, poorly staffed and totally out of control. Why is it every time we try to help our children the professionals can't or won't help?

Emily sees her new psychologist three days later. He is a no-nonsense level-headed expert in dealing with adolescents. Emily tries to snow him and gets nowhere. We are greatly encouraged. Maybe she's found her match. Emily falls back on her old standby—she shuts him off cold. He gives a good outline of Emily's mental state—conduct dis-

order, with all that implies—and tells us he will be available
if and when she's ready.

The only way Jon and I have survived any of this is by stay-
ing in touch 24 hours a day. We have a pact that there will always
be consultation with one another before an action is taken. But it
seems like the crises come almost hourly. Jon has already taken
much time off from work, though his boss is most understanding
about our situation. Jon looked at his calendar, cleared what he
could, and arranged to work out of our home for the rest of the
year, nipping out only to attend meetings. It is a huge relief to
have him home.

We begin our involvement with Barbara VanSlyck,
Dr. Dupre-Clark, and the Parenthesis organization. We now
consult with Barbara as each new crisis arises. We continue
to be frustrated in our attempts to attend the education sessions; the children are still all over the place, and now we
are about to miss the last series of this year. Barb suggests
that we just come to the sessions ourselves. We are able to
attend the three in the middle of the series, and find them
most helpful. It is so good to know that we are others with
these problems.

We have, at her suggestion, started seeing Dr. Dupre-
Clark as a couple. Hey—we need our own therapy in order
to deal with this mess. We saw him only three times, but
it was enough to keep us on keel, along with Barbara's sage
advice sessions on the phone.

December: Emily's 16th birthday. Normally, when we
think of 16th birthdays, we think of a special party and
a special gift, and catching daddy with a tear in his eye
as he sees his little girl officially growing up. Obviously
that scenario would not be taking place. We couldn't give
Emily gifts on the usual scale, because we now knew she
would just hock or trade them for drugs. Emily did not
come home on her birthday. I had a special cake for her. I
called Marilee (on her neighbor's phone) to ask where Emily

was; Marilee mentioned a family party that night (of course never considering us as Emily's family). I asked if we could bring Emily's gifts, and we settled on a time to deliver them. We arrived at precisely the appointed time. Neither Emily nor Marilee were there.

Christmas: Under the circumstances, we were not looking forward to these hitherto special holidays. Jon and I just didn't have the heart for celebrations.

Elizabeth came home from college. Tom and Emily ran again on the 20th. Fifteen minutes before we left for Midnight Mass on Christmas Eve, Tom and Emily came home, fresh from a birth family celebration. They remained for a few days, and fled again on the 28th. Jon went to the police station to file the police report. On the evening of the 29th we receive a phone call from the local hospital's emergency room. Emily was there with abdominal pains. The physician diagnoses possible flu symptoms.

Upon returning home, Emily stages a pre-planned tantrum in her room, kicking out a glass pane in her closet door, roughly pushing me so that I almost fall, then running downstairs and outside like the wind - pretty agile for someone with abdominal pains. Tom informs us that Emily had planned the entire episode. He leaves on the night of January 1st. It was my turn to give police the missing report.

1995. Jon notes: "We thought our situation couldn't possibly get any worse, but it has. Our kids have picked up steam in the areas of running away, verbal abuse, and noncompliance with any sort of authority. Jon and I have been at odds for over a month now as to whether or when we should file with juvenile court to declare them incorrigible and unruly. He is more an optimist about improvements than I. I tell him that that's because I, not he, am the usual target of their anger.

"The aggressive behavior of both children seems to

be escalating and indicates a willingness to injure. Both children are big and strong enough that their mother is not capable of defending herself against an unrestrained attack. I fear for her safety because there is no predicting what these two may do. My business travel is scheduled to pick up drastically this year, and I am afraid to leave her alone to deal with this situation for the necessary extended periods of time."

Therefore, in January we file the unruly/incorrigible complaints on both children with juvenile court. Our legal action only served to spur them on to more intense activity. But now we are finding out that filing this legal motion and obtaining court jurisdictional services takes a heap of pressure off of us. And we find that we have filed this motion a scant week before the school would have done so.

End of January: The children come home very late in the afternoon, once again having not met me after school as arranged. They demand to be let into the house but I am weary of their verbal abuse, and tell them to wait outside until Jon gets home in about half an hour. They abusively yell their demands, but I tell them to stay on the terrace; I continue to prepare supper. They angrily bang on all of the windows in the dining room and kitchen areas, and I am afraid they will beat down the side door. Tom yells obscenities at me, and I become more afraid. They circle the house for about twenty minutes in this fashion, and the yelling is louder and more obscene as time goes on.

Jon comes home before I am aware of his presence, and before I can tell him what is happening, he walks in the door, followed by the children. I try to tell him what has gone down, but the children out shout me. Jon tells them to go to the porch and wait. I close the door just seconds before Emily can enter the house. With chilling speed, Emily used a small object to break the pane of glass closest to the door knob, and tries to reach in to turn the latch. I quickly step onto the pile of broken glass to grab Emily's wrist. Tom kicks a bottom pane of glass out as he grabs a bottle and smashes still another pane of glass out—this time one that is on a level with my face as I am attempting to thwart Emily's attempt to enter the house. I catch Tom's action a split second before the bottle hits the glass, and narrowly avert getting a batch of glass splinters in my face. Jon puts both children down on an old sofa and yells for me to call the police. Our children do not take this quietly, but Jon sees to it that they stay put until the city police make yet another visit to our house.

This time the charge is domestic violence, and they once again enter police custody, going to detention for three nights until a hearing is scheduled.

As we sit in the corridor outside the probation office, we are shocked to see our children in handcuffs and shackles. Tom comes first. He is slowly led along the corridor on the side where we are sitting. As he comes even with me, he yells "bitch!" at me and quickly kicks at my leg with his big, clunky boot before the officer can stop him. He is suddenly surrounded and subdued by three more officers in such a manner that I am shielded from him. After he is placed in the holding cell, the officer apologizes profusely. Emily is brought up with two guards, walking along the other side of the corridor.

They have for many months now tried to force us to physically hit them as a consequence of their actions and words. We have refused to do this, and they have continued to goad us, yelling "abuse!" when denied what they want. They often have threatened to go to court and bring our "bad parenting" to the attention of the judge, whom they are convinced will see things their way and throw us in jail. Fortunately, the judge brooks no nonsense. They are ordered into individual foster care.

Their oppositional behaviors and truancies continued. Tom was placed in a foster home that had been in business for years. He quickly "nastied" himself out of the home, running away several times and piling verbal abuse on these good people, who declared they had never encountered the like in all their years of foster parenting. He was then moved to another home. He did a little better there, but he and Emily worked hard both together and independently to get back to the birth family.

Even though they were not with us, we were besieged regarding their frequent AWOLs. There were countless court visits over a two month period, when they were remanded back to foster care where they continued the pattern of truancy and defiant oppositional behavior.

Barbara could see that we still needed major feedback for the situations we were facing, and suggested that we come to the monthly support group meetings. These turn out to be a lifesaver for us. The group had been together for ten years already, and we received much advice backed up by "been there, done that." They were important enough for us that Jon would change his travel schedule rather than miss a support group session.

In early April, it was quite clear that both the foster care network and law enforcement officials would tolerate very little more from them. Our social worker, the guardian ad litem, and we were up against a wall. How could we stop this constant running to the birth family?

The social worker called one day with an unexpected proposal. Why don't we give the oppositional players in this scenario what they want, and then see how things work out? In short, what they proposed was that Jon and I give the birth mother temporary custody of the children. They decided that 90 days was a reasonable length of time for such an arrangement. Random drug checks, regular school attendance, regular med. regimen for Tom, and compliance with court orders and the stipulations of the custody agreement were to be integral parts of the arrangement.

The more we thought about it, the more appealing it became to call their collective bluff and see where the chips would fall. We drew up a list of our requirements, and saw our lawyer. We ran the agreement past the guardian ad litem, social worker, and probation officer. Marilee was approached with the plan. She happily added her signature to ours and everyone else's.

Tom had a foolish, unbelieving look of triumph on his face when he heard the news—and we breathed what? A sigh of relief? Apprehension? Guilt? Sadness?

May/June: How did things go? Here are some points:

- When I called the school I learn that they have not been attending.
- The probation officer tells that Marilee is working as a bartender at a downtown bar from 6:00 p.m. to 2:00 am.
- On Friday Emily and Tom were at Marilee's house, baby-sitting two little cousins. Two juvenile boys were also there, and all four were smoking pot. Police came to the house because one of the visiting juveniles had broken arrest by destroying his electronic ankle device.
- Drug test results: Marilee told the probation officer what her test would show: Alcohol, marijuana, and crystal meth (a hallucinogen).
- In questioning Marilee about compliance with the custody agreement, it comes to light that she has not administered all of Tom's med—just the transdermal patch (we discover later that she has told Tom that we sedate him for our own convenience.) The magistrate orders her to comply fully with the med requirements.
- The P.O. tells us that they are not prosecuting Marilee because so far there is insufficient evidence that she is supplying them with drugs. The social worker thinks that the children should be removed because of Marilee's drug abuse. The P.O. disagrees, feeling that Marilee's perfor-mance (or lack thereof) as guardian will offer us much

valuable leverage when Tom and Emily are returned to our custody. Mandating return to our custody at this point would negate any such leverage. It was the children's choices which led to this action, and it should run the course. They must hear Marilee say to their faces that she no longer wishes to parent them · · · .

- The guardian *ad litem*. She offers an interesting anecdote of her own; She recently encountered Marilee, Tom, and Emily coming out of the bar where she works. It was a school day.

How did we feel about all this information? We certainly had trouble morally justifying their staying with Marilee, in view of her drug use. Yet where would they be if they were back with us? Would things really be better? They must hear from Marilee herself that she cannot parent them. Nothing less will make an impression on them.

Mid-June: One day we learn Marilee has, in effect, kicked them out of her house by locking them out, and they are at that very moment sitting in the probation office waiting for us. Now we must re-integrate them into our household. We had assumed that the custody period would last to the end of July, and we had been too tired and depressed to give it much thought.

End of temporary custody agreement

While the agreement was in force, Marilee chose to ignore most of its provisions, notably Tom's medication. (It is unfortunate that she shared this philosophy with Tom, because he now refuses to take his medication, nor does he consider that his ADHD psychologist, can help him.)

Behavior of children after return (6/95)

Overall, Tom has been reasonably cooperative and at most times civil. There was one instance where he became verbally physically abusive to Anne (spit a mouthful of carrots at her and pushed her). He has since apologized and has been able to discuss the incident. Unfortunately, he refuses to resume his medication. Tom chose to stay home when Emily ran away. He did not go with her because she had stated an intention of getting stoned. He is concerned about her drug use, and refuses to participate with her. Emily thinks she is pregnant, but left before she could be tested.

There is no way to delicately say that for the past 12-18 months, Emily has been aggressively seeking to become pregnant. With each failure, she informs the young man that she has had a miscarriage. She then terminates the relationship. This has occurred at least four times.

Emily continues to be more difficult to reach and to deal with. Her attitude is one of "if you give me everything I want, I'll be civil. But I won't tell you what I want and I'll be mad if you don't give it to me in spite of that."

Emily just will not allow us to parent her or help her. The focus of her running away, behavior, and attitude have changed from "You can't keep me/us from our birth family" to "We want to be on our own and live independently—now." She mentions this at every opportunity.

Emily ran away June 21 followed by a week in detention. She is now using sex as currency for drugs. We attempt to obtain detox/substance abuse treatment. She was sent for an assessment and outpatient treatment is court ordered. Emily has been ordered into foster care and starts school followed by truancies and house arrest.

Tom is suspended for truancy. We did not let Tom's presence in our household deter us from attending our monthly support group meetings. Barb helps us set up a respite arrangement with Parenthesis, and twice this summer, we are able to leave Tom, 15, at a foster home while we attend meetings.

Analysis

Both Tom and Emily feel they should be able to do

anything they want without limit or control and that we should ignore their past behavior. Neither of these children are emotionally and mentally ready to be on their own. Two such beautiful, intelligent, and potentially talented young people could indeed be anything they want to be with just a little effort—what a waste!

October 1995: Emily has spent the last 3 weeks in a detention center due to runaways and drug use. She begins 45 day residential treatment for substance abuse. We begin the post-adoption education series. Tom dodges the first two sessions by running outside the building. However, he observes the activities through the window and decides to participate in the third session. He is amazed that there are others his age with the same concerns. He now looks forward to each of the remaining classes, and is actually upset when the series ends. He has participated fully and has come away with some new perceptions about adoption. We, however, gain far more. We learn other families also have these problems and that we have done the best we could. We regain some feelings of self worth.

December: Emily (17) returns to high school. The residential facility had placed her on Zoloft to level her moods. She runs again December 8. Tom rushed to Emily's defense with the school and got a 10-day suspension. On December 22, after her return, she is placed under house arrest.

1996. Tom is permanently expelled from high school. We help him apply for GED, naively thinking he will then lead a productive life. He gets a job at a men's clothing store. We realize Tom has a growing interest in "white witchcraft," and Merlin/druid-type beliefs. This is a new and frightening turn of events.

Emily is skipping school and is verbally abusive. We have a deep feeling of foreboding that she will not attend regularly again.

—

In March, Emily is in court for the third time in 5 business days. The judge reads the riot act to Emily. He said that the courts and county had poured enough money into futile rehabilitation efforts and were unwilling to house her in detention until her 18th birthday in December. He then wiped out all charges. He said her father and I could make any living arrangements we wished for her in our house or out. I was stunned!

She moved out that night and has not lived here since. Emily bounces from place to place, surfacing when she wants something. Tom stays home most of the time. The job did not last. He still disappears to the birth family to get them to buy his cigarettes. Tom receives his GED, scoring six-tenths of a point below the national median for graduating seniors taking the same test.

Emily begins a pattern of Emergency room visits. We get calls about treatment for a variety of minor ailments. After 7 or 8 visits, one in August, showed a positive test for pregnancy. We had feared this possibility. Bringing an innocent being into her sphere of destruction was unconscionable to us. We plead with her to eliminate drug and alcohol use, but she scoffs at our concerns. We arrange for prenatal care.

November and December 1996; Anne's mother, who lives 500 miles away must go to a nursing home. Anne moves to her home and stays until the end of the year. Emily's eighteenth birthday comes and goes. She is in advanced pregnancy and living with a friend.

Jon brought Beth and Tom for Thanksgiving. On the trip he learned information that he wanted to share. After the kids went to bed he told me that Elizabeth had revealed to him that she is a lesbian. The shock was too much to bear on top of the situations with Tom and Emily. Elizabeth is my oldest, the most affectionate, gently humorous and lovable, sensible one, the one who will make such a fantastic wife and mother. Could my baby, who wants to be a professor and write books, be a lesbian?

It was a difficult night. I sobbed into the blankets most of the night. By unspoken mutual agreement Beth and I stuck to mundane conversation until after the family visits ended. All we had was a brief, emotional discussion in a cold, windy parking lot before they left.

There are incidents relating to Tom that need to be mentioned because they show the lack of help we got from the police, children's services, hospitals, doctors, and the managed care umbrella under which the medical, mental health industries operate.

May 1st through August 1996. Tom is increasingly difficult to live with, has stepped up his witchcraft studies and has become involved via the internet. He refuses to see a counselor or resume medication. We believe now that it was during this period that he began using marijuana and other drugs, obtaining them from Emily and his birth family. His internet use ran up phone bills of several hundred dollars. We locked the computer room and secured the phones again. He just picked locks and used them anyway.

He ran away in July to a large city in northern Ohio, supposedly to study the "craft." We involve the police but they will not help. We discover later that the witchcraft story was a ruse to cover the real reason he left. Tom has run away to live with homosexual friends. We had no clue to his interest in homosexuality until this incident. We attempt everything we can to extract him from this potentially dangerous environment, but to no avail.

Several weeks later, while Emily is staying with their birth mom, Tom arrives. He is to be picked up by a "friend" and returned to his group. We call the police as he is listed as a runaway. When the friend comes, an altercation occurs and the police intervene. Tom is taken into custody. The adult male "friend" of our underage boy is released. (Why? We still don't understand to this day). Against our urgent pleas, the police release our son back to the birth home. He and his friend go back north.

All we wanted at the time was to break the connection with this unknown group. We felt if the police or children's services could have held Tom overnight that we might have been able to find a locked facility to hold Tom until he got some counseling. We got no help at all.

November: Tom, now 17, did return home several weeks later after a falling out with the group. We endured several crises with him including one in which Tom was involved with a major theft. Finally, it all exploded in his face and he returned to the only place that would still accept him—home. It was an uneasy time. He did nothing, either outside or inside the home. He was aggressive and angry.

We did make one last major effort to get help for Tom. A series of incidents occur which lead us to believe Tom needed critical psychiatric care. It came to a head one night when his anger overcame him and he attacked us both. The most important thing that happened is that he asked for help. We call our EAP(Employee Assistance Plan) and they say the only place that can help is the public psych clinic. They say they will set up an intake evaluation for us. Bring Tom and everything will be ready.

The center had not been informed that we were coming, and send us to Emergency where we wait. And wait. And wait. After a time we are put into a psychiatric waiting room. It is a tiny, dimly lighted room, with two chairs for the three of us. We wait. Thirty minutes later a resident comes in for a minute and leaves. We wait. Twenty minutes later he returns with a senior resident. He elicits from Tom that he had been using a street drug that could have contributed to his behavior. They say some one from the psych. unit would have to assess Tom for admitting purposes. We wait some more. Forty-five minutes later the doctor arrives, spends five minutes with us and says. "Unless there is immi-

—

nent potential for suicide we don't admit anyone. Here is a child asking for help and people saying to him—"you've got to try to kill yourself before we will help you." Hours and hours of waiting—for this.

The doctor says we should stay until someone comes to release us. We wait. After thirty minutes we leave, disgusted.

On the way home, Tom leaves the car. He figures if no one will help him he might as well get drunk with his birth mother. This was absolutely the final blow. This last futile try for help really frustrated us to the point of total loss in faith in the health care community. Our pleas for help were met with indifference and bureaucratic stonewalling. Nobody even tries to help us save the fragments of our family.

Current state of affairs—1997

Elizabeth, (25) is committed to earning a master's degree. She is essentially on her own but we still help out a little financially. We have not completely come to grips the news that she is a lesbian but have decided to deal with it when we have more strength. Meanwhile, we are communicating on an amicable surface level.

Emily, 19, had a beautiful baby girl earlier this year. Emily married three weeks after the birth. Her husband is not the biological father. He has had a rocky life, including addictions, violence, and several skirmishes with the law. His temper and attitude seem to get in the way of holding outside employment. There has already been one arrest for beating Emily. She refused to press charges.

We decide that we will do all in our power to not get involved with the daily aspects of their lives. We will help the baby, but on our own terms. We fear for this child at the hands of our daughter's limited parenting skills, but are powerless to do much to assure the baby is not abused or neglected. Emily is working for the first time in her life and leaves the baby in the questionable care of her husband. Their poor financial decisions keeps them at the edge of homelessness.

Tom, 18, is living with an older man in another state. He talks a good game about getting a job or further education, but admits he is using drugs. He claims he is happy, but we believe that is because he is given access to the internet, a TV, and spending money.

Overall: We tried to raise three children. We feel we lost three children. Not a good tally for 25 years of hard work.

Charting the Course

We still rely heavily on Barbara's (Charting the Course support group) wisdom and experience. Writing this biography was most difficult because we had to relive everything we had tried to put behind us. Barbara currently helps us with the whole new territory in which we find ourselves now: trying to protect our baby granddaughter and trying to come to grips with the distorted lives of these three strangers who lived with us for a while.

Issues and feelings about adoption

Adoption in itself is beneficial. However, the system as it presently exists is flawed, dooming more adoptions to failure than need be. Major modifications are necessary if the adoption process is to keep pace with the changes in society and the needs of the children.

A big pet peeve of ours was having to educate the professionals, with the consequence that we received little or no help from said "professionals." Comprehensive education and ongoing training must be required for social workers, counselors, teachers, clergy, physicians, court personnel, and all others who touch the lives of adoptive families. We need knowledgeable help and compassion, not ignorance, and criticism,

Prospective adoptive parents should receive mandated comprehensive education. Empower parents to make appropriate decisions early enough to avert devastating emotional and financial crises and teach them about rights and responsibilities regarding the children. Ongoing education must be mandated and taught by thoroughly qualified professionals.

Educate the media to assure that adoption situations are accurately presented. Today's media are powerful education forces that can be utilized to assist the adoptive family. Consider:

Adoption Subsidies: Moneys should be allocated at finalization to each family. Mind boggling crises erupt years after finalization. Families can be strengthened and supported with a subsidy system that allows the parents to obtain help for their children as the need arises.

Support groups: A support group network system should be in place for all adoptive families. We would not have survived without ours. We mean this literally, not figuratively.

What worked overall?: Very little except the support group, Dr. Rose, and our faith in each other.

What didn't work?: The overall adoption infrastructure, the school systems, the courts, the media and the misguided uninformed do-gooders with their guilt trips.

Our Feelings

We feel abused by the system, used by the children, and angry that so-called professionals know so little that they do more harm than good. Everyone was guessing with our kids; experimenting, trialling, and in general using them as laboratory animals to prove the professionals' pet theory "du-jour." We also feel that trust is a virtue no adoptive parent can afford. We have none left at this point. Every one of the institutions, bureaucracies and other systems which we believed would help us, failed to provide a solution and were definitely part of the problem.

Now, after 30 years of marriage, we must chart our own course alone, feeling that none of our children will be there to help us when we are older, the way we have been helping Anne's mother. We are bitter and sad as we watch our children's peers go on to attain the goals of their "normal" lives.

Were we "collies raising bulldogs?" No. Our children are more like female black widow spiders. After getting what they want from the male they kill him, suck him dry, and throw away the husk. Right now, "two husks dangling in the wind" is not a bad description of Anne and I. At least we are together.

Editors' Note: This is the longest and most detailed of the stories. It allows the reader to watch as a hoped-for traditional family deteriorates into frenzied attempts to just maintain safety for themselves and their children.

These parents, like the others, whose lives you have shared in these stories, are intelligent, loving, stable people who have borne much adversity incurring terrible scars, yet they persevered.

As you will note from the end of their story, they have not reached the peace or resolution that many others have found as their children have matured. We struggled with Mr. Brach's ending words and then decided to let them stay. We could think of no better way to convey the pain than to express it as written.

She
She's always happy,
      laughing,
           and carefree.
Never worried,
      upset;
           She's trouble free.
Oh, my friend,
      can't you see?
It's a mask...
        not me.

12

The Fremont Family
by Joan Fremont

T he big decision came after much thought and self questioning, when I was 33. In 1979, becoming a single parent was not as acceptable as now. I waited three years through our county adoption agency for a child under five. Being single, I had to be realistic and admit I could not handle children with certain disabilities or a child who was medically fragile.

In 1982, after another single friend adopted privately through an attorney, I contacted him myself. In September I received the most exciting call of my life. There was an eight week old baby girl available for adoption! The next few days were a blur. After being "pregnant" for over three years, how does one prepare for a child in three days? You can't prepare ahead of time, and I had told only close friends that I was planning to adopt.

On Friday, September 10, I arrived at my attorney's office to pick up my baby daughter, and from the first moment I held my daughter Lily, I loved her, but transition from a single person to a single parent in a matter of days was overwhelming. Suddenly someone was totally dependent on me.

The fifteen years we've been together have been a roller coaster ride: sometimes scary, sometimes exhilarating. She was always a challenge and a delight, walking and talking early. As a toddler she began demonstrating her formidable will. She began daycare at 13 months, and was soon trying to run the place. At age four, there were serious difficulties with her behavior at the daycare. I had her tested, and learned that the determined daughter I loved so much had ADD, with hyperactivity and oppositional/defiant disorder. At last I understood where her behavior was coming from, and Lily's anger about her birth family's abandonment added more complications.

From her infancy we had talked about how we became a family, because children realize early that "normal" families have a mother and a father. At age six, Lily asked once again about her birth mother. For the first time, I saw the light bulb go off in her head. She suddenly realized her birth mother was single and gave her up for adoption, *but I was single and had adopted her.* I could almost hear her asking herself: "Why, Why?"

Throughout school years, the dreaded "family tree project" brought recurring upheavals to our house. Few teachers understand the effect this project has on adoptees. Each time adopted children have to confront the missing information about their background, while the rest of their class can easily access generations of information easily, at home.

Despite Lily's problems, I found such delight in being the parent of such a bright, energetic child. What a joy, watching her discover the wonders of the world, and rediscovering with her so many beautiful things I'd stopped noticing, like the polished smoothness of a weathered rock in our yard. In order to nurture and develop my gifted daughter, I enrolled her in every enrichment program known to man. Art classes, music classes, anything that would encourage her. During the years I discovered that she sang like an angel, and her natural artistic talent has been held back only by her refusal to take much advice from anyone. She draws beautifully, and works in pastels and oils.

But there were serious problems too. And when other mothers could say, "No wonder she's behaving that way. My sister did that when she was the same age." I couldn't attribute my daughter's behavior to old Aunt Mary, and sometimes I wanted to tell the world that her behaviors weren't my fault; I hadn't contributed to her genetic makeup.

I rarely talked about my child's problems with most friends or family. I assumed that since some people never understood why I'd adopted in the first place, they sure wouldn't feel like listening to me complain when things got difficult. Did they assume, I wondered, that I'd simply failed to discipline my child and that was causing all the bizarre acting out behaviors?

As time went by, Lily grew more and more defiant. I wanted the best for my child. How was I supposed to react when she did everything she could to prevent that from happening? Handling everything alone, sometimes grief and guilt overwhelmed me, and I had to fight to remember that there had been good times before, and there would be good times again. But when Lily reached nine, I hit the wall. How would you confront the following situations:

1. Your daughter hanging head first from her bedroom window, threatening to let go and drop eight feet to the ground.
2. Walking into the kitchen and finding her with a carving knife to her throat.
3. Discovering that after dark she's leaving the house by climbing out of her window.
4. Receiving a call from her daycare center and hearing that your nine year old had a razor in the van going to school.

She was cutting her arms with it, and they had to remove the other children from the van in order to get the razor away from her.

One evening, in the presence of someone from social services, Lily threw a tantrum, and it took both of us, two good sized women, to physically restrain my 40-pound daughter. For years she'd been physically aggressive with me, hitting, kicking and punching when she flew into one of her rages. Now, with both Lily and her anger stronger, I had to face the real possibility that she would do harm to herself or to me. I couldn't handle the fear that she might seriously injure herself, and I had her admitted to a psychiatric hospital.

Overcome with numbed disbelief, I signed the reams of papers at the hospital, feeling as if an evil spell had been cast over our home. My child was admitted; next came the long drive home to a house filled with an emptiness that devastated me. What in the world had I done?

No parent brings a child to any hospital lightly. The questions, doubts and guilt cascaded over me. Along with the questions, though, came an unsettled relief. At least now she was in a safe environment and I didn't have to be her constant gatekeeper and watchdog. I realized for the first time that I'd been running a 24 hour psych ward on my own, single handedly. In the hospital they had three shifts of psych techs, social workers, a psychologist, and a psychiatrist.

Along with the heartache and relief came the sad knowledge that the dynamics of my relationship with my child had changed, and it would never be the same. In Lily's eyes, I'd abandoned her, leaving her against her will with strangers who frightened her. Sick with the knowledge that in a way she was right, I prayed that our relationship could be restructured into something healthier from this experience, and emerge healthier and stronger.

—

Lily's mother, as is the case with many adoptive parents, was totally burned out and psychologically drained by the time she had her daughter placed in the hospital. When she came to our parent support group the first time, she could barely speak. She said about three words, then sat there looking dazed while the group leader explained her situation. Several of the group took it upon themselves to call Joan and keep in touch with her. It took months for her to get to the point where she could interact in group and to talk about what was going on in her home.

In the middle of a crowded room I'd find myself feeling totally alone. Why couldn't I handle a nine year old? What had I done wrong? What should I have done that I neglected to do, that could have averted this situation? Thoughts like these spiraled me into a serious depression. In our wildest dreams, none of us ever expects things to get this bad.

I've learned so much since then. You can't always make it alone, and the support of other adoptive parents can be essential to your survival. The problems we all have to face are unique, totally different from the problems our friends confront in their homes.

Unfortunately, the social workers felt that all of our problems had been caused by my behavior, and that I just needed parenting classes. I wanted to scream at them, "I don't need parenting classes, Lily needs classes on how to be a child!"

Lily adamantly believed that no rules applied to her. Hormones had kicked in when she was trying to decide if she was supposed to be patterning herself after her birth family or after me, and the combination of teen age hormones and an identity crisis was lethal. We began seeing an attachment therapy counselor, in Cleveland, who specializes in bonding issues. He helped me tremendously, because he made me understand, finally, that I wasn't the cause of the problem. Although he couldn't change Lily's behavior, he helped me to change my reaction to it. Lily yelled at me once, "I hate that doctor!" When I asked why she said, "Because he made you strong."

After her first hospitalization, Lily and I went through three years of hell. She had to be put back in the hospital several times, in an attempt to get her medication regulated, but nothing seemed to help. Because of totally unruly behavior at home, with repeated incidents of shoplifting, constant lying, and many.physical assaults on me, I was forced to put her into foster care at one point for fifteen months. Then we tried living together again, but her behavior deteriorated quickly and we were back where we started.

After a few months of Lily being home, I had to accept the fact that although I'd told myself adoption was forever, forever was about over for now. Most days brought another violent rage from Lily. After she came at me with scissors, I had a bolt lock installed on my bedroom door so I could sleep at night. She constantly skipped classes, wouldn't be at the library when I came to pick her up, and would stroll into the house around ten with some elaborate story about where she'd been. She'd insist she'd been at the library when I got there, and that I just hadn't looked for her. Around this time, Lily told me that it was her house. I could remain in the house as the cook, laundress and housekeeper, but I was to impose no restrictions upon her, as she intended from then on to do as she pleased. Meanwhile, Childrens Services kept saying I was dealing with "normal teenage behavior"!

Sleep deprived, defeated and exhausted, I was forced to place my 14-year old daughter in temporary foster care again. In front of Lily, children's services told me I should give them permanent custody so that she could be adopted by another family and get on with her life. Lily looked as if someone had kicked her in the stomach. Furious, I totally, unequivocally refused. I also hired a lawyer to protect Lily and me from any further attempt by Childrens Services to tear our family apart.

—

I'm sure you won't be surprised to hear that Lily didn't do well in foster care. She couldn't handle parent-child dynamics any better in foster homes than she could in mine. She's now in a group home nearby, with other girls her age. She has to stay at a certain level to be able to come home for weekends, and lately her behavior is improving, but with many peaks and valleys.

My advice to any single adoptive parents reading this would be to first seek out an adoptive parent support group. If none exists in your area, form one yourself. Knowing you're not alone and that you're not crazy either, can get you through some difficult times. The meetings provide the help you need when things aren't going well, and when they are going well you can help someone else in need. It's also extremely important to be able to pick up a phone and call someone who's "been there."

My thoughts on single parenting

The transition from being a single person to being a single parent in a matter of days is overwhelming. Suddenly I found myself holding a baby, totally dependent on me. Although I later learned that was overwhelming for couples too, at least they had each other. What have I done? I thought. Am I ready, on my own, for this kind of responsibility? I allowed myself a moment of panic, and moved on.

In the early years I was alone with the baby. I couldn't just say to someone, "You watch her while I take a break." To add to the difficulty, Lily was hyperactive. There was no escaping, to go anywhere or do anything. And forget spontaneous outings when you have an infant.

I searched for a babysitter I could trust because I lived in a city with no family nearby for support. As Lily got older, it became impossible to find anybody willing to babysit this whirlwind of mine. She violently refused any parental direction, and she certainly wasn't going to listen to a babysitter. When I found the adoptive parents group, I also found a source of respite care so that I could get an occasional, badly needed break.

My single parenthood journey has been challenging, joyous, miserable, daunting, heartbreaking and sometimes funny. Lily has her own special way of seeing the world. One example is how she views food. Once when she asked for dessert and I told her that she hadn't finished her chicken, she informed me that her chicken compartment was full, but there was space left in her dessert compartment.

When I visited Lily's group home recently one of the other girls, whose parents don't visit her, asked me for a hug and wanted to know if she could call me "Mom," too. I told her she could, but Lily said, "No, you can't. She's my mom!"

I know now that I'll always be her mother, but not necessarily be in the same home. Lily and I, and our relationship will continue to evolve with time, so the story will never be over.

PART FIVE

*SPECIAL
SERVICES*

13

The Adopted Child and School Issues
by Ellen Wristen

Ellen Wristen is an attorney in private practice in Columbus, Ohio. Her practice involves the representation of children and families in special education and legal matters in public elementary, junior high, and high schools. Ellen is the single adoptive parent of two special-needs boys.

Adoptive parents can find that their children's educational experience is extremely challenging to both their children and themselves. They must, therefore, have a good grasp of the rights and protections available to children in the public schools. The difference between adoptive families and those with birth children is a frequency in which serious school problems occur as well as the intensity of such problems. Adopted children, because of genetic make-up, life experiences and/or self image as an adopted child, frequently struggle with traditional educational settings and goals. Adoptive parents must arm themselves with knowledge so they can effectively advocate for their childrens' needs and preserve the proper role of school as the educational setting and of home as the nurturing and supportive setting.

Help! —School has taken over our lives

Parents who adopt nonspecial-needs children at birth simply do not expect to confront school learning and behavior problems with any greater frequency or intensity than their counter-parts who are parenting birth children. Unfortunately, much to the surprise of the adoptive parents, the truth is that their adopted children may be educationally much more needy. For many adoptive parents of these "nonspecial-needs" infants, confronting school problems is very troublesome. It causes many of them to question their ability to parent effectively. The school staff frequently feeds the sinking parental self image and implies faulty parenting.

Parents who adopt older or special-needs children, likewise experience challenges in their childrens' educational experience. These parents, however, depending upon the child's special needs may expect learning difficulties, physical challenges, adjustment difficulties and behavioral challenges. These parents could anticipate meeting these challenges and helping the child adjust, learn, and behave. These parents dream of overcoming their child's pre-adoptive hardships so that the child becomes the individual that the child could have been but for the difficult pre-adoptive life. Academic improvement and school behavior become the measuring stick for the adoptive parents' success in parenting such a challenging child.

Unfortunately, many adoptive parents find with amazing frequency that their life is totally controlled by their child's school needs. The needs may take the form of either learning problems or behavior problems, but often the needs are a combination of both. The child is attention deficit, disorganized, suffering from untaught skills, learning disabled, academically slow, or a discipline problem. The parents want to help their child. The school staff desires to have the problems solved. The most convenient solution appears to be for the parent to be responsible and do quality parenting so that the child will be successful. According to many school staffs, all solutions to the problems lie at home with the parent. The parent is made to feel responsible. The educational tasks seem to be easily transferred from the school to the parent—after all, what good parent would not help their struggling child learn? The child's homework, learning, behavior, and even faulty memory slowly cease to be the responsibility of the school staff and become the burden of the adoptive parents and to a lesser extent the child. Home life deteriorates into an away-from-school educational setting in which the parent is supposed to correct all of the child's misbehavior, missing skills, and accomplish an increasingly large pile of homework. All available parent/child time and interaction becomes focused on school.

All parents, particularly adoptive parents, when confronted with such frustrations, should seek help from the school and should stop shouldering the entire burden for their child's education and school behavior. These parents should exercise their rights and their children's rights under federal law. Most adopted children who exhibit distressing learning problems and behavior problems can qualify for federally mandated identification and individualized services. Once identified, these children are entitled to appropriate interventions at public expense. Families can return to peaceful home environments instead of school-centered "war zones." Troubled children can learn appropriate family relationships when academics are removed as the central issue. The often heard statement of educators that "parents need to work with and support school staff," is correct. But the competing statement, "school staff needs to work with and support parents" is also correct. Parental support of school staff does not mean blindly following the well meaning but perhaps misguided mandates of school staff that the parent is totally responsible for the child's academic success and school behavior and that parents must shoulder that responsibility to the exclusion of all other family relationships and responsibilities. That kind of demand and thought fails to honor the school staff's responsibility of working with and supporting the parent in the parent's role of parenting.

A parent who finds himself or herself in the unfortunate position of being "responsible" for the child's school learning and behavior needs to act quickly and legally properly. There is help out there. Once parents become knowledgeable about their legal rights and begin acting on such knowledge, they will be perceived differently by the school authorities. Positive change can happen at school. Positive change can happen at home.

Federal law

IDEA — The Individuals with Disabilities Education Act, P.L. 101-476, formerly the Education for All Handicapped Children Act of 1975, P.L. 94-142, guaranteed all children with disabilities from ages three to 21 an appropriate, free public education designed to meet their individual needs.

The Education of the Handicapped Amendments of 1985, P.L. 99-457, extended special education services from birth. The extension was reauthorized in 1991 and amended as part H of P.L. 102-119, the Individuals with Disabilities Education Amendments of 1991.

In June of 1997, the federal law was again reauthorized in legislation known as the Individuals with Disabilities Education Act Amendments of 1997. This new legislation modified discipline that might be imposed upon special education students, parent involvement in the identification process and certain educational planning processes.

SECTION 504 — The Rehabilitation Act of 1973 contains a section commonly known as Section 504. The Rehabilitation Act establishes rights and entitlements for people with disabilities. The law simply prohibits discrimination on the basis of disability in all programs that receive federal financial assistance. This legislative protection is not limited to education.

This legislation was put into effect through federal regulations. The legislation and implementing regulations created our national approach to the education of handicapped children. Before this legislation was passed, schools could and often did refuse to educate handicapped students.

How to have your child evaluated for services

The most common parental frustration expressed when the child is experiencing school learning and behavior problems is the inability to obtain meaningful school help. The parent is directed by school staff to help the child at home, to medicate the child, to discipline the child, to tutor the child, and to monitor all assignments for timely completion. The school staff does not typically volunteer that it also has responsibilities for evaluation and accommodation.

The parent can quickly and effectively seek school intervention by requesting in writing; evaluation and services. Please note: an oral request does not mandate compliance with the federal law. The school might undertake evaluation and implementation of services in response to an oral request, but there is no obligation to do so.

A parent can present an image of a knowledgeable parent aware of the federal requirements by simply sending a letter requesting evaluations and services with the following form letter:

_____ (Date)

_____ (Principal)

_____ (Address)

_____

_____

—

RE: Student - _____

Grade - _____ DOB - _____

Dear _____ :

I am the parent of the above student. My child is enrolled as indicated in your school.

My child is experiencing great difficulties in school. I believe that my child suffers from a handicapping condition as set forth in Individuals with Disabilities Education Act. Please evaluate my child by performing multifactor testing in order to determine eligibility for special education services, Section 504 of the Rehabilitation Act of 1997 adaptations, and Americans with Disabilities Act accommodations.

This letter will serve as my consent for the appropriate evaluation and testing. If you need any additional consent signed, please make it available to me without delay so that I can sign it as soon as possible.

I request that the testing be completed in a timely fashion as required by the special education rules and that a meeting be scheduled at the conclusion of testing so that I may be informed of the results and of what interventions are necessary and appropriate in order to help my child in school.

Sincerely,

_____ (Parent)

_____ (Address)

_____

Phone _____

cc: Superintendent of Schools

The letter contains several necessary elements. It specifically requests testing as mandated in IDEA and contains a consent to testing. A consent is necessary for testing. Failure to execute a consent prevents testing, and failure to execute a consent at the time testing is requested can delay testing by as much as 30 days. A parent is best served by simply copying the form letter verbatim, and filling in the appropriate blanks.

The letter should be sent by certified mail, return receipt requested, to the child's school principal. A copy of the letter should be sent in the same fashion to the superintendent of schools. In large school districts it is helpful to also send a copy to the school's department of special education.

Once received, the school district must act upon the request. Under IDEA, school districts must complete action upon the request within 90 days after receipt. Testing must be completed, reported, and, if eligible, a special education plan developed within the time frame. The days are counted as calendar days—not school days. Weekends and school vacation days are counted. The day count is only extended if the last day falls on a weekend or holiday, in which case the last day becomes the next normal business day (not school day). Normally school districts respond by testing but if the district believes that the testing is unnecessary and inappropriate there is a procedure for informing the parent of the refusal to test. Rarely is this done.

Testing requested in the Spring needs to be completed so that the child has appropriate services for the beginning of the next school year. Typically school districts are understaffed or understaffed during the summer vacation. The staffing concern is a school district problem and not a parent problem. Reality is that if the parent is sure that the student qualifies for services and appropriate services are going to be provided, then there is no harm in delaying signing the final paper work until the school staff arrives back from vacation. Caution should be taken, however, to ensure that services will be provided from the beginning of the school year. Most school special education staff administrators arrive back at work one to two weeks before school starts. At least, initial documents qualifying a child for services and placing the child in a program can be completed before the teachers are back at work. An addendum can be completed a week or two into the school year. If, however, a parent is not confident that a child will be qualified for services and that appropriate services will be offered, then the parent should insist that the time-line be followed. If the parent intends to dispute an ineligibility determination or the nature of services, the dispute resolution process can be started and perhaps be concluded before the start of school.

A parent should disclose to the school all known facts concerning the child's learning disabilities. Prompt disclosure assists the testing process. The parent should inform the school of any medical problems such as attention deficit disorder, uncorrected vision problems, visual perception problems, auditory problems, auditory perceptual problems, and mental health problems (depression, obsessive compulsive disorder, etc.). A parent should write a note giving his or her best description of any problems. If there are medical or psychological reports available that could asset the evaluation process, the parent should quickly supply a copy.

To be eligible for service under IDEA, a child must fall into one of the designated categories. The categories are as follows:
1. Mental retardation
2. Hearing impairments (including deafness)
3. Speech or language impairment
4. Visual impairment (including blindness)
5. Serious emotional disturbance
6. Orthopedic impairment
7. Autism
8. Traumatic brain injury
9. Other health impairments

10. Specific learning disabilities
11. Developmental delay (for children 3 to 9)

These categories are all specifically defined in the law or regulations existing for the implementation of IDEA prior to the reauthorization. The regulations for the reauthorized IDEA have not, as of this writing, been published. The old regulations should be followed unless they are in clear conflict with the reauthorized IDEA. There is no reason to believe that the new regulations defining these categories will modify the definitions. Because there is always much confusion and misunderstanding about the nature of the handicapping condition suffered by children eligible for services under the categories of serious emotional disturbance, specific learning disability and other health impairment, the definitional language is being quoted in full here.

Serious emotional disturbance is defined as follows:

1. The term means a condition exhibiting one or more of the following characteristics over a long period of time and to a marked degree that adversely affects a child's educational performance

   a. An inability to learn that cannot be explained by intellectual, sensory, or health factors;

   b. An inability to build or maintain satisfactory interpersonal relationships with peers and teachers;

   c. Inappropriate types of behavior or feelings under normal circumstances;

   d. A general pervasive mood of unhappiness or desperation; or

   e. A tendency to develop physical symptoms or fears associated with personal or school problems.

2. The term includes schizophrenia. The term does not apply to children who are socially maladjusted, unless it is determined that they have a serious emotional disturbance. 34 CFR §300.7(b)(9).

Specific learning disability "means a disorder in one or

more of the basic psychological processes involving understanding or in using language, spoken or written, that may manifest itself in an imperfect ability to listen, think, read, write, spell, or to do mathematical calculation. The term includes such conditions as perceptual disabilities, brain injury, minimal brain dysfunction, dyslexia and developmental aphasia. The term does not apply to children who have learning problems that are primarily the result of visual, hearing, or motor disabilities, of mental retardation, of emotional disturbance, or of environment, cultural, or economic disadvantage" 34 CFR §300.7(b)(10).

Other health impairment "means having limited strength, vitality or alertness, due to chronic or other health problems such as heart condition, tuberculosis, rheumatic fever, nephritis, asthma, sickle cell anemia, hemophilia, epilepsy, lead poisoning, leukemia, or diabetes that adversely affects a child's educational performance." 34 CFR §300.7(b)(8).

Children suffering from attention deficit disorder (with or without hyperactivity) may qualify under serious emotional disturbance, other health impairment, or specific learning disability. Frequently these children have the ability/performance discrepancy needed to qualify as learning disabled. Children with ADD/ADHD often suffer the emotional disturbances needed to qualify under that category. Children with severe cases may also qualify under the category of other health impairment. If qualification is not achieved, the parent should seek services under Section 504.

Which children should be referred for testing?

Any child that you believe is educationally handicapped or disabled should be referred for testing. It is not necessary that you know for certain that a child will qualify. A good faith belief is sufficient.

Obvious "red flags" for the need for a referral and

services are a proposal of retention, failing grades, expressed dislike of school, multiple behavior problems in school and/or multiple imposition of in-school suspension, out-of- school suspension and/or expulsion, more than normal disorganization and/or a medical or mental health problem giving rise to school related problems (e.g. attention deficit disorder, depression, anxiety, obsessive compulsive disorder, narcoleptic, Tourette's syndrome, etc.).

A referral for testing can help determine if a proposed school retention will assist the child or be detrimental. Children with educational disabilities are often retained. Generally, no real benefit is achieved by retaining these children. Real benefit is accomplished only by determining the learning problem and addressing it.

School related behavior problems are often the result of undiagnosed and unaccommodated learning problems. Children, like all individuals, become defensive when asked to do tasks that they do not have adequate skills to accomplish. These children find ways to act out and distract attention from their academic frustration. Such children quickly develop real problem behaviors. It is amazing how quickly problem behaviors subside when academic tasks presented to the child are within the child's skill/ability level.

Adopted children, particularly special-needs adopted children, often do not have the skill background expected of a child at a particular age level. Children who have suffered, (prior to adoption) abuse, neglect, multiple custody changes, and emotional losses, present to the educational environment emotional challenges that many schools are not truly ready to accommodate. It is hard to focus on academic tasks when the child's primary need is for safety, identity, security and predictability. Educators, not part of the adoption triad, do not understand that the primary needs of adopted children are not necessarily satisfied by placement in a good adoptive family. The child's haunting adoption-related issues and problems may reappear at any time, even long after what appears to be a successful adoptive placement. Unmet emotional needs may cause serious behavior problems and greatly interfere with the educational process. Special education services may assist in servicing the child's emotional needs.

After deciding that a referral for evaluation is appropriate and necessary, parents should resist attempts by school staff to be talked out of the referral. All too many parents are, after making the written request, convinced by school personnel that the child is not "bad enough" for services, is not retarded, will only learn more troublesome behaviors, is simply immature, needs to "grow up," or will suffer from being "labeled" handicapped. Many of these same parents return to their initial conviction to request testing after the child continues to suffer as a result of not being properly served.

Special education service under IDEA

The reauthorized IDEA and its predecessors established a federal grant program to assist states in providing free and appropriate public education to all students in need of special education. IDEA sets forth specific requirements that must be met in serving handicapped children in order for states to receive the funds. IDEA's student qualifications for special services are clearly defined and limited. The procedures for identification, planning, servicing, and limits on discipline are set forth in IDEA. All states, in order to receive the funding, must comply with the guidelines of the legislation.

Evaluation of the child

Federal law mandates that a child must be tested in a full and individual evaluation before the initial offering of special education and related services. The testing process is normally called "multifactor" testing. The testing must determine if the child is an educationally handicapped child as defined under federal law and must determine the child's educational needs. Reevaluation occurs every three years, but the recently reauthorized IDEA, unlike its predecessor, does not mandate full retesting every three years. The only retesting necessary is that which the education team determines is necessary unless the parent requests full testing.

The initial testing must use a variety of assessment tools and strategies to gather relevant functional and developmental information about the child. No singular procedure or test may be the sole criterion for determining if a child suffers an educational handicap and determining appropriate education programming. Testing must be completed with technically sound testing instruments that access the relative contributions of cognitive and behavioral factors in addition to physical or developmental factors.

The tests must be selected in a manner free of racial or cultural bias, be in the child's native language, be validated for the specific purpose for which the test is used, be administrated by trained and knowledgeable personnel, and be administrated in accordance with any instructions provided by the test's producer.

The purpose of testing is to determine the child's eligibility for services under IDEA. The determination of eligibility is the decision of the child's educational team. The team consists of qualified educational professionals and, under the newly reauthorized IDEA, the parents.

An individual education program team (IEP team)

Membership in the child's individual education program team is provided for by Federal law. The team is composed of the following persons:

1. The parents of the child;
2. A least one of the child's regular education teachers (if the child is or may be participating in the regular education

program);
3. At least one special education teacher or one special education provider;
4. A representative of the local education agency who
   a. Is qualified to provide or supervise special education instruction;
   b. Is knowledgeable about the general curriculum, and
   c. Is knowledgeable about available resources;
5. An individual who can interpret the instructional implication of the evaluation results;
6. Other individuals who have knowledge or special expertise regarding the child. (The parent may bring nonschool individuals, such as counselors.)
7. The child, when appropriate.

It is vital that a parent attend individual educational program team meetings. These meetings are typically called IEP meetings. Parents may bring individuals such as case worker, counselors, ministers, grandparents or other significant individuals in their or the child's life to the meeting.

It is essential that the parent have adequate emotional and knowledgeable support in order to effectively advocate for the child. The parent may seek information and support from special education parent mentor programs, knowledgeable parent advocates, knowledgeable attorneys in private practice representing families in educational disputes, or legal services corporations involved in special education litigation. Knowledgeable parent advocate organizations are federally funded nationwide. Likewise legal services corporations are federally funded and available in every state. Parent advocates will generally help parents with the case and may even attend some meetings in support. Legal service attornies (generally not legal aid or public defenders) will frequently provide limited legal information but will normally only undertake "target" representation designed to "make law" or establish precedent.

—

The needs of educationally handicapped children are only a small portion of the target populations represented by legal service corporations. These organizations can typically be located within each state by contacting the local school district special education department or a neighboring school district's department and requesting this information; contacting your state department of education, division of special education, and requesting this information; or by contacting a local congressional representative's office and requesting information as to what organizations have been funded by the federal government to provide this assistance locally. A local legal aide chapter or bar association might be aware of the area's parent special education advocacy organization and legal services corporation. Parents should take the necessary time and seek out the support organizations that lie within their geographic area.

Individual education program (IEP)

The Individual Education Program is commonly called the IEP. An IEP is required for a child to receive special education services. It is a written statement setting out the special education plan for the child. The IEP should include a statement of the type of services to be provided, educational goals, educational adaptations and other special services appropriate for the child.

It is important that there be both short- and long-term goals and that the goals be measurable. The IEP should set forth who is responsible for what. A good IEP document does not simply set forth general statements and general goals that could be said about every child's educational plan. Further, a good IEP document does not place the entire burden of the adaptations upon the child. After all, teachers run the classrooms—teachers should be responsible for the fashion in which the education is presented.

It is critical for parents who have found themselves

"doing school" at home to have specific expectations and limitations placed in the IEP about what school work will be done at home. It is appropriate to demand that the child's reading material and all assignments be presented at the child's reading level. It is extremely *inappropriate* for the parent to spend hours reading schoolbooks to a child because the child cannot read the material. The child, perhaps with help, should be doing the reading. This can be accomplished with modified reading assignments. If the school staff believes that reading particular materials, which exceeds the child's reading ability, is necessary to the child's educational development, then the school should supply tape recordings of the material. Under *no* circumstances should a parent develop the expectation that he or she will read to the child all overly difficult assignments. Isolated reading for assistance in understanding is different—such as reading of poetry aloud when the child can read the words. Going beyond that may actually prevent learning, particularly the learning of reading skills.

Homework, if appropriate at all, is designed to provide reinforcement of material learned at school. The parent is *not* the primary teacher. The IEP should clearly specify the appropriate roles of home and school. The parent should not feel guilty at refusing to engage in a daily role of primary teacher.

When the child has educational problems and is not accomplishing all desired educational goals within the school day and with a reasonable period of parental help, the parent and school staff should select the skills and knowledge most desirable for the child to learn and focus on them. Obviously it is more desirable for the child to learn to read than that the child learn the content of all the school books. Therefore, the focus should be on having the child read and not having the child listening to someone else read. That same philosophy should be applied to all academic expectations.

—

Homework and related issues can destroy adoptive homes and family relationships. When homework rises to a level of destroying family life and family relationships, homework should be reassigned to its proper role secondary to family life. Parents may demand and obtain a statement in the IEP that the parent will supervise for 30, 45, or 60 minutes (whatever time is age and developmentally appropriate) of homework per evening and then the parent's and child's responsibility is over. The parent signs a note saying the time has been spent doing assigned homework and the balance was not completed. It then becomes the teacher's responsibility to assign meaningful homework that can be completed within the appropriate time. Parents should simply not accept school staffs' positions that all homework is essential and the assignments cannot be modified for their child. The parents should maintain that having their adopted child develop appropriate family relationships and an understanding of family life is important. Without the ability to reside within a family, the child may not have a home. It is difficult to impossible for many school staff members to understand the intensity of the "homework war" that takes place in many adoptive homes. Winning the "homework war" by simply not doing the battle can save a home for a child in jeopardy of being placed out of the home into residential care. In the big picture, is it more important that the child complete the prescribed number of homework pages or be maintained in a loving, nurturing, supportive home?

Admittedly, this position will not strive to have the child achieve the greatest possible academic development at the earliest age—a normal parent and school goal. An adopted child may have developmental and emotional issues that prevent this goal from being a reality. For the adopted child with these issues, academic achievement may be delayed or not achieved at the fullest. The parent and school must accept this fact as reality. The adopted child may have other more basic learning to do (learning to be a part of a family and society) that delays academic achievement.

Continuum of alternative academic placements

Once a child is identified as eligible for special education services, the child must be placed in the "least restrictive educational environment." No educational handicap is served in only one kind of educational placement. The limiting of available educational placement settings is particularly true when seeking placements for children with emotional or behavioral issues.

All special education children can be served in any one of the following placements:
1. Regular classes
2. Supplemental services
3. Individual/small group instruction
4. Special classes/learning centers located in
   a. A public school building
   b. A separate school in the district
   c. A separate facility specifically designed to serve a special population such as a developmental center or youth penal program
5. Home or hospital instruction

The continuum of placement options should be viewed starting from the "least restrictive." The "least restrictive" option reasonably calculated to meet the child's needs should be selected.

The placement option is decided by the IEP team. The parent is a part of the team and should feel free to express wishes, beliefs, and desires about the most desirable placement option.

Disputes about placements and enforcement of an IEP

The newly reauthorized IDEA mandates that all states make mediation available as a dispute resolution option. Parents should be encouraged to use the mediation process.

However, parents are not required to do so.

If parents elect to engage in mediation, they should have in clear focus the issues in dispute, the issues on which they are willing to give, and the issues on which they are unwilling to give. In order to meaningfully understand legal reality prior to mediation, the parent should consult with a knowledgeable person who can advise parents of the likely outcome should the matter be litigated. Mediation does not require legal counsel but the services of knowledgeable legal counsel or parent advocate are extremely helpful in the mediation process.

Federal law sets forth a formal dispute resolution process known as due process. Due process is an administrative hearing process in which the parent and school each have the opportunity to present their case. A hearing officer presides. A parent may elect not to be represented by counsel but must understand that the hearing is conducted like a trial and that the hearing officer is the presiding officer—not their advocate or assistant. Due process proceedings are appealable through administrative appeals and eventually to the local, state, or federal court.

School expulsion and suspension

Limits are placed upon schools in using suspension and expulsion with students served under IDEA. The newly reauthorized IDEA requires that a "free and appropriate public education" be made available to all children with disabilities, including those who have been suspended or expelled from school.

As of this writing, the new law has not yet been tested as to the exact limits on the amount of time a child may be suspended or expelled. An argument can be made that services must be continued during all days of suspension and expulsion. The old law was interpreted to allow each special education identified child to be removed from services for disciplinary reasons for a total of ten days each school year. The regulations implementing this new law have not yet been written and published. It is believed that the new regulations will again authorize a 10-day removal. The validity of the regulation, in light of the statutory language will surely be tested and the interpretation of the legislative language will ultimately be decided in the courts. Parents, however, can be reasonably certain that the number of days a child may be removed from services will remain ten days per school year and perhaps less.

The reauthorized IDEA clearly specifies that a child who brings a gun or other dangerous weapon (including a knife with a blade of 2.5") may be removed from school and placed in an alternate educational setting for 45 days. Likewise, a child who knowingly possesses or uses illegal drugs or sells or solicits the sale of a controlled substance while at school or a school function, may be removed from school and placed in an alternate educational setting from 45 days. Even if the parent objects to the removal and the alternate setting and requests due process proceedings, the child remains in the alternate setting for the 45 days.

Other removals from programming or changes to alternate school placements, if opposed by the parent and objected to by the filing of due process proceedings, must be delayed until after the hearing officer determines the appropriateness of the change or the parties agree to the change. The child remains in what is known as "stay put" or the last agreed upon placement.

The newly reauthorized IDEA requires educational teams to consider the child's behavior if the behavior is significantly problematic, to establish a behavioral plan if one is not in existence, to revise an existing behavioral plan if it is not working, and to consider the child's present placement for appropriateness. The approach is that the team can change the child's educational environment and create

—

conditions that may cause the child's behavior to improve or at least be less problematic.

Services under Section 504

The Rehabilitation Act of 1973, which includes Section 504, was developed and passed in the 1970s. It established rights and entitlements for people with disabilities. The law is brief and simply prohibits discrimination on the basis of disability in all programs receiving federal financial assistance—many programs other than educational services are covered under this legislation.

The legislation was implemented through regulations written by the U.S. Department of Health, Education, and Welfare (HEW). The legislation and its implementing regulations created the U.S. approach to the education of handicapped students. Before that time schools legally could, and often did, refuse to serve students solely on the basis of disability.

Section 504 is not an education law nor is it a federal program. Under Section 504, states do not receive federal money to be used to prohibit discrimination and to provide reasonable accommodation. Section 504 provides that discrimination and failure to provide an appropriate public education to eligible children is a violation of a basic civil right. Violation of this basic civil right can jeopardize the federal funding that states and other recipients receive from the federal government.

Section 504 provides a guarantee of the basic right of reasonable accommodation in educational settings to a much broader spectrum of children and in a larger scope of activities than does IDEA. Many children can achieve accommodations under Section 504 who are not entitled to services under IDEA. Among adopted children, as among nonadopted children, the largest group of children eligible for services under Section 504 and not IDEA are those suffering from attention deficit disorder. Section 504 is particularly useful for obtaining assistance for children suffering from attention deficit disorder who present few symptoms other than remarkable disorganization and forgetfulness.

Eligibility under Section 504

Section 504 includes a much broader population of children than does IDEA. The definition of who qualifies as an "individual with a disability" is more inclusive than the eligibility requirements under IDEA. Many children found not to be eligible for services under IDEA are eligible for services under Section 504. Under Section 504 a disability is a physical or mental impairment that substantially limits one or more major life activities. Education is considered a major life activity. An individual is considered as having a disability under Section 504 if the individual has only a "history of" or is "regarded as" having a disability. The disability eligibility continues even if there is not disability in fact so long as there is the "history" or perception of disability.

Section 504 states:

> No otherwise qualified individual with a disability in the United States · · · shall, solely by reason of her or his disability be excluded from the participation in, be denied the benefits of, or be subjected to discrimination under any program or activity receiving Federal financial assistance · · · 29 USC §794 (as amended 1992).

Section 504 provides accommodations for students with physical disabilities or sensory impairment who may only need accommodations for physical access or alternative methods of communication. Children with health needs such as asthma, diabetes, attention deficit may be served under Section 504. Children who are HIV positive and asymptomatic, who are excluded from school activities because of fear, could be served under Section 504.

Children eligible under Section 504, even if they are

found to be ineligible for special education services, must be evaluated by the school district to determine whether a free, appropriate education for them requires any type of special services. Section 504 children are to be identified and provided a free appropriate public education regardless of the nature or severity of their disability.

Section 504 requires that children be evaluated in order to determine appropriate education services and to guard against inappropriate placement. An evaluation under Section 504 is not necessarily a full scale multifactor evaluation as required under IDEA. The parents should supply to the school staff any medical or other information available regarding the child's handicapping condition. A letter from a physician or other medical provider is helpful in establishing eligibility. Under Section 504, the school has an affirmative duty to conduct an evaluation before any significant changes are made in the child's educational placement.

Obtaining Section 504 services

Many of the accommodations needed by children should be offered by the regular support services available to children. For example, medicine needed by a child with attention deficit disorder should be administered and tracked by school staff. "Forgetful" children should be reminded to take their medicine in a reasonably timely fashion. For many families, the first approach is obtaining information about the child's need from the child's health providers and then meeting with school representatives in order to describe the child's needs together with what the parents believe to be services the child needs. This approach can result in satisfactory interventions being put in place.

If the simplistic, straight-forward approach of meeting, discussing, and agreeing to accommodations for the child does not provide the necessary accommodation, then the parents should make the request in writing. The written request can be a simple request directed to the principal and or superintendent stating the handicapping condition, the need and the requested accommodations. The letter may, but does not necessarily have to be, a request for evaluation for services under both IDEA and Section 504. If the parent is uncertain of the child's needs and believes that there might be eligibility under IDEA, the parent should send the formal letter as set forth earlier in this chapter

Types of services available under Section 504

It is not uncommon for school representatives to understate the type of services available under Section 504. Many believe that the only services available under Section 504 are extended time for testing or projects. That is simply not true. Many types of services can be required under Section 504.

Children can be provided extended time for test taking, tutoring, modified instruction, assistance in organization skill, homework monitoring, enlarged reading material, computer access and many other services. It is not uncommon to have the school place a limited number of services on a 504 Plan and other services on some other type of intervention plan. Case law has determined that the handicapped child is entitled to "whatever it reasonably takes" as 504 services. Placing some accommodations on another form does not eliminate the accommodations as required under Section 504.

Suspension and expulsion

Children identified and served under Section 504 have some protections and considerations when facing serious student discipline such as suspension and expulsion. Section 504 requires that before a school may change the educational placement of a child, the school must conduct an evaluation. The evaluation does not have to rise to the level of a multifactor evaluation.

If the incident giving rise to the suspension or expulsion is related to the child's handicap, then the school may not use discipline which would change the child's placement. Unfortunately, the law does not clearly identify when the disciplinary removal under a suspension or expulsion amounts to a change of placement. The child's educational team, however, can in a "nondisciplinary" decision, change the child's placement in order to accommodate the child's needs. Services would still have to be provided so that the child receives a free appropriate public school education.

If the child's education team determines that the incident giving rise to the discipline was not related to the disability, the school may use its regular form of discipline including suspension and expulsion. There is no requirement in Section 504 that a school must continue providing educational services to a child during the period of removal.

Section 504 provides no protection for children who are currently using illegal drugs from enforcement of laws, regulations, and school rules about illegal drug use. Furthermore, Section 504 provides no "stay put" provision as in IDEA that requires the child to remain in placement while the propriety of the removal, suspension or expulsion is litigated.

Procedural safeguards

Each local school district and state is required to have procedural safeguards in place for dispute resolution. The law requires that procedural safeguards be established to allow parents to influence and contest decisions regarding their children's evaluation and placement. Parents need to be given notice of actions regarding educational placement.

Parents may address complaints to the Office of Civil Rights (OCR) of the U.S. Department of Education. Offices that investigate complaints are located throughout the United States. To find your local office, contact the Department of Education, your local congressman, representative, or a local attorney who does either handicapped education litigation or civil rights litigation.

Why seek services under Section 504?

Some parents prefer to seek services under Section 504 rather than IDEA. The primary reason is that many more students qualify for services under Section 504 than under IDEA. Many parents, however, feel that the "labeling" under IDEA as disabled and frequent grouping of students in special classes, is undesirable. Section 504 also mandates in some cases (such as when there is a need for medical services), services that IDEA does not provide.

Parents should carefully consider these concerns and evaluate the advantages of proceeding under IDEA if those services are available. The IDEA requirement of "least restrictive environment" allows for services in the regular education setting to the extent possible. If the child presents discipline issues that might result in suspension and expulsion issues, then clearly services under IDEA are much preferable.

The Americans with Disabilities Act of 1990 (ADA)

The Americans with Disabilities Act of 1990 (ADA) requires that "no individual shall be discriminated against on the basis of a disability in the full and equal enjoyment of the goods, services, facilities, privileges, advantages, or accommodations of any place of public accommodation by any person who owns, leases (leases to), or operates a place of public accommodation."

The ADA utilizes a three-prong definition of a disability. For purposes of coverage and protection under ADA, a person with a disability is defined as an individual who;

1. Has a physical or mental impairment that substantially limits one or more major life activities, or
2. Has a record or history of such an impairment or
3. Is perceived or regarded as having such an impairment.

Learning is one of the major life activities described in the ADA. Generally, any student protected under Section 504 would also be protected under ADA. The ADA, however, would protect students not covered under Section 504. For example, a student feared of having AIDS, because of association with a family member with the condition, would be protected as would also be a student who is HIV positive but symptom free.

Educational Services For Adopted Children

As the single parent of two special-needs adopted children, I was forced to learn about educational services available in the public sector. This learning came about as a necessity when my oldest son was approaching compulsory education. Fortunately, my legal training made learning the federal mandates implemented in my state easier, but still not easy. Most schools do not "get it" when it comes to the needs of children suffering the effects of traumatic pre-adoption experiences, attention deficit disorder, hyperactivity disorder and/or problematic genetic mental health issues.

My oldest son was adopted at the age of twelve months and is now fifteen years old. His learning problems presented (at the age of compulsory education) a perplexing educational dilemma. He seemed bright but was delayed in normal early educational skills. He had difficulty socially interacting with peers. He "hoarded" stuff. He loved various fairy tales and seemed totally absorbed in them. He was totally mute if frightened and often reacted at what seemed nonfrightening events. He was OK as long as he believed that the adults were in charge, but terrified and nonfunctional if the adults did not take charge. He was afraid to take risks, even the normal risks necessary for successful learning. He avoided tasks requiring risk taking. He developed fears associated with his body and the environment. He demanded much adult attention.

I approached my oldest son's enrollment in kindergarten firmly, politely, but aggressively as an attorney. I insisted on an appropriately selected free educational program suited to his needs. A program was selected, but free only happened after due process proceedings were instituted.

My son has been served well most of the time by his public school. He attended a separate mental health/educational facility during his elementary school years. The facility was especially suited to provide a secure, supportive environment necessary to service him. His emotional needs took precedence over his educational needs.

He began attending the regular public school in the sixth grade. At that time he was served in the regular educational system with the support of an educational aide. The aide provided the necessary emotional support and some academic intervention. Emphasis shifted from providing emotional support to providing educational instruction. Emotional support was still, however, very necessary.

Today my son is in high school. He has overcome most of the educational delays present in the elementary school years. His emotional needs are still, however, quite great. He began his high school career in mainstream classes in all subjects except math. Fortunately, he gained the support of an educational aide. In spite of his ability to achieve academically, and the emotional support of an aide, the first few weeks of high school proved to be a disaster.

My son has experienced a lot of teasing during his public school experience. The severity of the problem escalated substantially in the high school. Unlike the junior high staff, the high school staff did not undertake a genuine effort to correct the behavior of the tormentors. My son "marches to the beat of a different drummer." His driving interests are theater, music, and art. His high school peers determined that he was gay—an opinion not necessarily shared by my son. Tormentors used every opportunity to make unkind remarks about my son being gay using a variety of unacceptable language. The situation and my son's reaction to it substantially interfered with his educational achievement. After all, it is really hard to educationally achieve, when one is so upset that one spends many class periods talking to counselors and other school staff about being teased. I read the school situation as not fixable in the time frame necessary to meet my son's needs and quickly made alternative school arrangements for him.

Approximately one month into the academic year, I requested that he be placed on home instruction. The special education staff understood my distress and reluctantly agreed.

My son is now on a home instruction plan. The school provides a tutor who meets with him on a regular basis. I have accessed the local home school network and have arranged for my son to participate in a number of programs designed for home-schoolers or adults (but welcoming home schoolers). My son now comes to my office and occupies his "office" in an otherwise unused room. He works on school related material from 9:00 a.m. until noon. Two mornings a week he participates in a tutoring program run by a local church. The tutoring program is really designed for high school dropouts desiring to acquire basic skills or study for the GED. My son's situation is different than most of the participants but the program has welcomed him and is assisting him to achieve. My son has found fellowship with other youth of similar interests in a theater program operated by the community parks and recreation program. He is artistically achieving in two adult community park and recreation programs. He participates in our church choir. My son is finding acceptance among home-schooled youth— many of whom experienced the same type of taunting in the public school setting. He is finding support and understanding from the adult leaders and participants in the art programs.

The test of time will ultimately determine if my decision to opt for home instruction with supportive programming is the correct choice for my son's high school career. Certainly success was not going to be achieved within the public high school. There is one other educational setting in my community that might be successful. I opted for home instruction with supportive programming rather than the more traditional program because the more that program has no art and music component. At this time and for several years, my son sees himself only in the total art arena (graphic, theater and music). A program without these components seems like a misfit.

I am confident that the early emotional problems, and learning deficits would not have been overcome without my aggressively asserting my son's special educational rights early in his school experience. Likewise, I am confident that my son would have fallen into deeper and deeper emotional and behavioral difficulty if I would have allowed him to continue in the high school setting. The inevitable lashing out at the tormentors had began to occur. The regular school setting successfully served my son for only a very few years of his mandatory educational experience. I can only hope that he can and will continue to educationally and emotionally develop removed from the daily trauma of fellow student inflicted abuse.

I have approached the withdrawal of my son from the regular educational program with sadness that successful accommodation was not achieved. The marshaling of forces to address the problem simply did not happen quickly enough to meet my son's fragile emotional state. I believe that if the teasing were about something other than his perceived sexuality, action would have been taken or at least attempted. The prevailing attitude among the high school administration was but a mild wringing of hands, maintaining that,

—

"We cannot control hallway behavior." I am sure that hallway behavior cannot be totally controlled and am equally sure that hallway behavior cannot be controlled if control is not made a priority. There did not even seem to be an interest in changing the behaviors. My distress was shared by the special education staff whose students apparently experience this type of situation often. If I had had an emotionally stronger son, I would have "gone to war" to correct the problem. My "war," however, could have destroyed my son, so I did not begin the battle.

My younger son was adopted at eight days and is now twelve years old. He did not experience pre-adoptive trauma and does not have a seriously problematic genetic background. He is, however, profoundly attention deficit and hyperactive. Fortunately, his condition is well controlled with medication. He also suffered from speech and language deficits. Those deficits have been addressed privately through speech therapy and have been significantly remediated. He has been educationally served in private parochial schools. I elected to send him to the Catholic schools, even though I am non-Catholic, due to the obvious effect that my aggressive assertion of my older son's educational rights had had on the school teaching staff. My original intent was to send my younger son to the public schools.

At public school enrollment, I was asked by three staff persons doing kindergarten evaluation if he was a special-needs student. When asked why the question, I was told that it was because my other son was special-needs. The superintendent of my school district later told me that I was the only parent as of that time who had ever filed for due process proceedings, so the staff all knew who I was. That information was sufficient for me to seek another educational opportunity for my younger son.

It is probably desirable that my younger son not suffer whatever preconceived notions that teachers may form from

—

their familiarity with my older son's problems. The Catholic school program has successfully served him. The school staff have been cooperative and the placement has worked.

Final thoughts

Professionally, I now primarily serve clients who have children with special education needs. A significantly large number of my clients have adopted children. These children have an array of learning and emotional needs. I note that the families with children who are fully educationally served are doing better as families than those who come to me having no services.

Many of the adoptive families, when I first meet them, are truly are on the verge of not being able to maintain the child in the home. The school and learning conflict so dominates life that no other aspects of life are addressed. In some families, the conflict is so great that the total family and the child's placement in the home can not be salvaged. I can only wonder if the outcomes would have been different if the school and learning problems would have been addressed earlier. Some families can and do successfully access appropriate services and stop "doing school." Preserving the family must be the adoptive family's primary goal.

14

Therapeutic Considerations

The following segments have been contributed by Dr. Alan Dupre-Clark and Dr. Richard Mague. Dr. Dupre-Clark has been a major contributor to the writing and presentation of our psycho-educational series for adoptive families. He has taught the parent group series for ten years and has a clinical practice that serves adoptive children and their families. Dr. Mague was a middle school and high school counselor for over thirty years and has a private practice that serves adoptive families. He also co-leads an adoptive parent support group.

Clinical interpretations of issues in adoption

The adoptive child confronts a number of psychological issues not faced by a child who is raised in a healthy birth family. Four of the major psychological issues that affects the adoptive child are abandonment, rejection, identity, and control. Traumas suffered by the child who is separated from the birth family are of greater magnitude. The greater extent of the trauma is due to the compounding of each hurtful new event with the adopted child's prior experiences of abandonment, rejection, abuse, and or neglect.

These traumatic experiences and concerns lead some adoptees behave in a dysfunctional manner. However, when the adopted child is behaving dysfunctionally, caretakers are better able to parent if they understand the origin of and the course of the behaviors. Hopefully, this knowledge will aide the parent to know when to seek professional assistance.

Part I:
Four Major Psychological Issues in Adoption

Abandonment—The sense of abandonment becomes a driving theme in many adoptive children's lives. The consequences of abandonment in the life of a child are often serious. The adopted child with abandonment as an overriding issue may suffer from low self-worth, low self-esteem and may feel responsible for the separation from the birth family. This child feels defective, flawed, or bad.

The emergence of abandonment as a major issue for the adopted child is frequently seen in closed adoptions. When the child permanently leaves the care of the birth mother, this loss may give rise to the emotions of anxiety, fear, and anger. A very harsh set of circumstances surrounding the separation of the child from the mother can lead to an array of psychological disorders, the most troublesome being attachment disorder. The long-term grief process associated with abandonment can lead to the development of severe depression of sufficient magnitude to cause even suicidal behavior. These conditions typically become more troublesome in the older child's or adolescent's life.

The remedies for a child whose main issue is abandonment are as follows: Assist that child who may believe that the birth mother was "good" and he was "bad" with a reappraisal of the birth mother's status and his own. The child will need help to appreciate both the limitations of the birth mother's situation and the child's natural innocence at the time of separation. It is important to normalize the child's needs at a young age. There was nothing that the child did that caused the birth mother to surrender the child. This discussion between the adoptive parent and child will need to be reviewed around this issue at times when the child or adolescent is struggling with low self-esteem, lack of confidence and showing depressed feelings.

Rejection—Rejection is an adoption issue when the child feels unwanted and deserted due to some "evilness" or flaw in the birth mother. The child feels the victim of the "evil" or "bad" circumstances of the birth mother's life. The birth mother is viewed by the adopted child as dangerous and may view anyone controlling his or her life in the same light.

The adopted child traumatized by the notion of rejection may develop another major handicapping thought process. The child may view himself as a victim who needs to be protected at all costs. The adopted child may even perceive as threats, events not seen at threatening by others. He or she may view the rejection as a rage producing event.

The child suffering from rejection may, in the extreme, suffer attachment disorder. The latency age child may already have a pattern of extreme self-centeredness and boundary violating behaviors—the worst of which are violence, fire-setting, and a variety of other "ignore you, I will do as I will" behaviors. Less problematic behaviors can include such things as stealing and hitting.

Identity—The adopted child who has serious identity issues suffers a weakened sense of self. Lack of information about the birth family and an atmosphere of secrecy surrounding the adoption lays a foundation for identity issues. The genetic part of adopted child's identity is often hidden. As a result, the child lacks a readily available confirmation of who she is. This issue may be more significant for girls than boys. The lack of information generates a lack of trust. A lack of trust seeds a sense of self-doubt about one's origin and one's place in the world.

The practice of some adoptive parents of withholding information about a child's birth origins may aggravate identity issues. In some cases even the gradual release of information by the adoptive parent to the child creates conflict between the parent and the child. Self-doubt and uncertainty about one's role in the family can lead such a child to seek emotional distance from family members through passive or aggressive means. Many adoptees with severe identity confusion may be highly unpredictable in mood and in behavior—sometimes resulting in impulsive behaviors such as running away or suicidal gesturing to get attention for their plight. Stealing and lying may also be present.

Therapeutic interventions for abandonment, rejection, and identity issues. When an adopted child's life is substantially disrupted over a significant period of time with the personal inner conflict of issues of abandonment, rejection, or identity, professional assistance should be sought. The professional should help the child understand and deal with the reality of his or her losses and subsequent adoptive placement and help the parent understand and deal with the internal struggles of the child. An experienced professional who is knowledgeable of adoption issues should be selected to provide this assistance.

The adopted child needs to be cognitively lead through the reality of his or her birth and adoption history. The child needs to understand that the birth mother did not place the child due to some "evil" or flaw within the child. The child will need help to appreciate the limitations of the birth mother's situation as well as the child's natural innocence at the time of separation. The child should be helped to understand the developmental needs and abilities of a typical child at the age he or she was at the time of placement.

—

The child needs to understand the human side of the birth mother. She may not have made good decisions but her humanity (youth, poverty, habits) might have prevented any other choice. Demonstrate that they are connected by mutual grief by exposing the child to stories of mothers who grieve for their children. It helps the child when the adoptive parent demonstrates empathy for the child's grief.

The child who feels rage can be assured that feelings can be expressed without the child or anyone else being injured. The child can be guided to release aggression through physical activities such as sports, running, organized self-defense training, and use of home-made kicking or punching boxes. Use contracts and rewards for showing prosocial behavior. Sharpen consequences for antisocial behavior so they are specifically designed for the wrong-doing and not lengthy so as not to build up resentment. Be consistent in setting behavioral expectations so the child knows the boundaries. Giving in to demands will only increase negative behavior.

The child needs to understand when only limited birth history information is available. The child may need to reconstruct all of the known information to gain understanding and a comfort level. Additional information may be available upon request from the agency that placed the child. Parents can recontact the placing agency at any time to ask for additional, nonidentifying information. Although some children may press for a search or reunion with birth family, only rarely is a search recommended before the child reaches age 18. Counselors specializing in adoption can be of assistance when search becomes an issue. The support of search by the adoptive parents can be very comforting to the young adult adoptee and lead the adoptive parent and child to an even closer relationship.

Control—The overly competent and self-reliant child. Some children enter adoptive homes prematurely competent or self reliant. These children have become convinced that they can not count on adults to keep them safe and/or provide for their needs. Some birth parents may have encouraged and supported premature mastery and competence in their children as if they were adult companions or partners rather than children with normal demands of immaturity. Children who develop adult-like mastery over their environments, refuse help from others. These competent and self-reliant children clearly demonstrate that they can handle situations independently and do not have visible control issues. Such children may grow into adults who are likely to be isolated and lonely, having developed a wall of defenses that keep others out. As children, they may not be able to ask for help, support or comforting. This is their paradox; their behavior puts others off further, thus re-enforcing their feelings of needing to be in control to be safe from emotional or physical pain.

Some recommendations for change in such children are to help the child set attainable goals, acknowledging their need for control by giving it where appropriate. Parents can foster this change by developing good listening skills. When parents try to understand what it might be like to be in the child's place, the child's needs can be better served, thus reducing feelings of distress or isolation.

The caretaking child. Some adoptive children attempt to master life by making themselves indispensable to others so that they will never be abandoned again. These children become caretakers. They usually forego their own needs so they can be totally serving to others. They become so outwardly focused that they grow increasingly unsure as to who they really are. They become unable to figure out or say what they truly think or feel because they have not been encouraged to develop or express their own thoughts or feelings or to even think for themselves.

The caretaking child attempts to buy friends with excessive flattery, gifts, money or by doing favors. These children often feel inadequate, depressed, and anxious when they cannot accommodate the needs of others. Caretakers project their needs onto others. They look for someone to rescue or love as they wish to be rescued or loved. This is one reason that many such children find their way into gangs, cults and/or unhealthy adult relationships.

As adopted children, these caretakers tend to be the older siblings. They may try desperately to maintain the role in the new adoptive home. They overrule and reject parental guidance. An older child that has been separated from the siblings for whom care was given and thrust into a role of younger child, may have great difficulty finding his/or her place in the adoptive family.

Recommendations for change in the caretaking child are to praise the child often for appropriate behaviors, and ask them for their ideas and suggestions when making family decisions. An optimum word for parents to keep in mind when parenting a caretaker is sensitivity. The parents need to be sensitive to the child's needs to feel attached to the parent/family. This will require the parent to be observant to cues that will allow them to anticipate the child's needs.

The oppositional child. In an attempt to maintain control over their lives, some adopted children become oppositional. These children feel used by life and attempt to control their environment. They fear if they lose control they will suffer even greater emotional or physical pain. In their struggle to maintain control, their lives become one battle after another.

These children refuse to accept limits, fight, and argue about any and all rules. They refuse to comply with reasonable requests and demands. No matter what limits are set for the child, he or she will overstep those limits. Their message to the parent is clear, "I don't need you or anyone telling me what to do or what I can't do." "You can't make me do anything." "I do not care what you say or think." These children are terrified of being under the control of any adult, including doctors, nurses or athletic coaches.

These children hide their feelings of hopelessness and depression by their aggressive, controlling behavior. They may show signs by sleeping more than normal, have school problems with peers and teachers, exhibit poor academic performance, suffer from physical complaints, and/or become involved in delinquent behaviors.

These children need parents to set firm boundaries or limits. They need physical activities without goals of winning or losing. The parent needs to establish a pattern of inviting himself or herself into the child's space. The child needs praise for each successful effort.

The passive or compliant child. Passive and compliant behaviors are one way children use to maintain control. These children simply give in to the feelings of helplessness and loss. These are the children that are picked on by their peers or are excluded from the activities of their peers. They do not ask for help in school or at home nor share their problems with anyone. They deny their problems and shortcomings until confronted with failure.

These children have little or no emotion for serious matters. They tend to ignore problems or issues and act as they are funny. These children often grow into passive-aggressive adults.

The passive/aggressive child needs to be drawn into activities that build self-concept and develop self-awareness. Child/parent activities that allow some physical contact are desirable, i.e., swimming, tennis, dance, martial arts, etc. These children are good candidates for group therapy.

Summary—Adoptive children who are working on the pain of loss will constantly need help recognizing their defensive shields. They need to learn how to control and redirect the thoughts, feelings, and behaviors. As they learn to make decisions that empower, they learn to accept authority of others. Many children who need to be in control find that when their environment is secure, the rules and consequences are constant, and authority figures are consistent, they can begin to develop healthy choices for control over themselves.

We all parent based on our own experiences. Adoptive parents may not have had to face difficulties in growing up that their adoptive children confront and therefore, must learn new methods for parenting. Hopefully, parents learn that the establishment of options allows choices, which in turn teaches empowerment. This is the development of caring—love. Love may not be enough for some adoptive children, but it is a great foundation on which to build the road for our children to travel onto adulthood.

Part II: Other Treatment Issues and Methods toward Resolution

Lying and stealing within the adoptive family — Two troublesome adoption-related behaviors are lying, (even about obvious things) and stealing (within the home). These two behaviors are often related to an adopted child's conflict, anger, confusion, or preoccupation about his/her differentness from the adoptive family or the need to establish control in a family that has assumed control over him. Lying and stealing can be pervasive in the child's life and quite strikingly different from the behaviors that have been modeled and instilled within the adoptive family.

Primary process lying and the adoptee—A pattern of not telling the truth even when the circumstances obviously show the person is lying, is known as primary process lying. This type of lying is a common symptom in a child with identity issues. Usually children know they are lying but seem unable to stop themselves—and only admit lying after being worn down with insistence about the truth.

Primary process lying stems from adoptee's dilemma of living what the adoptee feels is a lie by being adopted. They feel they are an impostor in the adoptive home. Out of resentment from this internal conflict, adopted children may begin to lie to their parents extensively in order to achieve emotional distance from them.

Primary process lying is also connected to other identity-related issues. Lying may result from a concern that the adoptee senses she is acting too much like the adoptive family. Lying can set the child apart. Adoptees may lie to assert their differentness. Some adoptees believe that the control about where they would be raised was taken away when non-blood relatives took over to make the adoption happen. These adoptees may lie to exert control over their lives—a lie being something parents cannot control.

Lying behavior can also be tied to feelings of abandonment. Lying becomes a means to hide inadequacies and at the same time to bring attention to them. Lying confirms the despair inherent in the child's deep sense of unreliability she feels toward adults—especially the adoptive parents.

Lying can also be a reflection of the anger that the adoptee feels from being rejected by the birth family. The anger is manifested in lying and is a means of punishing adults that were allied in the adoption conspiracy.

The lying web that follows, was created to illustrate the connections that primary process lying has with adoption issues. It also depicts the trapping effect that extensive lying creates for the adoptee. When adoptees struggle with adoption issues, lying may be a way that he or she uses to isolate himself or herself from the adoptive family. Because of the resentment, anger, and self-doubt that longs for expression, lying becomes a convenient symptom to bring attention to what seems to be an unsolvable plight.

—

The Adoptee's Lying Web
Developed by Dr. Alan Dupre-Clark

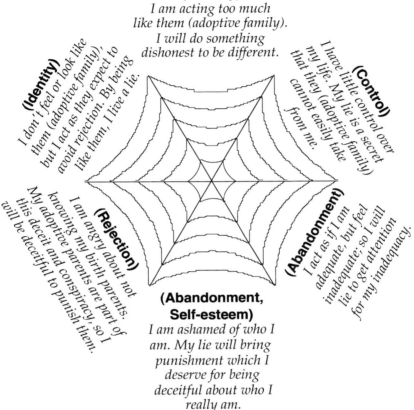

(Identity)
I am acting too much like them (adoptive family). I will do something dishonest to be different.

(Identity)
I don't feel or look like them (adoptive family), but I act as they expect to avoid rejection. By being like them, I live a lie.

(Control)
I have little control over my life. My lie is a secret that they (adoptive family) cannot easily take from me.

(Rejection)
I am angry about not knowing my birth parents. My adoptive parents are part of this deceit and conspiracy, so I will be deceitful to punish them.

(Abandonment)
I act as if I am adequate, but feel inadequate; so I will lie to get attention for my inadequacy.

(Abandonment, Self-esteem)
I am ashamed of who I am. My lie will bring punishment which I deserve for being deceitful about who I really am.

Lying can be handled productively in several ways. It is important to realize that lying may be difficult for the child to remedy. Great effort may be required by the parents and the child to process the parents' loss of trust, hurt feelings and feelings of betrayal. When lying is a chronic problem the adoptive parents must view diminishing the behavior as a long-term process.

A strategy for dealing with lying involves giving consequences for the concrete effects of lying rather than the lying itself. Most adoptive parents report that giving consequences for the lie does not successfully eliminate lying. The adoptee needs to be confronted with the results of the lie. Consequences work better when they are given immediately.

Parents can make a definite statement that lying has occurred rather than asking for the truth. The demand for truth simply invites another lie. The parent should stay low-key when presenting evidence. Praise, when the child least expects it, for telling any truth may change feelings about lying. Sometimes, saying "I believe you," in circumstances when the evidence is inconclusive may place some paradoxical pressure on the child to tell the truth. With frequent, persistent lying on a daily basis it may help to assert that the parent will assume the child is lying until evidence convinces the parent otherwise. This position should be re-evaluated if the child begins to speak truthfully.

Deprivational stealing—Stealing within the home demonstrates a lack of trust that adequate resources will be provided. Resources normally are material things which the child uses to take the place of an internal sense of emotional security. The adoptee implies through the behavior, that: "I cannot really depend upon you to give me what I need, so I'll take what I need." This stealing is associated with the need for self-sufficiency and secrecy from the adoptive family. Stealing can arise as the child, who has been well taken care of in a loving home, begins reacting to the loss of birth origins. Constitutional factors such as risk-taking temperament and impulse control problems may contribute to the development of stealing behavior.

Many adoptive parents are dismayed by stealing (especially those who adopted their children as infants or toddlers). When the value system taught in the home has been totally inconsistent with stealing behavior the parents have difficulty understanding how the stealing behavior developed.

In one case, the Ellisons adopted an infant after having three biological children. By the time Marcus was 13, he had been stealing money and hoarding food for many years. The parents could offer no logical reason why Marcus would act as he did as food was always available and he was given a weekly allowance. In fact, there was no logical explanation for the stealing within the values and moral limit-setting practiced in this adoptive family. The parents were quite correct in being confused about how this could arise within their family.

The characteristics of deprivational stealing as presented in many children include:
- the stolen items are stashed
- the stolen items are given away
- stolen money is quickly spent
- items are moved back and forth between home and school
- the stolen items are easily discovered
- the stolen items are fleeting in value
- the child denies the theft even when evidence is obvious

Commonly, the child lacks a genuine remorse for the theft. The stealing is usually related to a survival mentality. The child steals from adoptive family members because they are the source of supplies. Moral judgment is obscured by the need for "supplies" for emotional survival. Conventional morality and the need for approval from the parent is suspended and superseded by the needs of the moment and the emotional value of the taking of the goods. When the child is confronted about the stealing, genuine remorse is prevented by the satiated feeling that the act of stealing provides for the child.

For younger children, ages three to ten, rewarding constraint (not stealing) is a major teaching and socializing method. Liberal use of positive reinforcement such as stars on a chart or token economy systems will usually help within the home. This should also be combined with pay-back consequences—logical consequences and natural consequences. Oversupplying the child's needs with surprise snacks and full access to certain foods may reduce the child's motivation to hoard and steal.

Over the long-term the energy of the parents may become too depleted to invent consequences. The depleted parent needs the assistance of a knowledgeable professional to effectively devise, monitor, and evaluate approaches and consequences to counter stealing behaviors. Approaches to the problem that could be used on an ongoing basis include the following:

• teach impulse control methods such as deep breathing
• develop "cue" words to prevent stealing
• help the child memorize self-control statements
• have the child use his/her past means to avoid stealing
• role-play to enact situations where the child uses restraint

When a child verbally abuses a parent—Many of the families' stories contained in this book involve parent reports of verbal abuse by the child. Verbal abuse usually takes the form of name-calling, prolonged demands, harassment and threats. It is important to be very clear with the child about what is unacceptable verbally. Anger that is really meant for the birth parents is often misdirected toward the adoptive parents.

For younger children (ages five to about eight or nine), verbal abuse may be handled through some form of behavior management techniques such as rewarding periods of no verbal abuse or on-the-spot time-out procedures. Verbal abuse may be associated with several adoption issues including control, identity, fear of rejection, or abandonment.

Presenting the possibility that the verbal abuse is con-

—

nected to adoption issues may help children make vital connections between the behavior and the underlying reason for the behavior. One adult adoptee reported that she began verbal abuse toward her mother at age thirteen. Her mother insightfully associated the anger with the pain of the loss of the birth mother and feelings of abandonment. As the young girl began to understand the source of her anger, she was able to end the verbal abuse toward the adoptive mother.

There are various effective pro-attachment responses to verbal abuse. Some parents have been able to use a rapid challenge to "nip it in the bud" and quickly return to a supportive style with their child. For example; an eleven year-old boy who had been abandoned by his birth mother would suddenly become verbally abusive. The mother's response was to quickly cut him off by saying, "Jason, enough!" She would then move into a softer tone as if the incident had not occurred. Her technique was effective because she cut off the verbal abuse and asserted a dominance that the boy needed to allay his abandonment fears.

Many adoptive parents report being ineffective when engaging in strong verbal exchanges with their child. Softer statements acknowledging the child's concern may help. In some situations, adoptive parents have relied on a pre-discussed silence that the parent enters when verbal abuse begins. In many cases, parents have simply said that "Verbal abuse does not help us and I will not engage you when you are using it." For older children and adolescents, consequences imposed by the parent rarely work for long. Any method that is selected to diminish verbal abuse will only work if used consistently. The parent must maintain the same response pattern for some time to gain the desired behavior.

Prolonged periods of verbal abuse toward the parent can dangerously erode the relationship and the commitment the parent feels for the child. Early intervention through the assistance of adoptive parent education and counseling can keep this problem from escalating and help the parent and child regain balance.

When a child physically strikes out against a parent Physical hitting is never an acceptable means of expressing anger or frustration. When the child strikes the parent it is often because:

- The parent has become engaged in a verbal battle,
- The parent has touched or grabbed the child in a heated moment, or
- The parent has intentionally or unintentionally blocked a child's path of movement.

When a child hits a parent, the child is seeking a strong reaction from the parent. The situation sought by the child is one that reenacts the earlier birth parent-child relationship when the parent had utter dominance over the child. Physical hitting must be brought under control and/or used to develop attachment through holding. The attention needs of a child who hits are immense. The need for success experiences and rewards for delayed gratification are also an important part of the treatment for the violence-prone child.

Several of the parents in our support groups have reported that their child has hit them, even to the point of injury. Parents tend to be in a state of disbelief when it happens the first time. They talk with the child about ways to control anger and hope it doesn't happen again. When it happens the second time, a fear develops in the parent that the violence will further escalate. The episodes are usually several months apart. When it happens again, the parent's alarm leads them to seek assistance from counselors or the courts. The striking of a parent and subsequent fear of worsened behavior may lead to placement of the youth outside the home.

The above behaviors of lying, stealing, and verbal and physical abuse are significant factors in out-of-home placement and the erosion of parental attachment. The inability to parent a child who maintains oppositional behaviors including school failure, drug and alcohol abuse, sexual promiscuity, repeated runaways, and suicide attempts also play a significant role in out-of-home placements.

Early intervention should be sought as physical violence from a child escalates in the same manner as spousal abuse. There are usually cues to the onset of such behavior and parents need to consult a professional at the first sign of physical violence. It is much easier to extinguish violent behaviors at the onset than years after they have become a part of the child's or adolescent's coping mechanism.

When a child has attachment disorder

Rejecting affection and holding. All adopted children, even infants, can experience attachment difficulties. Some babies who are adopted at only a few weeks of age reject cuddling. The new parents of a "porcupine" infant should be encouraged to find ways to hold and give affection just as they would if they had adopted an older child who is rejecting and prickly.

The adopted child may experience attachment difficulties at various stages of his development, i.e. when he realizes there must have been a loss in order to gain an adoptive family. One period of potential detachment may occur in the teen years when identity, loyalty issues, and thoughts of search come to the fore.

It cannot be determined that adoption in infancy will insure bonding and attachment. Some teens, adopted in infancy, report feeling like "outsiders" at family gatherings. Extended families that refuse to accept the adopted child as a "real" member of the family compound the likelihood of this issue. Detachment of the adopted child from the adoptive family can be viewed by the child as a way of maintaining loyalty to his or her "lost" family.

—

Attachment Disorder from a clinical perspective In the mental health field "attachment disorder" is not yet an established psychiatric designation in the DSM-IV. However, the characteristics describing the behaviors are well known to a few treatment specialists. To those clinicians, attachment disorder is a distinct, complex phenomena that requires extraordinary efforts to modify. It is a collection of symptomatic behaviors that together define a child who shares a similar background with other children who have experienced significant neglect by the birth mother ranging from the prenatal period up to age two.

Reactive attachment disorder is an established psychiatric diagnosis for infants that have experienced severe neglect by the birth mother. This psychiatric diagnosis is the framework for the development of further enumeration of symptoms of behaviors in children as they grow older and adapt to the effects of earlier neglect. As Greg Keck, drawing from the work of Foster Cline and others, relates in his book, Adopting the Hurt Child, that children with developmental interruptions leading to the evolution of attachment disorder have some of the following symptom behaviors:

- superficially charming and engaging
- indiscriminate affection with strangers
- not cuddly on parents' terms
- poor eye contact
- persistent nonsense questions
- demanding and clingy behavior
- lying about obvious things, stealing
- destructive behavior to self, others and material things
- abnormal eating patterns
- poor impulse control
- lags in learning
- abnormal speech patterns
- poor peer relationships
- lack of cause and effect thinking

- lack of conscience
- cruelty to animals
- preoccupation with fire

Preoccupation with blood and gore might be added to this list along with bedwetting and soiling when seen in combination with other symptoms.

Children may develop attachment disorder with varying levels of severity. The age of the child when the symptoms first emerge is the first criterion for evaluating the severity of the disorder. The younger the child is at the emergence of symptoms, the more striking is the disorder. Attachment disorder symptoms that emerge after age ten or eleven are less ominous in their implications of early damage.

Another criterion for measuring the prominence of attachment disorder is the number of symptoms. For example, a child with six or seven symptoms may be considered in a mild range, eight to 14 symptoms a moderate range, and 15 or more in the severe range. These are, of course, estimates.

Another important criterion is which symptoms are most prominent. A child who is exhibiting aggression (without genuine remorse), preoccupation with fire, bedwetting, and cruelty to animals will command more serious consideration for attachment disorder even if there are few other symptoms. Another important consideration is identifying symptoms that have improved, stayed the same or gotten worse. Improvements are important to note as they suggest that corrective influences have held sway. Improvements also indicate the child has been amenable to positive family and environmental influences.

Adoptive parents may come for services with confusion about what their child's behaviors and symptoms indicate. Some conditions such as attention deficit disorder (ADD) and with hyperactivity (ADHD), major depression, fetal alcohol syndrome (FAS) or fetal alcohol effect (FAE), conduct disorders, and symptoms related to such things as early childhood trauma and sexual abuse will present complicated pictures to sort out for both parents and clinicians.

The most important feature of attachment disorder is the longevity and constancy of its symptoms and that they may not improve with outpatient psychological and psychiatric services or get worse despite them. Since a number of the other conditions have some overlap with the symptoms of attachment disorder, it requires careful attention by the diagnostician to determine if attachment disorder is the primary condition. For example, attention deficit disorder may share poor impulse control as a symptom of behavior with attention deficit disorder, but lying about obvious things and stealing are not directly associated with ADD. Severe tantrums may be a symptom of major depression in children and are also a symptom of attachment disorder.

The following table distinguishes attachment disorder from ADD/ADHD and Fetal alcohol syndrome (FAS). It illustrates which symptoms are similar to ones found in attachment disorder. By observing the symptoms one can see the distinguishing characteristics of attachment disorder. The table clearly indicates that fetal alcohol syndrome and fetal alcohol effect share a number of the same symptomologies as attachment disorder.

It is important for the clinician and the adoptive parents to know the attachment disorder symptoms. When the evidence supports the existence of a moderate attachment disorder (a mild attachment disorder is more likely to be evidence of another disorder or the symptoms of a child's adoption issues), outpatient therapy can be effective.

Behavior or Symptom	ADD ADHD	FAS FAE	Attachment Disorder
Low self esteem/self worth	★	★	★
Poor/abnormal eating pattern	★	★	★
Poor peer relationships	★	★	★
Depression	★	★	★
Tantrum tendency	★	★	★
Feels different from others	★	★	★
Developmental delays	★	★	★
Poor impulse control	★	★	★
Doesn't learn from mistakes	★	★	★
Lacks cause & effect thinking		★	★
Friendly to strangers		★	★
Superficial charm		★	★
Lying about obvious things		★	★
Stealing		★	★
Lack of conscience		★	★
Destructive		★	★
Demanding/clingy		★	★
Not cuddly			★
Poor eye contact			★
Nonsense questions & chatter			★
Abnormal speech patterns			★
Preoccupation with blood & gore			★
Cruelty to animals			★
Preoccupation with fire			★
Chronic procrastination	★		
Distractible	★	★	
Hyperactive	★	★	
Poor motor function	★	★	
Clumsy	★	★	
Poor management skills	★	★	
Low frustration tolerance	★	★	
Tendency to addiction		★	
Poor sleeping pattern		★	
Short memory		★	

Table compiled by Barb VanSlyck and Alan Dupre-Clark, 1997

Some recommendations given to adoptive parents for addressing an attachment disorder at home are
1. Establish firm limits for the child
2. Present clear boundaries (right and wrong)
3. An emphatic approach in reassuring that the child's needs for food, clothing, and shelter will be met
4. Simultaneous use of touch, eye contact, and verbalization with the child
5. Prolonged periods of holding and hugging the child
6. Strong messages from parent to child about appropriate behavior in "live" social situations with on-the-spot confrontations, if needed

Part III:
Issues and Concerns Expressed by Parents

The parent who has realistic expectations of the child's development and is educated about the causes of adoption related feelings and behaviors is more likely to be able to maintain attachment to the child and fend off mutual detachment when crises and extreme behaviors occur. Participation in post adoption education series, participation in support groups, reading books about adoption, and seeking out knowledgeable professional resources can be of great assistance.

Sudden behavior changes occur without forewarning A characteristic of adoption issues is that problematic behaviors can erupt suddenly and without warning. This type of sudden outbreak of behavior problems is mostly reported in latency age (6–12) or early adolescent adoptees. Parents report major changes of disposition that may remain in force for successive months, or even years. Sometimes the change occurs because the child has come to a developmental point cognitively, and emotionally, to reflect on birth origin questions. Sometimes the change occurs because the child hears or learns something at school or at play that triggers strong feelings about her adoptive status. Or, the child may come across a piece of information about the birth parents. When an adopted child suddenly changes, the parent needs to investigate the possibility that adoption issues (i.e., loss or grieving) have arisen. It is also not uncommon for children to suddenly escalate acting out behavior when parents or professionals attempt to alter behaviors.

Severe behaviors may be seen only in the home or expand to the community A cardinal characteristic of adoption issues is that behaviors such as lying, stealing, severe tantrums, and verbal abuse begin within the adoptive home and may be conspicuously absent in the child's behavior at school or in the community. However, the more serious the adoption issues the more likely that they will appear in other settings. The most common reason that behaviors characteristic of adoption issues are manifested primarily in the home is because the child may be struggling to work out his identity. He may present himself at school or to the community as if he feels a normal fit with his adoptive family. It may look to others that he feels no conflict or shame about his adoptive status. It is only when the pain and anger become overwhelming that problems may begin to appear outside the home.

Opposition to core family value systems feels like an assault Children with significant adoption issues may oppose what the adoptive parents hold most dearly in their value system. For example, the Blakes adopted their daughter, Mary, at age six and would work nightly with her on her school work until it exhausted all of them. Education was among the most important things to this upper middle class couple. By the time Mary reached age 12 she refused to do homework at all, returned no assignments, and announced that "School is boring and I hate it." The child and parents had reached a state of crisis and most of the sixth grade was spent in an unproductive power struggle. Mary was actually expressing a common adoption issue. She was not going to become too much like them, her adoptive parents. She refused to perform academically at a level they dearly wished for her. An improvement in school work would cause her to surpass the image of herself which was reflective of the humbler origins of her birth parents. The identity she felt belonged to her did not fit the image of scholastic success.

What to do when adoptive parents feel like giving up The development of total helplessness and demoralization of adoptive parents in the face of an uncooperative and acting out child is, unfortunately, all too common. When an adopted child "turns on" the family or fails to respond to parental and/or professional attempts to modify the acting out behaviors, desperation can set in. The adoptive mother frequently becomes the victim of the adopted child's misplaced anger about his adoptive status.

Parents need to develop a capacity to depersonalizing the attacks within their own emotional frame of reference. Adoptive parents can cripple themselves emotionally when they feel they either caused the problem or should have full power to change what is happening. Some adoptive parents in our education/support groups have called this parental stance "detachment", but it is only detachment from being responsible for a problem they did not cause. It is not detachment from the needs of the child or from the child.

Adoptive parents who successfully wrestle with "parental stance detachment" are closer to being able to more effectively manage the child. Successful adoptive parenting has some new features in this case. They are:

- Becoming aware that the child has adoption issues that are not caused by the adoptive parents
- Learning and practicing a set of skills that addresses the child's behavior problems as reflections of adoption issues
- Measuring success based on taking actions that meet the needs of the child even if the child continues to act de-

structively

- Taking affirmative steps to assure that the child's behaviors do not ruin the adoptive parent's lives, i.e., marital strife
- Providing for adequate stress breaks and relief for both parents

Re-energized, effective, adoptive parenting seldom produces quick results but will produce immediate changes in interactions between parent and child which, due to the parent's changed perspective, can lead to lasting results.

In 1991, Carol Demuth, CSW-ACP (then Director of Adoption Education and Support at Hope Cottage Adoption Center in Dallas, Texas), wrote an article called Biological Clock. This insightful piece spoke of the "key times" that may trigger a need for information, or have an emotional impact due to earlier losses and traumas. She pointed out that what many children think of as positive events may be seen negatively by the adopted child.

Our findings expand on that theme:

- In first grade, the child who previously thought adoption made him special in a positive way, may unexpectedly find that others will point him out as different or tease him
- When the child has an opportunity to go to camp, or any sleep-over, he may fear that his parents will leave him there and not return
- On his birthday or Mother's day, the child may feel sad rather than enjoy the occasion as it reminds him of the loss of birth family Other traumatic events include:
- The child whose friend moves away, or the adolescent who breaks up with a girl friend may suffer profoundly
- The adolescent who has taken years to attach, struggles to perform the normal detaching expected of an older teen
- If a parent suffers severe illness, the child may lash out in anger rather than be empathetic, as he fears abandonment if the parent should die

—

- The teen may (mistakenly) believe that adoption ends at age 18 and that he will be without a family. These teens may sabotage their senior year in high school in order to fail so that they can stay home longer
- The adopted youth that insists on going away to college finds that the separation from parents has come to soon.

Part IV: Special Treatment Techniques

Adoption Sensitive Therapy

Effective outpatient counseling for adoptive families requires that the professional providing the service be sensitive to adoption issues. The professional must have a clear understanding of an adopted child's difficulty in dealing with control, rejection, abandonment, identity and attachment and how these issues impact on the entire family.

The modalities that have appeared to be most effective with adoptive families involve parent guidance sessions and individual or group sessions for the children. Family sessions may be used to compare growth on both the parents' and the child's parts, to capitalize on and enhance attachment rather than for conflict resolution.

Parents of severely acting-out adolescents may, at times, be too overwhelmed and angry to care about causes and reasons for the behaviors. They may require additional efforts to relax them and strong cognitive interventions and emotional support to help them assimilate and use the information about their child.

Discussions about how the child deals with loss and attachment may help the adoptive parents focus on the child's own internal issues apart from the adoptive family. As the parents see their child's difficulty more as a product of loss and problems with attachment or "fit" with the adoptive family, they are likely to feel better about themselves and be more able to participate in their part of the solutions for the child.

—

The adopted child may often feel confused and angry with the adoptive family. The child knows that something is not right but mistakenly sees the adoptive parents as the problem. An adoption counselor can ask questions that push the adoptee to consider his or her birth origins and early experience which may tap into an area that the child may not have previously considered. Some adoptees give fleeting attention to birth origin concerns while others spend considerable time and interest exploring things that they feel but rarely talk about. Asking adoptees questions about their thoughts on their surrender by their birth mother and their fantasies about her and the birth family, may bring up an arena that contains some of the roots for current conflicts. Asking adoptees to consider that their current conflicts may have something to do with unresolved issues with birth origins may help children look at different causes for their behavior that the ones they currently see.

As parents encounter problems with their children, they are usually trying to find out what is going on with their child while also exhausting their own parenting resources in trying to solve the problem. In many cases separate work is required by the child on adoption issues and birth origins and by the parents in recovering from their own self-recriminations and unjust blame from others about them as parents.

The adoptive parents will need to reassert themselves as parents and provide more informed and effective help for the child. In later stages of counseling the goal is for adoptive parents and child to be more accepting of one anothers' limitations and therefore, more able to make progress with attachment to each other. The last stage may take much longer than anyone imagined—sometimes requiring the maturity of adulthood or the enduring patience and love of the adoptive parents well beyond emancipation of the adopted child from the nest of the adoptive family.

One newer treatment used in conjunction with conventional counseling is Eye Movement Desensitization and Reprocessing (EMDR). We have included this specific treatment as it has seen some recent success in treating traumatized children.

Eye Movement Desensitization and Reprocessing

EMDR is a new clinical treatment that has been shown to be effective for victims of trauma. Since its introduction in 1989 by its founder Francine Shapiro, EMDR has been shown to be a time efficient, comprehensive methodology for the treatment of the disturbing experiences that underlie many pathologies found in the distressing behaviors of the adoptive child. Dr. Shapiro theorizes that its effects are connected to the same processes that occur in REM sleep. EMDR is an eight phase treatment approach that includes using eye movements or other left–right stimulations. EMDR helps the traumatized child to reprocess disturbing thoughts and memories. The eye movements seem to stimulate the patient's innate information processing system to transform dysfunctional, self-denigrating thoughts into less threatening, more palatable information.

Specific applications for EMDR are physical, sexual, and emotional trauma, academic performance, memory lapses, self-esteem, communication issues between child and authority figures, motivation issues, inappropriate behaviors, self-sabotaging behaviors, and the belief that the child is unloved or unlovable.

The system in the adoptive child becomes unbalanced due to the traumas of abandonment, loss, separation, and grieving. Once EMDR is appropriately activated it brings negative experiences to a state of therapeutically appropriate resolution. Behavioral and emotional modification are then achieved by the child.

An adoptive family parenting a child with past trau-

matic experiences may seek out a trained EMDR professional to determine if the treatment modality may be helpful.

Psychoeducational parent-child parallel support groups

Adoptive parents as a group have many questions, and
a thirst for effective solutions. So many times I have said to
an adoptive couple "I cannot give you all you need, but there
is a place that can provide a good deal of it." This was, of
course, reference to the ten-week parallel group series for
adoptive parents and children.

This education and support series was created to assist
families in crisis. The purpose was to diffuse crises, assist
parents and children to understand their emotions and behaviors and then lead them to a healthier relationship. Approximately 300 families have been served by the education
series.

The opening session of the parallel group series has
always begun with members sharing why they came. There
are always expressions of surprise and then relief around the
circle as parents share experiences that are, in many cases,
similar to one another. Typical comments are:

"I didn't know others were having similar struggles. I
feel like I'm not crazy now."

Many parents say that they feel they have found a
haven or "come home at last" when beginning the series
or our support groups. Such comments reveal that parents
came to the series fearing that they would be judged. Our
facilitators are sensitive to the years of emotional build-up
from confusion and lack of direction in parenting.

Many parents move from frustration and despair at the
beginning of the series to hopeful, renewed, and energetic at
the end of the series. Others have begun with confusion and
ended with more knowledge and great appreciation for the
support. Initially, in the parents' group we look at expecta-

tions, hopes and dreams that parents held for their children. We dispel the myth that children adopted during infancy are immune to developing serious adoption issues. The parents could not believe that their child, adopted as an infant or toddler, could have been so hurt so quickly in his life.

Although adoptive parents expressed fears about the paths the children were on, the hard work of some parents or statements of resolve for the future helped others to reaffirm their commitment to their children. As one parent said it, "I know that no matter how hard it has gotten, there is no turning back. We are his only opportunity for a chance in life. I couldn't abandon him."

Among the concepts that prove useful is the establishment of entitlement to parent their child. Some have felt that even their legal entitlement to parent was not a surety anymore, especially when the courts and children services had become involved. Most have lost confidence as a parent. Once entitlement is discussed as a right and also a necessity for the security needs of their child, some parents are able to regain more resolve to parent. These parents need more tenacity and morale to keep going. As one parent stated, "I know what I need to do. I just need the permission to do it", referring to setting limits for his adolescent son.

One mother told of a 16 year old daughter who had been stealing from family members for many years. She had tried persuasion, consequences, giving the benefit of the doubt, ignoring the thefts, and locking up belongings. She tried discussing adoption issues with the girl. Nothing seemed to work. The mother finally illuminated a new principle by which she would parent and live. She stated emphatically, "From this point forward I am going to accept that my daughter is someone who is capable of criminal behavior. This stealing does not define all of who she is and I still love her, but I am not going to let her stealing be a reflection of what kind of parent I am. I am past disappointment and disillusionment with her to a place where I am going to enjoy my life again."

Handling such adoption issues as control or abandonment with the child while at the same time trying to carry out the normal disciplinary duties of a parent is a tightrope act that many parents need time and help to refine. Some parents report that they see the need to be sensitive to their child's adoption, loss, and grief issues and yet be prepared to insist on certain kinds of conduct. To do this successfully requires versatility and courage to follow through with consequences that can often result in strong backlash responses from the child. Parents are often in need of much emotional support to continue to do what is needed. They learn that if they persist in being informed and available for the deeper issues in the children's lives, eventually there can be positive results.

Parents often follow up the series with regular attendance at support groups, and sometimes seek renewed therapy for the family with fresh vigor and determination.

The parents who wrote about their experiences for this book all entered adoption unprepared for the severity of the behaviors they faced. All blamed themselves for the problems of the children. They had different parenting methods and philosophies. They sought help from professionals who were not able to provide a workable course of action. They needed full information from the placing agency or attorney, and ongoing education, and support.

We would like to see the future of adoption directed in such a manner that the pain and confusion and self-blame of the parents and pain, confusion and emotional upheavals suffered by the children can be avoided through the commitment of placing agencies and helping professionals.

References

Barth, R., and Berry, M. (1988). *Adoption and Disruption: Rates, risks, and responses,* NY. Aldine de Gruyter Press.

Cordell, A. S. Nathan, C & Krymow, V. P. (1985) *Group Counseling for Children adopted at older ages,* Child Welfare, 64, 113-124.

Goodman, Denise. *Here Today, Gone Tomorrow: An Investigation of the Factors that Impact Adoption Disruption. Dissertation,* (1993). Ohio State University

Janus, N. *Adoption Counseling as a Professional Specialty Area for Counselors,* (Mar/Apr 1997) Journal of Counseling and Development.

Howard, J., and Smith, S. (1995) *Adoption Preservation in Illinois: Results of a Four Year Study,* University of Illinois.

Keck, G., and Kupecky, R. (1995). *Adopting the Hurt Child: Hope for Families with Special-Needs Kids,* Pinon Press. Colorado Springs, CO.

Ng, N. S., & Wood, L. (1993) *Understanding Adoption: A guide for educators,* Palo Alto, Ca: FAIR.

Shapiro, Francine. (1995). *Eye Movement, Desensitization and Reprocessing: Basic Principles, Protocols, and Procedures,* Guilford Press.

Smith, S. and Howard. J. (1996) *An Analysis of Child Behavior Problems in Adoptions in Difficulty,* Illinois State University.

VanSlyck, B. and Dupre-Clark, A. (1995) *Charting the Course, Vol I: A therapeutic Manual for Post Adoptive Families,* Columbus, Ohio

Suggested Reading

Professionals

Bourguignon, Jean Pierre, & Watson, K. *After Adoption: A Manual for Professionals Working With Adoptive Families*, year, Pub?. A resource regarding attachment disorders and other issues of post-legal adoption services.

Brodzinsky, D. M., & Schecter, M. D. *The Psychology of Adoption*, 1990. New York. Oxford Press.

Howard, Jeanne, & Smith, Susan. (1995) *Adoption Preservation in Illinois: Results of a Four Year Study*. University of Illinois, Normal, Ill.

Lindsay, J. W., & Monserrat, C. P. (1989) *Adoption Awareness: A Guide for Teachers, Counselors, Nurses, and Caring Others*. Buena Park, CA. Morning Glory Press.

Smith, S., and Howard, J. *An Analysis of Child Behavior Problems in Adoptions in Difficulty*. 1996. Illinois Department of Children and Family Services. An excellent compilation of information regarding difficulties in special needs adoptions and the needs for services.

vanGulden, H., & Bartels-Rabb, L. M. (1994). *Real Parents, Real Children*. New York. Crossroad.

VanSlyck, Barbara, & Dupre-Clark, A. (1995) *Charting the Course, Vol I.: A Therapeutic Manual for Adoptive Families*. A ten week educational series for adoptive families. Columbus, Ohio.

VanSlyck, B., & and Dupre-Clark, A. (1996) *Charting the Course, Vol II.: An Educational Manual for Pre-Adoptive Families*. A twelve hour training for use by adoption agencies. Columbus, Ohio

VanSlyck, B., Mague, R., & Dupre-Clark, A. (1996) *Charting the Course, Vol III,: An Educational Manual for Adoptive Families with Children (Ages 6-10)*. A six week series to explain adoption to children and help parents understand their childs issues.

VanSlyck, B., & Dupre-Clark, A. (1996) *Charting the Course, Vol IV.: An Education Manual for Adoptive Parents of Pre-school Age Children*. A six week course to prepare parents for childrens changing needs and stresses how to talk the the adopted child. Columbus, Ohio

Delaney, Richard, & Kunstal, F. *Troubled Transplants, Unconventional Strategies for Helping Disturbed Foster and Adopted Children*. 1993. National Child Welfare Resource Center, University of Southern Maine.

Fahlberg, Vera. *Separation and Attachment. Putting the Pieces Together*. 1984. Michigan Department of Social Services, DDS Publication #429. An excellent workbook and overview of attachment and separation issues.

Magid, McKelvey. *High Risk: Children Without a Conscience*. 1989. Bantam Books. A frightening look at the impact of attachment disorder on conscience development.

Parents and professionals

Arms, Suzanne. *To Love and Let Go*. 1983. Stories of birth parent experiences and feelings about their pregnancy and placement of child.

Askin, J., & Oskim, B. *Search: A Handbook for Adoptees and Birth Parents*. 1982. Harper & Row, NY. A guide for use in searching. Includes current state policies and techniques for searching.

Brodzinsky, Schecter, & Henig. *Being Adopted, The Lifelong Search for Self*. 1993. Doubleday. A book to help adoptive parents and adoptees understand the struggles and stages of developing an identity when an individual experiences separation from his roots.

Davis, Diane. *Reaching Out to Children with FAS/FAE*, 1994. Offers support and hope and serves as a comprehensive resource to professionals and families

Delaney, Richard, and Kustal, Frank. *Troubled Transplants: Unconventional Strategies for Helping Disturbed Foster and Adopted Children*, 1993. University of Southern Maine. Conventional approaches to parenting do not work for many foster and adopted children. This book is easily understood and should prove useful to parents at the end of their ropes.

Dorris, Michael. *The Broken Cord*, 1989. Harper Collins. A single adoptive father writes about his experiences in parenting a child with fetal alcohol syndrome.

Dorner, Patricia. *Talking to your Child About Adoption*, 1991. The booklet emphasizes that communication about adoption is an ongoing process.

Dusky, Loraine. *Birthmark*, 1979. M.Evans & Co., NY. Ms Dusky, a birth mother, tells the story of her experiences and adjustment over the years since making an adoption plan for her daughter. (Lorraine and her daughter are featured in *How it Feels To Be Adopted, After Reunion*).

Homes, A. M., *In a Country of Mothers*, 1993. Alred A. Knopf. A novel which examines contemporary myths surrounding adoption and motherhood.

Jewitt, Claudia. *Adopting the Older Child*, 1978. Harvard Common Press, Harvard, Mass. Dr. Jewitt, an adoptive parent of older children and a psychotherapist, provides various case histories and experiences of families formed by older child adoption as well as information on the decision

---

to adopt and preparation for children and families.

Jewitt, Claudia. *Helping Children Cope with Separation and Loss*, 1982. Harvard Common Press, Harvard, Mass. Very specific guide about helping children cope with separation, loss, and grief. Can be used by professionals and parents.

Keck, Gregory. *Adopting the Hurt Child: Hope for Families With Special-Needs Kids*, 1995. Pinon Press. Addresses Attachment disorder, early issues and strategies for healing the hurt child.

Kirk, David. *Shared Fate*, 1964. Free Press, NY. Dr. Kirk is an adoptive father who sensitively writes about adoption and develops a theory of adoptive relationships based on ten years of research.

Komar, Miriam. *Communicating With the Adopted Child*, 1991. Walker, NY. A guide to the how and what of talking about adoptive issues.

Magid, Miriam. *High Risk: Children without a Conscience*, 1989. Bantam Books. A frightening look as the impact of attachment disorder on conscience development.

Melina, Lois Ruiskai. *Raising Adopted Children*, Harper & Row. This book provides a guide for adoptive parents to assist them with many questions and situations in parenting a child who is adopted. Appropriate for both families who adopted infants and older children.

McNamara, Joan. *Adoption and the Sexually Abused Child*, 1990. Addresses needs.

Melina, Lois. *Making Sense of Adoption*, 1989. Practical help for parents in how to talk to their children about adoption.

Musser, Sandra Kay. *I Would Have Searched Forever*, 1979. Jan Publications, Division of AIM Inc. Capa Coral, Florida. Sandy explores the struggle for all in the adoption

—

triangle in reconciling with each other, creating comfortable relationships among all in search situations.

Pohl, C., and Harris, K. *Transracial Adoption: Children and Parents Speak*, 1992. Watts, NY. Issues of transracial adoptions through words and experiences of families.

Rosenberg, Elinor. *The Adoption Life Cycle: The Children and Their Families Through the Years*, 1992. Free Press, NY. Looks not only at the issues of adoptees, but also at those of birth parents and adoptive parents.

Schaffer, Judith, & Lindstrom, Christina. *How to Raise an Adopted Child*, 1989. Crown Publishers. A comprehensive how-to book anticipating nearly every situation adoptive parents may encounter. Chapters cover specific age groups, from infancy to teen years.

Schooler, Jayne. *The Whole Life Adoption Book*, 1993. Pinon, Colorado Springs, CO. Realistic advice for building a healthy adoptive family.

Schooler, Jayne. *Searching for a Past*, 1995. Pinon Press. Adopted adults unique process for finding identity.

Sheehy, Gail. *Spirit of Survival*, 1986. Bantam Books, NY. Gripping story of the journey of Gail's adopted daughter from Cambodian work camps to her adjustment in her adoptive home.

Sorosky, Arthur. *et al, The Adoption Triangle: The Effect of Sealed Records on Adoptees, Birth Parents and Adoptive Parents*, 1978. Anchor Press/Doubleday, NY. A detailed study complied over five years, covering all perspectives of the triad, including portions of letters received in this extensive study. This book is highly recommended to give an overview of experiences of members of the triad.

—

Books for Children and Teens

Brodzinsky, Ann Braff. *The Mulberry Bird*, A story of a mother bird and her baby explains why a birth mother would make an adoption plan, with careful attention to the child's self-esteem.

Brown, Irene Bennett. *Answer Me Answer Me*, Bryn Kenney's search for her parentage begins after the death of her Gram when she is unexpectedly provided with a fortune and a clue to her roots.

Crook, Marion. *Teenagers Talk About Adoption*, Based on interviews with more than 40 adopted teens in Canada, this book conveys the feelings they have about their birth parents, being adopted, and the attitudes of others toward adoption.

Gabel, Susan. *Filling in the Blanks, A Guided Look at Growing Up Adopted*, 1988. Perspectives Press. A workbook to help pre-adolescents (ages 10–14) understand their own histories.

Ginsburg, M. *The Chinese Mirror*, 1988. A book (for readers 6–10) about a Korean child and identity development.

Girard, Linda Walford. *Adoption is for Always*, 1986. Celia feels alone, angry and insecure about being adopted. But with her parents' patience and understanding, she accepts it and makes her adoption day into a special family celebration.

Gordon, Shirley. *The Boy Who Wanted a Family*, 1980. Michael's hopes, fears, and experiences with his new mom are explored during the one year waiting period to finalize his adoption.

Graville, Karen, & Fischer, Susan. *Where are my birth parents?: A guide for teenage adoptees*, 1993.

—

Greenberg, Judith E., & Carey, Helen H. *Adopted*, 1989. Sarah and Ryan are adopted. To help Sarah understand, her parents and grandfather explain about adoption and being a family member.

Krementz, Jill. *How it Feels to be Adopted*, 1982. Alfred A Knopf, NY. Nineteen adopted children ages 8–16, of various races and cultures are interviewed. Each describes feelings and thoughts about adoption.

Livingston, Carole. *Why Am I Adopted?*, 1978. Lyle Stuart Inc. Appropriate for early elementary age children.

Mandlebaum, Pili. *You Be Me, I'll Be You*, A bi-cultural child decides she dislikes her brown skin. Her father devises a creative alternative.

Mills, Claudia. *Boardwalk With Hotel*, 1985. Eleven year old Jessica becomes angry about her adoption and starts to feel competitive with and jealous of her siblings who are not adopted.

Nerlove, Evelyn. *Who Is David?*, 1985. Child Welfare League of America. An excellent novel about an adolescent adoptee struggling with identity who participates in a support group for adopted adolescents.

Rosenberg, Maxine. *Being Adopted*, Helpful for children, ages 5–10, when they first have questions about adoption. Three children relate their adoption stories.